Teaching the Educable Mentally Retarded

SUNY Series in Special Education
DAVID A. SABATINO, EDITOR

Teaching the Educable Mentally Retarded

Robert A. Sedlak and Denise M. Sedlak

State University of New York Press

Published by
State University of New York Press, Albany

© 1985 State University of New York

All rights reserved

Printed in the United States of America

No part of this book may be used or reproduced
in any manner whatsoever without written permission
except in the case of brief quotations embodied in
critical articles and reviews.

For information, address State University of New York
Press, State University Plaza, Albany, N.Y., 12246

Library of Congress Cataloging in Publication Data

Sedlak, Robert A., 1947 –
  Teaching the educable mentally retarded.

  (SUNY series in special education)
    1. Mentally handicapped children — Education.
2. Teachers of mentally handicapped children — Training of.
I. Sedlak, Denise M., 1947 –   .   II. Title.
III. Series.
LC4661.S37   1985   371.92'82   84-16344
ISBN 0-88706-055-2
ISBN 0-88706-056-0 (pbk.)

We dedicate this book to Carol and Phil Cartwright and Louise and Jack Cawley who have influenced our lives both personally and professionally.

Contents

Preface

The American public has come to expect excellence both from the performance of students in the schools and from the teachers who deliver the instruction. More accountability measures are being required for both students and teachers. The accountability for the special education teacher is even greater than for the regular classroom teacher since there are annual reviews of student progress and extensively written long- and short-term plans which must be completed by the special education teacher. Because of the high cost of special education, local school boards watch closely the impact of such programs.

The critical variable in the success or failure of the special education program is the teacher. The preparation of future special educators must include training which addresses the manner in which they can make themselves accountable and the range of problems which they will be expected to solve. We have attempted to include both of these aspects in this text.

This text is intended for students who are preparing to become teachers of the mildly retarded. The case studies and problem situations depicted in the text are actual situations that we have encountered in the classroom. We have tried to explain the theoretical base of teaching but always from the perspective of what is practical. The way things are can be quite different from the way they are supposed to be. Our greatest frustration in training future teachers has been to break them from the mind set that we live in a perfect world as far as programming for the mildly retarded is concerned. Our experience from working primarily in rural and suburban schools is that a full continuum of services is not generally available. The flow-chart system of how students are identified, referred, staffed, and educated in a systematic fashion may exist in the minds of special education administrators, but it is not so evident to the teacher working on the front lines of education. We have attempted to show the problems which exist in the day-to-day operation of a classroom and also some means to deal with them.

There are no adequate substitutes for planning and hard work on the part of a beginning teacher.

The hard work and effort of many people contributed to the completion of this book. The authors would like to thank: Sheila Davis for her help in locating resource materials; Sherry Watson and Jeanne Kussrow-Larson for their expert typing, art work, and editing; the graduate and undergraduate students at Southern Illinois University-Carbondale and the University of Wisconsin-Stout, who field-tested many of the draft copies of the chapters while taking our "methods" classes; and finally, Rob and Wendy, our children, who helped us learn how normal children learn and gave us perspective on what is possible.

Remember this . . .

1. All states do not define mental retardation in the same way.

2. Some students who have been categorized as being mentally retarded have been "cured."

3. Mentally retarded learners remember learned facts as well as you or me.

4. The primary problem related to learning for the mentally retarded may be "motivational" rather than "mental."

5. The problems of the mildly mentally retarded may be more controlled by environmental conditions than by an inborn deficit in the individual.

6. The responsibilities of the teacher of the mildly mentally retarded are different from the responsibilities of regular classroom teachers in programming for atypical learners.

CHAPTER I

The Educable Mentally Retarded: Characteristics and Issues

Who are the Educable Retarded?

Every student being trained to teach the mentally retarded will be taught the American Association on Mental Deficiency (AAMD) definition of mental retardation. In most training programs it is critical that students be able to state this definition from memory. Students teaching in the public schools within the United States quickly realize that while the AAMD definition is accepted by a segment of the professional community, that other definitions exist and that the usage of even the same definition varies widely among school districts and states. Figure 1.1 shows a state-by-state breakdown of selected com-

Figure 1.1
States' Guidelines Concerning Definitions of Mental Retardation

State	Date of Guidelines	Type of Definition	Intelligence Criteria	Include Adaptive Behavior in Definition
Alabama	1973	Other	30-80 IQ	No
Alaska	1975	Other	Not Specified	Yes
Arizona	1977	Other	Not Specified	No
Arkansas	1977	Other	≤ -2.0 S.D.	Yes

Figure 1.1 (Con't)

State	Date of Guidelines	Type of Definition	Intelligence Criteria	Include Adaptive Behavior in Definition
Colorado	1976	Similar	≤ − 1.75 S.D.	Yes
Connecticut	1976	Other	Not Specified	No
Delaware	1974	Other	Not Specified	No
District of Columbia	Not specified	AAMD & BEH	≤ − 2.0 S.D.	Yes
Florida	1976	AAMD	≤ − 2.0 S.D.	Yes
Georgia	1975	Similar	≤ − 2.0 S.D.	Yes
Hawaii	1966	Other	Not Specified	No
Idaho	1975	Similar	≤ 75 IQ	Yes
Illinois	1976	Other	Not Specified	Yes
Indiana	1973	Other	≤ 75 IQ	No
Iowa	1974	Other	≤ 1.0 S.D.	Yes
Kansas	1976	Other	Not Specified	Yes
Kentucky	1975	Other	Not Specified	No
Maine	Draft	Other	Not Specified	No
Michigan	1973	Other	Not Specified	Yes
Missouri	1976	AAMD	≤ − 2.0 S.D.	Yes
Montana	Not specified	Similar	≤ 75 IQ ≤ − 1.6 S.D.	Yes
Nebraska	1975	Other	Not Specified	Yes
Nevada	1976	Other	≤ 75 IQ	No
New Hampshire	1976	Other	Not Specified	No
New Jersey	1976	Other	≤ − 1.5 S.D.	Yes
New York	1975	Other	≤ − 1.5 S.D.	No
North Dakota	1976	Other	≤ 75 IQ	No
Ohio	1973	Other	≤ 80 IQ	No
Oklahoma	1976	Other	≤ 75 IQ	No
Oregon	1976	AAMD	≤ − 2.0 S.D.	Yes
Pennsylvania	1976	Similar	≤ 80 IQ	Yes
Rhode Island	1973	Other	Not Specified	Yes
South Carolina	1972	Other	≤ 70 IQ	Yes
South Dakota	1974	Similar	Not Specified	Yes
Tennessee	1976-77	Other	Not Specified	Yes
Utah	1975	AAMD	≤ 75 IQ	Yes
Virginia	1972	Other	≤ − 2.0 S.D.	No
Washington	1976	Other	≤ 75 IQ	Yes
West Virginia	1974	AAMD	≤ 75 IQ	Yes

Figure 1.1 (Con't)

State	Date of Guidelines	Type of Definition	Intelligence Criteria	Include Adaptive Behavior in Definition
Wisconsin	Not Specified	AAMD	≤ −2.0 S.D.	Yes
Wyoming	1975	AAMD	≤ −2.0 S.D.	Yes

AAMD   = American Association on Mental Deficiency
BEH   = Bureau of Education for the Handicapped
Other   = definition other than AAMD & BEH
S.D.   = standard deviation(s)
Similar = similar to AAMD definition, with only minor variations

Adapted from T. J. Huberty, J. R. Koller, T. D. Ten Brink, Adaptive Behavior in the Definition of Mental Retardation. *Exceptional Children*, 1980, *46*, 256–261. Copyright 1980 by The Council for Exceptional Children. Reprinted by permission.

ponents of their definitions for mental retardation. Even within these states, different agencies use different definitions and criteria for mental retardation to determine eligibility for services. Figure 1.2 shows several different definitions recommended by agencies or professionals. You will note that even the AAMD definition has changed over time.

Figure 1.2
Definitions of Mental Retardation

Source	Definition	Concerns
American Association on Mental Deficiency (Grossman, 1983)	Significantly subaverage general intellectual functioning resulting in or associated with current impairments in adaptive behavior and manifested during the developmental period	*IQ cutoffs:* 50-55-75 mild (EMR) 35-40-50-55 moderate (TMR)
American Association on Mental Deficiency (Grossman, 1973)	Significantly subaverage general intellectual functioning existing concurrently with deficits in adaptive behavior and manifested during the developmental period	*IQ cutoffs:* 52-67 mild (EMR) 36-51 moderate (TMR)

Figure 1.2 (Con't)

Source	Definition	Concerns
Bijou, 1966	A retarded individual is one who has a limited repertory of behavior shaped by events that constitute his history	Function of observable social, physiological, and biological conditions
Mercer, 1973	The individual's social system determines retardation	Child does not "officially" become retarded until deficits in social interactions are observed

The definition of the condition (in this case mental retardation) is a critical step in the decision process. Classroom teachers may have some influence regarding a student's eligibility for placement in a class since they are a part of the multidisciplinary team that makes placement recommendations and disability decisions. Knowing the state and local definition of mental retardation helps immeasureably to the contribution a teacher can make as a member of the team.

The educable mentally retarded (EMR) constitute the third largest category of handicapped youngsters, with a prevalence of 3%, which places them just behind the learning disabled and the speech impaired (U.S. Office of Education, 1975). Over the last ten years the incidence of learners classified as educable mentally retarded has decreased substantially (MacMillan and Borthwick, 1980). In California, for example, EMR enrollments have decreased by 50%. A number of factors have operated to contribute to this decline, including:

1. Court decisions questioning the overrepresentation of ethnic minority students in EMR classes (Hobsen and Hansen, 1967)
2. The redefinition of the educable mentally retarded which lowered the IQ limit
3. The implementation of PL 94–142

The net effect of this shift has resulted in:

1. A reduction in the number of self-contained classes for the EMR

2. A lower functioning population in the EMR classrooms
3. An increase in students being served by learning disabilities (LD) or cross-categorical resource programs
4. A greater sensitivity to placement of ethnic minority group children in EMR classes
5. Increased use of adaptive behavior measures in placement decisions
6. A reluctance by school psychologists and multidisciplinary teams to categorize students as educable mentally retarded

In general, educable mentally retarded individuals are expected to have a recorded IQ between 50 and 75 on individual intelligence tests; e.g., *Standford Binet* and *Wechsler Intelligence Scale for Children*. The content of these tests is to some extent culturally biased, and contrary to a commonly held belief, IQ is not a fixed phenomenon. McCall, Applebaum, and Hogartz (1973) have shown that in a group of middle-class, normal children there can be an average IQ shift of 28.5 IQ points (plus or minus) between the ages of 2.5 and 17 years. The extent to which such a shift is possible with a group scoring in the "retarded" range is unknown.

Garrison and Hammill (1971) studied the assessment process for identifying the mildly mentally retarded. Using five measures which included the *Slosson Intelligence Test*, the *Test of Social Inference* (a measure of social comprehension), an *Informal Reading Inventory*, and the *ITPA* subtests verbal expression and auditory reception, 698 eleven-year-old students in either classes for the educable retarded (N = 378) or regular classes (N = 319) were assessed. The study found that at least 25% of the students in these classes were misplaced and that an additional 43% may have been misplaced. Only about 31% of the students in EMR classes were placed correctly. Only one child in the regular class was located who probably should have been placed in a class for the EMR. What can we conclude from this study? First, making a diagnosis on the basis of a single test score is not appropriate. Second, there were children placed in classes for the EMR who did not belong there. Since the Garrison and Hammill study, the percentage of children placed in classes for the educable mentally retarded has decreased dramatically, while the field of learning disabilities has grown to represent the major categorical placement in special education. By today's standards, many of the "misplaced" students in the Garrison and Hammill study would probably now show up in classes for the learning disabled. Of course, the creation of the learning disabilities category has not solved the problem of misplacement. In fact, currently there is great concern that too many students are misplaced into classes for the learning disabled.

Since this is a textbook which provides methods and curriculum for teaching the mildly mentally retarded, it will not delve deeply into the placement question but merely make the reader aware of the problems. The operational definition of mild mental retardation from which the authors operate is quite simple. For the purposes of the information in this text, the mildly mentally retarded are defined as children and/or youth who are found in classes for the mildly retarded or educable mentally retarded in public school programs. Because students in these classes will exhibit a wide range of behavioral characteristics, the methods and curriculum discussed in the text will address their diverse needs in order to provide an appropriate educational program.

Learning and Behavioral Characteristics

While this is not a text on the characteristics of the mentally retarded, the teacher must understand these characteristics in order to provide an appropriate educational program for the learner. The mildly mentally retarded cannot be served best by "cookbook" approaches where the same strategy is good for all learners, but rather teachers must develop programs which are based upon the unique learning and behavioral characteristics of the learners.

Learning Potential

Budoff (1968, 1969) conducted research on the assessment process for identifying mentally retarded individuals and used a procedure which tests a student's ability to "learn" a new task as compared to the conventional system which requires a student to answer questions or perform tasks which are heavily based on *prior* learning. Budoff has termed the procedure a test of "learning potential." Budoff differentiated between labeled mentally retarded children who truly have a learning deficit from those who initially scored low on a task but could be taught to perform the task in a short period of time. Budoff used a test known as the *Kohs Block Design*, which is a subtest in the *WISC*, in order to differentiate between these groups of learners. The students looked at a picture of a design and then were required to reproduce the design with a set of colored blocks. The test was selected because it was highly unrelated to past learning experiences. If a student failed to perform satisfactorily on the task, training was undertaken and then the student was retested. Students who achieved well initially or who made significant gains on post-testing were considered students with high learning potential.

The fact that they were categorized as mentally retarded was due to an absence of *achievement* or performance and not due to a problem in *learning*. Budoff refers to these students as *educationally* retarded rather than *mentally* retarded. Unfortunately, few schools use alternative assessment procedures in the testing of students for placement. As a result, students in special classes for the educable mentally retarded will represent a real "mixed bag." Some students will have problems related to the variables associated with learning, while others will have deficits in achievement due to inadequate prior experience or poor instruction. For both of these groups of youngsters, the teacher can create a program which increases their achievement and learning rate. An understanding of methods for circumventing behavioral deficits or motivational limitations is critical. These are described in portions of the following material and also in Chapter III.

Attention and Memory Deficits

A major myth surrounding the performance of the educable mentally retarded is that they forget things easily or that they have poor memories. There is a voluminous body of research which indicates that *retarded children do as well as nonretarded children once they learn the correct solution to a problem* (Robinson and Robinson, 1970; Zeaman and House, 1963). The problems faced by the mentally retarded are those of *attention* and *employment of learning strategies*. Fortunately, these are two problems which can be addressed by the classroom teacher.

ATTENTION. A student must be able to attend to the task at hand before he can be expected to learn it. The research of Zeaman and House (1963) strongly suggests that attention deficits may be the basis for many of the learning problems of the mentally retarded. An attention deficit does not necessarily mean that the student is out of his seat or not paying attention (although it might) but might also mean that in a new learning task the student focuses his attention on *all* attributes of the problem without being able to screen out what is unnecessary. It is the classic symptom of the student's being unable to see the pine tree in a forest of elms. Examples of this occurring are the student's looking at page 25 while the teacher is talking about page 27, the student's looking at the tens column in an addition problem while the teacher is talking about the units position, or the student's looking at the teacher but evaluating the teacher's jewelry rather than what is being said. When the student is *taught* to *focus attention* on a particular attribute of a task, the problem can be minimized. The teacher must be certain that the student is attending to the same information as is being discussed. The teacher does this by asking questions often, regularly checking work, and seeing that the students are manipulating the right materials.

MEMORY. The mentally retarded, as a group, perform poorly on tasks which require them to answer questions about or remember lists of words, sounds, events, or pictures that were initially presented to them a few seconds earlier (Borkowski and Wanschura, 1974; Brown, 1974). Once they have learned the material they are able to remember it as well as nonretarded individuals. Thus they are said to have a deficit in short-term, not long-term, memory. The short-term memory deficit is the result of a failure to use *mediational* or *organizing* strategies (Borkowski and Wanschura, 1974; Brown, 1974). Strategies such as reciting the list of words out loud (mediational strategy) are used by nonretarded individuals as techniques which help them remember. Retarded individuals do not spontaneously use these strategies. Research has demonstrated, however, that instruction in clustering and rehearsal strategies increase the short-term memory capabilities of the retarded student. The critical issue here is that for many of the performance deficits there are instructional strategies which can be used to teach the retarded learner so that the effect of the deficits may be minimized.

Incidental Learning

Related to the area of attention is the deficit noted by retarded students in terms of incidental learning. Incidental learning involves the acquisition of information peripheral to or incidental to the main point of attention. Retarded individuals often do not spontaneously attend to these peripheral pieces of information. Consequently, the teacher cannot assume that students possess specific information or have attented to peripheral types of facts in situations that most of us would take for granted. This particular trait became evident to one of the authors when he was teaching in a junior high EMR class. Several of the students referred to all of the female teachers in the building as "Miss _____." I corrected them (for those teachers who were married), but they continued to use the term "Miss _____." I finally realized during an English lesson on the use of abbreviations that the students pronounced "Mrs." as "Miss," and also that they didn't realize that the term "Mrs." meant that the woman was married. In our society this probably wouldn't be a problem, and they could refer to everyone as "Ms. _____" without anyone's catching on.

To compensate for this deficit, the teacher should question students often and call their attention to "peripheral" events on a field trip or in an instructional film. Questions related to their everyday environment should also be asked such as "What are the colors of the flowers in front of the school?" or "What color was the banner hanging in the gymnasium?"

Motivational Characteristics

MacMillan (1971) has argued that the educational programs for the educable mentally retarded have focused almost solely on the *mental* deficits of the learners. He points out that the research of Zigler and Butterfield (1968), Zigler (1966), MacMillan (1972), and others have identified that the problems of performance in many of these children have a motivational rather than a cognitive basis. MacMillan argues that a program for the educable mentally retarded which treats cognitive deficits to the exclusion of the problems originating in the motivational sphere is doomed to failure.

Motivation when viewed from the perspective of a teacher simply means that a student will have a desire to learn and will put forth effort in a task to achieve that end. People become "motivated" as the result of numerous interactions with their environment. These interactions start at birth and become more complex through adulthood. People become more competent as they gain control over their environment. The technical term for this satisfaction which is gained from the successful completion of a challenging task is *effectance* (Harter and Zigler, 1974). People are driven by the successful completion of difficult tasks and they gain a sense of personal reward from their completion.

With the mentally retarded, however, the natural development of effectance motivation does not occur, because rather than being successful in the completion of tasks through childhood and in school, many of the mentally retarded have a history of failure which results in feelings of frustration and even escape from challenging tasks. School-related tasks which others of the same chronological age find challenging are overwhelming for the retarded. Behaviros which some would categorize as "lazy," "unmotivated," "uncooperative," "incorrigible," "unresponsive," are often attributed to the mentally retarded. These terms focus on the student although these behaviors develop as the result of the students' unsuccessful interactions with the environment and not as the result of an inborn condition. The motivational problems of the mentally retarded can be categorized under three headings: expectancy of failure, positive and negative tendencies, and outer directedness.

EXPECTANCY OF FAILURE. There appears to be a functional relationship between the "histories of failure" experienced by these children in academic areas and their approach to problem solving which is characterized by the need to avoid failure rather than to achieve success. Failure occurs so often in their lives that each new learning task is approached with an *expectancy to fail* even before attempting the task (MacMillan and Keogh, 1971). Such a failure set interferes with the acquisition of new skills which are slightly beyond the learner's present level of performance. Fortunately, teachers can control the circumstances which contribute to breaking this failure set. For example, providing prompts or cues to the correct response to a problem may provide a means of guaranteeing success while still challenging the learner.

POSITIVE AND NEGATIVE REACTION TENDENCIES. Children who have had a history of social deprivation (i.e., not received enough affection and attention from the important adults in their lives) desire an extraordinary amount of adult attention. When faced with a challenging cognitive task (or even a less than challenging task), they are not motivated to solve the problem confronting them but instead use the situation to gain attention from adults in the form of seeking help. EMR students have two forces pulling at them simultaneously in these situations. They have a desire to interact with an approving adult but are simultaneously hesitant because of the many negative encounters with adults.

Related to this conflict is an understanding of the child's reinforcement hierarchy. With nonretarded middle-class children, being correct is higher on their hierarchy of reinforcement than it is for EMR learners (Zigler, 1968).

OUTERDIRECTEDNESS. According to Zigler (1966), repeated failure can result in a problem-solving style which is outerdirected. The retarded child distrusts his solutions to problems and begins to over-rely on external cues. This extreme reliance on adult approval and feedback runs counter to the development of nonhandicapped children. Acceptance of such behaviors in a child by other teachers and adults in the environment is questionable. The results are more negative interactions with adults, more failure, and less independence.

TEACHER STRATEGIES. Teachers must structure educational programs such that the level of material challenges the student but does not lead to excessive frustration. Tangible or strong social reinforcers may be required to attract a student to a task and its completion. Tasks then can be increased in difficulty commensurate with a gradual fading of contrived reinforcing events. The ultimate goal is a greater reliance on the part of the student to initiate challenging tasks without these external rewards. This change will not be brought about in a year to two; remember, the student has had six, eight, or even fifteen years of unsuccessful interactions with school. Think small, proceed slowly, and plan thoughtfully.

Expected Academic Achievement

Not surprisingly, in traditional academic subject areas retarded children lag behind their chronological peers. They even tend to underachieve when contrasted to normal children who are their "mental age." Underachievement in EMR children is most pronounced in the academic subject areas of reading and arithmetic. While the major deficit area in reading is comprehension, the predominant deficit in arithmetic is in reasoning and problem-solving skills. Phelps (1956) found that in a group of 163 retarded children with a median IQ of 60.6, less than 5% graduated from either eighth grade or junior high school. The median reading grade level of the group was 3.9, and the median arithmetic grade level was 4.3. Robinson and Robinson (1976) indicated that *optimal* levels of achievement occasionally reach as high as the sixth grade level.

Language

Language difficulties are a frequently encountered characteristic of the mentally retarded. Structurally, their language is similar to that of normal children (O'Connor and Hermelin, 1963). Bizarre uses of language are not noted but rather a pattern which is frozen in a normal developmental pattern (Lenneberg, 1967). Jordan (1976) noted that a delay in beginning to talk is common in the mildly retarded, but a complete absence of speech (mutism) is rare. More information on language development and language problems can be found in Chapter XI.

Postsecondary Adjustment

Using indicators of job success and marital adjustment, the postsecondary adjustment of the EMR is mixed. While Kidd (1970) found that 86% of a group of mildly retarded former students were employed ful time, Dunn (1973) indicated that a trend was developing toward the availability of fewer of the unskilled and service jobs which were filled by the EMR in the past. The evidence is overwhelming that job success is related to *personality and social adaptation factors* rather than job competence (Huddle, 1967; McCarver and Craig, 1974). Work habits and getting along with fellow employees are critical areas for job success. Brolin, Durand, Kramer, and Muller (1975) found that EMR students who had a secondary program which followed a work/study orientation made a more successful postsecondary adjustment than did those who had received a school program emphasizing academics.

Marital adjustment is only slightly more of a problem for the mildly retarded than for the normal population (Smith, 1971). Marriage per se is not a problem, but rather the raising of children who might result from the union is. Issues related to birth control have been raised, and the arguments pro and con on the need for instruction in contraceptive measures have been advanced.

Personal/Social Skills

Many mentally retarded individuals have difficulty discriminating relevant social cues (Gardner, 1977). Mentally retarded persons have appropriate behaviors in their repertoires but fail to use them at appropriate times. They become assertive when they should be diplomatic; they are passive when they should be angry. Problems which arise could be related to the intensity, duration, or magnitude of their behavior. Moving rapidly from one class to another is rewarded, but running in the halls is not; blocking hard in football is appropriate, but fighting is not. Behaviors exhibited by poor models pose another problem for the retarded. Making the judgment of whether someone is a good or poor role model is difficult. They may attend to the behaviors of the "class clown" and "troublemaker" because of the intensity of such behavior or the kinds of consequences which result and thus attempt to imitate the behavior. The same individual will not always serve as the best role model in all situations.

The role of the teacher in the education program is to teach the student to attend to the relevant cues in a social situation and to act accordingly. It is also necessary to teach the student to observe the behavior of others and to identify the relevant circumstances surrounding the behavior. Training in social skills needs to be an integral part of the training program for the mentally handicapped. Such training takes place not only in the regular interaction within and outside the classroom but also through role playing and discussion of acceptable behavior in different social situations.

Recapitulation

The range of behavioral and learning characteristics discussed here can provide the basis for some of the decisions which a teacher must make in regard to educational programs for mildly retarded learners. Issues which arise that also may influence the programs provided for mildly retarded learners are integration into regular classes (mainstreaming), the permanency of mild mental retardation, and the responsibilities of the special education teacher.

Issues

Mainstreaming

MacMillan and Borthwick (1980) studied the extent to which the EMR population was being mainstreamed in California. Their findings were that the vast majority of EMR children were not integrated with nonhandicapped peers for any kind of instruction. When integration did occur, it was in subjects such as art, music, and vocational education. Of all fifty states, California had one of the lowest percentages of children classified as mentally retarded (.84%). This percentage included the profound, severe, and moderate ranges. Since there should be little state-to-state variability in prevalence rates of mental retardation within the more severe ranges of disability, the differences found among states should be attributable to the mild or EMR range. The differences among states ranged from an absolute low of .66% (retardation of all degrees) in Alaska to a high of 3.89% in Alabama. Several conclusions can be drawn from this data.

First, the definition of mental retardation is quite fluid and varies widely among states. Second, severity of retardation exhibited by students in EMR classes will vary widely between districts and states. In states with small overall percentages of mentally retarded youngsters, the degree of retardation should be greater than in states where the percentage is larger. Third, mainstreaming of EMR learners should be based upon student need and not sweeping generalizations that all EMR learners should be mainstreamed. All EMR youngsters are not alike in the degree of disability. Advocates for mainstreaming of EMR learners should take into account the overall percentage of mentally retarded individuals in a state. In general, the larger the percentage, the more able the population of EMR students and the greater the likelihood of successful mainstreaming. The major question is not "mainstreaming" versus "no mainstreaming" but rather in placement being made within an appropriate educational environment. "Paper programs" do not necessarily make for good instruction. Receiving teachers must be capable of competently carrying out the instruction. Placement of an EMR youngster in a regular fourth grade math class may be appropriate. Appropriate placement also carries with it the assurance that appropriate instruction will take place. Mainstreaming may work with Teacher B but not Teacher A. Not only the decision to place but also the decision of with whom the learner should be placed is of paramount importance.

Permanency of Condition

The extent to which the condition of mental retardation is curable is probably based more on the opinion of the professional being questioned rather than on the research that has been conducted. The follow-up research on persons who have been classified as educable mentally retarded reveals that after leaving school the traits most often associated with mentally retarded persons are not evident (MacMillan, 1977). By at least one standard then, many mildly mentally retarded persons could be "cured" simply by leaving school. The literature intimates that the condition of mild retardation is one which is school related. The President's Committee on Mental Retardation has written quite extensively on the "Six-Hour Retarded Child." Such a child is considered retarded only during the period of time during which he is in school. For the remaining eighteen hours of the day, the student is essentially unrecognizable as being retarded and, in fact, exhibits adaptive behaviors which indicate that the diagnosis of the condition of mental retardation is probably incorrect. Only about 15 to 25% of the cases of mental retardation have a known cause, and most of these youngsters are considered moderately, severely, or profoundly retarded. Most of the students who are classified as educable mentally retarded have no known etiology for the condition. Social class appears to be correlated with the incidence of mild retardation, but the causal link is not presently evident.

In the case of known etiologies there have been significant breakthroughs over the years. The use of diet to control phenylketonuria and other protein toxins has prevented mental retardation of many children. Surgical intervention to prevent retardation in the case of hydrocephaly is another case in point. In terms of educational interventions, the historic work of Skeels in the 1930s provides evidence that educational and environmental intervention could do much to minimize the effect of mental retardation. The lowest functioning orphans constituted the experimental group and a higher functioning group of orphans constituted the control group. The experimental group was placed in the care of middle-aged women in an institution for the retarded and then later placed out for adoption. The control group received the regular care of the orphanage staff. Thirty years later in a follow-up study of individuals who had been in the study, Skeels (1966) found:

1. All the adults from the experimental group were self-supporting.
2. Half of the control group were in institutions and only 15% were satisfactorily maintaining themselves in society.
3. The average grade level reached by subjects in the experimental group was twelfth with several going to college.

4. The average grade attained by the control group was third.
5. The cost to the state for the *control* group was 700 to 2,400% higher than it was for the experimental group.

One conclusion which can be drawn from all of this is that educational programs can make a difference. What the program is called is probably of less importance than what is actually done. The critical factor in the educational program of a mildly retarded learner is the teacher. It is the teacher who decides what a student will or will not be taught, when a student will be taught, how a student will be taught, and how it will be determined if a student has learned. In the authors' opinion, teachers have a great deal of responsibility regarding the success of educational programs for their students.

Responsibilities of the Teacher

The responsibilities of the special education teacher are considerably different from that of the teacher of nonhandicapped youngsters. Due to the nature of the behavioral and learning characteristics of handicapped youngsters, teachers of handicapped students must take a greater amount of responsibility for academic and social achievement or lack of it.

With nonhandicapped students, we expect a degree of self-initiative; we expect them to attend school regularly, arrive on time, be prepared for tests, complete assigned work in school and out (or at least attempt it), remain in their seats during class time, be attentive during class, volunteer answers to questions, and ask for help when it is needed. Handicapped learners often show deficits in each of these areas. The major question is whose responsibility is it to insure proper behavior in each of these areas? Teachers of nonhandicapped children will say that it is the *student's* responsibility for all or most of these behaviors. Special education teachers cannot transfer the responsibility for each of these behaviors to the student but must acknowledge that these are responsibilities of the *teacher*. By *definition*, handicapped students exhibit deficits in academic and social behaviors. The special education teacher's responsibility, therefore, is to teach appropriate academic and social behaviors.

We wish to stress this point because the perceived responsibilities of regular classroom teachers are different from special education teachers'. Those behaviors for which the *student* is responsible in the regular classroom are the responsibility of the *special education teacher* when displayed by exceptional students. A major responsibility of the special education teacher is to circumvent the deficits of the learner or to take these deficits into account when planning the academic program and instruction. Failure to do so places responsibility on the shoulders of the handicapped student. The student already has an inability to handle such responsibility and, therefore, we feel that the teacher must be the person who takes the initiative for insuring that an appropriate learning rate is established.

Remember this . . .

1. Testing and assessment are different processes.

2. The exceptional behavioral (noncognitive) characteristics of the mentally retarded may result in depressed scores on standardized tests, and nonstandard assessment procedures may enhance their performance.

3. The opposite of a right answer is not necessarily a wrong answer.

4. Students sometimes get correct answers for the wrong reasons.

5. You can predict how long it will take a student to learn a new task by using task analysis and graphing.

CHAPTER II

Assessment of the Mentally Retarded

This chapter will differentiate between the terms testing and assessment and describe some procedures a teacher can use to obtain maximum information from the assessment process so that the results will be readily interpretable for the design of an educational program. It will also highlight some problems which occur in testing situations. While most authorities identify five major purposes for testing (i.e., screening, classification, program planning, measurement of individual progress, and program evaluation) this chapter will focus only on the two aspects with which a classroom teacher will be most closely associated — program planning and measurement of individual progress.

The process of testing involves the administration of a task or series of tasks under predescribed conditions. Paraprofessionals can be taught to competently administer standardized or nonstandardized tests and to score them accurately in order to obtain quantitative information on a learner (e.g., 85% correct, 3.2 grade level equivalent, or 35th percentile rank). In contrast, assessment includes a larger process starting with the selection of the test or tests to be administered and culminating in an interpretation of the results. Testing is therefore only a small portion of the total process referred to as assessment. The assessment process involves the collection of both *quantitative* and *qualitative* information about the learner. Both are important and must be considered in the interpretation of results. Qualitative information may involve a professional's judgment regarding a learner's performance on a test. For example, the examiner may note hesitancy by the learner in making responses or an expressed desire to please the tester. Qualitative information could also involve an error analysis of student responses on a test (e.g., correct answers only on addition and subtraction problems or correct answers only on problems not requiring regrouping).

Qualitative judgments also include the hypothesized relationship between a learners prior opportunity to learn information or skills required on a test and their actual performance. For example, if being able to read is a necessary prerequisite to successful performance on a test, selection of that test is based upon the premise that the individual can indeed read. Qualitative judgments are a necessary part of the assessment process. If accurate, they can be invaluable. If biased or inaccurate, they can cause a major delay in programming or a waste of valuable time by programming for the wrong objectives or testing the wrong skills.

The Process of Assessment

Salvia and Ysseldyke (1981) cite three tenets to consider regarding the type of information to collect and the process to follow in making some decisions:
1. Information sources differ in specificity.
2. General information is collected more rapidly than specific information.
3. The amount of time available to assess any particular individual is limited and finite.

Making Decisions

Throughout this book we will refer to the critical variable of *time*. Tenet number three clearly reflects the need for teachers to limit the time spent in formal assessment and, conversely, increase the time in direct instruction. Given a finite amount of time, the teacher must select assessment procedures carefully and make judgments regarding the most salient areas to assess, and then determine which areas of performance need to be assessed in greater detail. The decision process begins with the accumulation and analysis of general information. This general information might be written reports from previous teachers, achievement test results, psychologist reports, or major concerns of parents. These pieces of information must then be organized. We have found it useful to make notes of major points found in these reports along with the dates and information sources in order to organize this information. Rereading these notes in chronological order helps to conceptualize the concerns of different individuals and the time periods during which problems were noted. By following this process, the teacher can see information gaps, contradicting information, and possible bias. If the available information is incomplete, out-of-date, of suspect validity, or generally sparse, the teacher must then do some additional assessment with an aim toward programming. At this point, some formal assessment by the teacher is probably needed.

Formal Assessment

The first step in the diagnostic assessment process depicted in Figure 2.1 is the administration of norm-referenced tests. In most cases this will be an achievement test which assesses a variety of areas, but in some cases it may be a scale of adaptive behavior or a norm-referenced test designed for a specific purpose, e.g., reading or math. A number of the more commonly used norm-referenced achievement and standardized diagnostic scales are listed and described in Figure 2.2.

Cautions Regarding the Use of Formal Tests

Norm-referenced tests do not generally provide information which would surprise a classroom teacher. In general, if the results of a formal test provide "surprises," the teacher might wish to more closely examine the items on the test or the manner in which it was administered. Norm-referenced tests do not provide *solutions* to a student's learning problem. In the hands of a competent examiner they provide some clues regarding the source of a problem. The solution however is clearly the domain of the classroom teacher and the strategies then used for instruction. Formal tests answer the questions "where does this student perform relative to a norm group?" and "which areas of achievement show the greatest degrees of deficit?" To learn more about the particular needs of a learner requires the use

Figure 2.1
Diagnostic Assessment Process

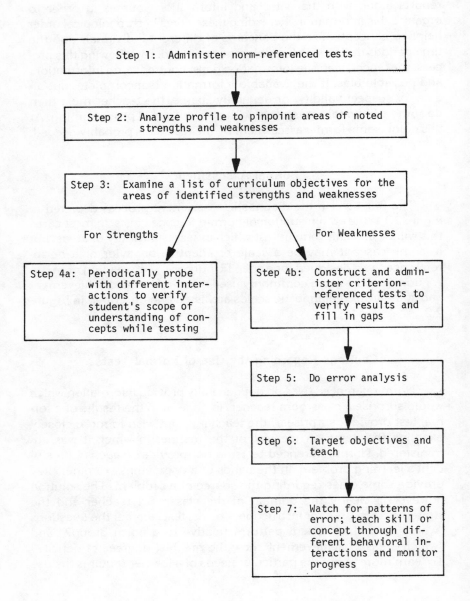

Figure 2.2

Test	Subtests	Brief Description	Age Range	Content and Scores
		Achievement Tests: Individual		
Wide Range Achievement Test (WRAT); 1978	1. Reading 2. Spelling 3. Arithmetic	The WRAT is a norm-referenced, pencil-and-paper test that assesses performance in the three listed subtest areas. The authors contend that the test is useful for diagnosis of disabilities of all ages in reading, spelling, and arithmetic as well as for comparison between school achievement and other individual abilities. Data on the normative sample is limited and reliability and validity measures are insufficient. The test was inadequately standardized so resulting scores should be analyzed with reserve.	Level one: under 12 yrs. Level two: over 12 yrs.	Three types of scores are obtained: a. grade ratings, b. percentile ranks, c. standard scores by age. A manual explaining theoretical constructs and approaches to testing is provided.
Peabody Individual Achievement Test (PIAT); 1970	1. Mathematics 2. Reading recognition 3. Reading comprehension	The PIAT is a norm-referenced test designed to provide a wide range screening measure over the five listed academic areas. The standardization of this test seems superior to	The test was standardized on grades K-12.	The test comes in two easel-kit volumes for easy administration. Age equivalents, grade equivalents, percentile

Figure 2.2 (Con't)

Test	Subtests	Brief Description	Age Range	Content and Scores
		Achievement Tests: Group		
	4. Spelling 5. General information	other individually administered achievement tests and reliability and validity measures are adequate for screening purposes. However, results should not be viewed in isolation for making important educational decisions and its validity should be assessed based on a teacher's own curricula.		ranks, and standard scores can be obtained for each subtest.

Keymath Diagnostic Arithmetic Test; 1971	1. Content
	  a. Numeration
	  b. Fractions
	  c. Geometry and symbols
	2. Operation
	  a. Addition
	  b. Subtraction
	  c. Multiplication
	  d. Division
	  e. Mental computation
		Keymath is an individually administered test designed to assess math skill development on three levels: content, operation, and application. Diagnostic information is obtained on four levels: total test performance, area performance, subtest performance, and item performance. The test can be used as either norm-referenced or criterion-referenced and can provide useful information for intervention and program planning.	K–8th grade	Stimulus materials and directions presented in an easel-kit. No formal training is necessary for administration. Scores can be interpreted for grade equivalent, relative strengths and weaknesses, subtest performance for deficiencies, and criterion-referenced performance.

Figure 2.2 (Con't)

Test	Subtests	Brief Description	Age Range	Content and Scores
		Achievement Tests: Group		

	f. Numerical reasoning
	3. Applications
	  a. Word problems
	  b. Missing elements
	  c. Money
	  d. Measurement
	  e. Time			

Woodcock Reading Mastery Test; 1973	1. Letter identification 2. Word identification 3. Word attack 4. Word comprehension 5. Passage comprehension	An individually administered battery to assess reading skills development uniquely providing a measure of reading proficiency at different levels of difficulty. The test can be used in a norm-referenced or criterion-referenced manner. The test is useful for providing strength and weakness data for remedial planning.	K-12	Complete test in easel-kit format. Two alternate short forms for quick administration are available. Raw scores can be converted to grade scores, age scores, percentile ranks, and standard scores for each subtest and a total score for all five subtests.

Figure 2.2 (Con't)

Test	Subtests	Brief Description	Age Range	Content and Scores
		Achievement Tests: Group		
Iowa Test of Basic Skills; 1978	1. Listening 2. Vocabulary 3. Word analysis 4. Reading comprehension 5. Language a. Spelling b. Capitalization c. Punctuation d. Usage 6. Work-study a. Visual materials b. Reference materials 7. Mathematics a. Concepts b. Problem solving c. Computation 8. Social studies 9. Science	A norm- and criterion-referenced test designed to provide broad general functioning assessment information. The test proposes multiple purposes including: 1) determination of student's developmental levels to assist in adapting instruction, 2) identifying strengths and weaknesses, 3) identifying readiness skills, 4) data for grouping students, 5) evaluating group performance, 6) evaluating individual progress. Reliability and validity data are limited.	K-9	Raw scores can be converted into national grade percentiles and stanines, standard scores, grade equivalents, age equivalents, normal curve equivalents, and special percentile ranks. Tests can be submitted to the publisher for printout analysis.

Figure 2.2 (Con't)

Test	Subtests	Brief Description	Age Range	Content and Scores
		Achievement Tests: Group		

SRA Achievement Series; 1978	1. Reading
	  a. Visual discrimination
	  b. Auditory discrimination
	  c. Letters and sounds
	  d. Listening comprehension
	  e. Vocabulary
	  f. Comprehension
	2. Mathematics
	  a. Concepts
	  b. Computation
	  c. Problem solving
	3. Language arts
	  a. Mechanics
	  b. Usage
	  c. Spelling
		A group-administered battery designed to assess academic skill development in basic curriculum areas on eight, nonoverlapping grade levels. The series is norm-referenced and has limited criterion-referenced value. The reliability measures are adequate for screening and group decision making.	K-12	Raw scores can be transformed into grade equivalents, stanines, national and local percentiles, and national percentile bands. Can also obtain normal curve equivalents; special percentiles for Title I, large cities, and non-public schools; growth-scale values, and percent and ratio of correct scores.

Figure 2.2 (Con't)

Test	Subtests	Brief Description	Age Range	Content and Scores
		Achievement Tests: Group		
	4. Reference materials 5. Social studies 6. Science			

Metropolitan Achievement Tests (MAT); 1978	1. Survey system
	  a. Reading comprehension
	  b. Mathematics
	  c. Language
	  d. Social studies
	  e. Science
	2. Instructional system
	  a. Reading
	  -visual discrimination
	  -letter recognition
		MAT is a two-component test that provides a survey test evaluating pupil skill development in academic content areas, yielding both norm- and criterion-referenced interpretation. The MAT survey test is used primarily for screening, monitoring group performance, and evaluating the overall program. The MAT instructional component provides useful information for instructional planning and curriculum evaluation. This component can also be interpreted in either norm- or criterion-referenced manner. Standardization, reliability, and validity are indicative of technical adequacy.	Survey: K-12
			
			Instructional: K.5 to 9.9
				Raw scores can be converted into six types of scores on the basis of subtests and components:
				1. scaled scores,
				2. percentile ranks,
				3. stanines,
				4. grade equivalents,
				5. normal curve equivalents,
				6. instructional reading levels.
				
				The scores can be obtained manually or by machine scoring.

Figure 2.2 (Con't)

Test	Subtests	Brief Description	Age Range	Content and Scores
		Achievement Tests: Group		
	-auditory discrimination -sight vocabulary -recognition of consonant and vowel sounds -vocabulary in context -word-part clues -rate of comprehension -skimming and scanning -reading			

Figure 2.2 (Con't)

Test	Subtests	Brief Description	Age Range	Content and Scores
		Achievement Tests: Group		
	comprehension			
	b. Mathematics			
	-numeration			
	-geometry and measurement			
	-problem solving			
	-whole-number operations			
	-law and properties operation			
	c. Language			
	-listening comprehension			
	-punctuation and capitalization			
	-usage			

Figure 2.2 (Con't)

Test	Subtests	Brief Description	Age Range	Content and Scores
		Achievement Tests: Group		
	-grammar -syntax -spelling -study skills			

Compiled by: Sheila Davis

of informal assessment strategies. Included in a teacher's bag of tricks for informal assessment are:

1. Nonstandard assessment strategies
2. Development of criterion-referenced tests
3. Error analysis
4. Task analysis

Informal Assessment

The process of informal evaluation is dynamic rather than static, involving the use of paper and pencil criterion-referenced tests, analysis of the student's errors, behavioral observations, checklists, and analysis of the student's responses to various instructional tasks. Informal assessment does not take place within a set period of time, but rather is a total part of the teaching process.

Assessment Rules

There are a number of rules which should be followed when undertaking an informal assessment. They are also valuable to consider when examining a student's performance on a norm-referenced test.

1. A wrong answer is not the direct opposite of a right answer. Students make errors for a variety of reasons and some wrong answers have a degree of "rightness."
2. Murphy's Law: "Anything that can go wrong will go wrong." Expect the unexpected from students in regard to the reasons given for their responses.
3. The answer given depends upon the question the student is answering and not necessarily the question the teacher asked. What a teacher perceives as errors could be the result of the pupil's differing interpretation of the question or problem (e.g., a student responds to one problem, $7 - 3 = \Box$ by saying "10." The teacher asked a subtraction question but the youth answered an addition question).
4. There is more than one way to make the same error. Two different students can arrive at the same answer by totally opposite procedures. They also can give totally different answers on a test but get the same percent of items correct.

5.   Students sometime get questions correct for the wrong reasons. Correct answers do not always guarantee understanding.

Nonstandard Assessment Strategies

One assumption which is generally made regarding a testing situation is that the assessment be made under optimally satisfactory conditions. What this generally means is that the examiner established rapport with the student, the testing was done in an area devoid of distractions, the administration procedures were followed, the test was properly scored, and the acculturation of the student was comparable to students on whom a test was normed. If you suspect that a student's score is unusually low it could be that one of the preceding conditions was violated. Factors such as race of the examiner, motivation of the learner, familiarity with testing situations, and language are also related to test performance.

Identified mentally retarded students generally do poorly on norm-referenced tests but not necessarily because of mental retardation. One of the characteristics of the retarded which has strong implications for assessment procedures has to do with their *expectancy for failure.* MacMillan and Keogh (1971) have written extensively about the "failure set" of the retarded. They approach new tasks or novel tasks with an expectancy for failure and quit easily. The fastest way for an individual to "escape" from a testing situation is to give all wrong answers or respond by saying "I don't know." A number of suggestions have been offered in the literature on nonstandard assessment procedures and there is some research to support their use, at least on a clinical level. Examples of nonstandard assessment strategies include:

1.   Token reinforcement for correct responses on a test
2.   Stating "correct" or "wrong" to learner after each item
3.   Elaboration by the examiner explaining after each item why it was correct or incorrect
4.   Prior training by the examiner to slow down the responding rate of the learner through modeling and verbal instruction
5.   Elaboration by the learner after each response to explain why that answer was given
6.   Rephrasing of instructions and substitution of formal vocabulary with informal vocabulary (dialect vs. standard English)

7.   Allowing a learner to respond in a different way from the
      manner required on the test
The use of these procedures invalidate the use of the conventional
norms, however, the research to date indicates significantly better per-
formances from handicapped, disadvantaged, and bilingual learners
than when administered under the standard conditions. We support
the use of nonstandard assessment procedures as an indicator of a
learner's optimal performance level.

Criterion-Referenced Tests

Criterion-referenced tests are commercially prepared or teacher-
prepared tests whose items are linked to behaviorally stated objectives. The purpose of these tests is to determine the extent to which
a learner has mastered the material and *not* to determine how one student has performed in comparison to another.
Teachers who wish to develop a criterion-referenced assessment
system should:
1.   Specify the goals of the program by curriculum area
2.   Delineate a sequence of subskills within each curriculum
      domain
3.   Delineate a sequence of objectives within each subskill area
      based on a developmental or behavioral analysis of the sub-
      skill (e.g., task analysis)
4.   Develop procedures such as a paper and pencil test, an
      observational checklist, or a rating/performance scale that
      adequately assess subskill objectives
5.   Cluster items on the test or scale that measure a common
      concept or objective to facilitate an error analysis of the
      learning performance
There should be a direct link between objectives and performance
items in the assessment.

Error Analysis

The teacher's ability to do an analysis of a student's errors and
to identify consistent patterns of errors is an extremely valuable dimension of the informal assessment process. While error analysis is not
the preferred means of assessment (since it allows a student to prac-

tice his errors), it is a common means of determining a persistent problem or skill deficit. Error analysis works particularly well in skill areas such as reading, spelling, math, and grammar.

To conduct an error analysis requires that the student perform the task. Preferably, this task results in a permanent product of his work so that an analysis can be made of the errors. The teacher examines the items on the test that are wrong and attempts to identify commonalities of the incorrect responses. Once some of these commonalities are identified, the teacher verifies the existence of the error pattern by requiring the student to take a test composed of a parallel set of items. If a similar error pattern exists, the teacher can then target the rule or skill that needs correction. Some examples of error patterns and alternative explanations for the errors are presented in Figures 2.3 and 2.4.

The process of error analysis, then, becomes an exercise in hypothesis testing. In some cases, it is valuable to have the student orally work through the problem or complete the assignment as he is writing it. In other cases, the teacher may wish to just observe the student and keep anecdotal records or ask the student to demonstrate his knowledge of the answer in a different way.

Figure 2.3
Sample Error Analysis in Arithmetic

46	32	38	49	50	43
+ 26	+ 46	+ 11	+ 12	+ 13	+ 27
612_x	78	49	511_x	63	610_x

Possible explanations: (1) Student adds from left to right.

(2) Student does not understand place value.

(3) Student does not regroup.

56	43	68	45	26	23
+ 14	+ 67	+ 27	+ 48	+ 19	+ 18
61_x	11_x	95	93	45	41

Figure 2.3 (Con't)

Possible explanations: (1) Student does not understand place value.

(2) Student does not understand zero as a place holder.

(3) Student does have a concept of zero and believes that it stands for nothing and therefore disregards it.

Figure 2.4
Sample Error Analysis of Written Expression

One day i seen a house that was on fire. The firetruck were (was) near when he ran into a tree. People they were running to see what happened. I ain't never seen anything like it. Today saw (was an) exciting day.

by billy

Analysis of Errors

Capitalization	Words
Beginning of sentences	Additions (they)
Proper nouns (Billy)	Double negative (ain't never)
Pronoun (I)	Substandard (ain't)
Verbs	Reversals (saw/was)
Tense (saw/seen; were/was)	Omissions (today was exciting day)
Pronouns	
Ambiguous antecedent (he, it)	

In order to minimize time spent in doing the error analysis, it is helpful for the teacher to construct the test or worksheet in a way that each group of items has a unique set of dimensions that differentiates one item from another. An example of this differentiation is shown in Figures 2.5 and 2.6. In these two examples, the items are differentiated by a single dimension.

Figure 2.5
Sample Math Test with Items Organized by Dimensions

Skill	Examples of Tasks				
Sum of two one-digit numbers < 10	4 + 5	4 + 2	3 + 1	5 + 3	6 + 2
Sum of three one-digit numbers < 10	4 2 + 1	3 3 + 3	2 4 + 1	1 3 + 1	1 2 + 4
Sum of two one-digit numbers < 10 horizontal format	4 + 2 = 5 + 3 =	6 + 2 = 5 + 4 =		2 + 1 =	
Sum of two one-digit numbers < 20	9 + 7	7 + 8	6 + 9	7 + 7	8 + 4
Sum of two two-digit numbers with regrouping	26 + 17	45 + 17	49 + 24	42 + 29	37 + 35

Figure 2.6
Sample Spelling Test with Items Organized by Dimensions

Skill	Example of Task				
	Direction: Teacher pronounces word and student writes and spells orally				
-at family	pat	mat	rat	fat	sat
-et family	pet	met	let	bet	set
-ing suffix with final consonant doubled	running	sitting	hitting	swimming	petting
-ing suffix with final consonant not doubled	kicking	fighting	jumping	writing	walking
final e silent: one-syllable word	bite	rate	late	pale	mute

In the error-analysis process, any aspect of the problem can create difficulty for the learner. The learner's error could be conceptual in nature, represent a skill deficit, or merely be the result of the presentation of the problem in an unfamiliar format. Format includes such aspects as a math problem being presented vertically rather than horizontally or written material being presented in cursive rather than manuscript form. Conceptual errors deal with the use of incorrect rules and are generally the result of incomplete concept formation resulting from poor instruction. For proper concept formation the teacher needs to provide examples of the rule or concept along with exceptions or negative instances of the concept. Skill deficits are usually easily recognized. Examples of skill deficits include nonmastery of basic math facts and nonmastery of basic vocabulary. For more information on error analysis there are several examples in Chapter XII.

Behavior Versus Content

Behavioral objectives are the foundation of criterion-referenced testing. Since behavioral objectives always specify both observable behavior (how the student is to respond) and the content (subject matter), a student's mastery or nonmastery of the objective can be assessed reliably. The problem encountered when directly applying the notion of behavioral objectives to mildly handicapped learners, and subsequently constructing criterion-referenced tests, is that *by definition* mildly handicapped learners have behavioral deficits. If a student fails the criterion-referenced assessment, the examiner (teacher) still does not know if the failure is attributable to a lack of knowledge of the subject matter or to the manner in which the objective was assessed. In order to solve this problem, content must be separated from behavior in the objective, and a range of behavioral response options for demonstrating mastery of the subject matter must be specified. Such a procedure is analogous to an error analysis on behavior.

An example of this problem might help to clarify the dilemma. Given the behavioral objective "from written directions the student will write in order the names of the last five presidents of the United States with 100 percent accuracy," the teacher may find that a handicapped student can fail this objective for a variety of reasons, none of which have to do with knowledge of the subject matter (history). For example, at least two nonhistory behaviors could interfere. The first behavior requires that the learner be able to read and interpret the printed word. The second requires that the learner be able to spell and write the names. A learner who is not competent in writing and/or spelling would not be able to successfully pass the objective even though the student might know the names of the last five presidents. A sensitivity on the part of the teacher is needed in order to discern whether the lack of mastery is attributable to a content or behavioral deficit.

The teacher who finds that the learner has failed certain items needs now to explore behavioral-response options in order to pinpoint the source of the difficulty. Several procedures can be undertaken at this point. The first is to consider the objective as a terminal objective that has subunits or subcomponents, commonly referred to as target objectives. The teacher can list the target objectives and assess the student's mastery of each. A second procedure would be to assess the student's knowledge by varying the behavioral demands. This second procedure would involve asking the student to tell you the names of the last five presidents, to spell aloud (or in written form) their names as they are dictated to her, or to name the presidents from pictures.

Task Analysis

Task analysis (TA) is a very useful technique to understand and use in the informal assessment process. It is defined as the process of identifying the sequential steps to be followed by the learner in the successful completion of a task. The process involves defining a skill or instructional objective, breaking that skill or objective into its component parts, and then sequencing these subtasks in a logical order.

Using task analysis in a classroom is a very efficient way to manage instruction. A variety of classroom activities can be task analyzed. Figure 2.7 lists some classroom activities and situations amenable to task analysis. Besides the obvious management advantages of TA's they are also helpful for evaluation, establishing a learner's level of functioning, reporting progress to parents, lesson planning, and for enhancing skill acquisition (Pancsofar, Bates, and Sedlak, 1982).

Figure 2.7
Task Analyzable Classroom Activities

1. Calculator usage
2. Math computation
3. Making change
4. Handwriting (letter formation)
5. Study skills procedures for math, spelling, social studies, etc.
6. Microcomputer operation
7. Speak and Spell® Operation
8. Cassette tape recorder operation
9. Classroom management procedures
10. Lesson preparation
11. Ruler usage
12. Firedrill procedures
13. Tornado drill procedures
14. First aid procedures
15. Opening ceremony
16. Dismissal or lunch practices
17. Map interpretation
18. Finding a book in library
19. Writing a check
20. Cooking a meal/snack
21. Comparison shopping
22. Writing a letter
23. Addressing an envelope
24. Reading a thermometer
25. Aide duties

EVALUATION. Having observable substeps allows the teacher to choose a measurement system that best represents the behavior.

Behaviors such as "picks up," "writes," and "points to" can be recorded by a frequency recording procedure (e.g., count the number of times the student performs the action). The use of words that are behavioral replaces terms that are not susceptible to precise measurement (e.g., "knows how," "appreciates"). The behavioral nature of each step directs the observer's attention to the actual nature of the task.

LEVEL OF FUNCTIONING. Pinpointing the exact steps that are interfering with a student's mastery of a skill is a valuable use of the task-analysis process. By identifying the exact nature of the deficiency, the teacher can either teach the subskill or use adaptive technology so that the goal can be achieved. Teaching the subskill is a matter of showing and telling the student the aspect of the task that he is not demonstrating. A deficit in one subskill may be inhibiting a learner's use of a skill that has as many as 15 or 20 subskills. Adaptive technology can be used whenever the teaching of the subtask is an unachievable goal in a reasonable period of time. The adaptive technology may be a calculator to solve word problems when the student can reason the problem through but is unable to consistently compute the answer mentally; it may involve using a tape-recorded copy of a history test for the student who cannot read the test, but knows the historical facts; or it may be an analog computer for the blind student who needs to measure chemicals in a science laboratory but cannot see the markers on the measurement beakers.

REPORTING PROGRESS TO PARENTS. Evaluative information about children should be in a positive form that is easily conveyed to professionals as well as parents. The use of a task analysis provides an optimistic goal-directed evaluation of a student's skills. Rather than saying that a learner cannot do long division problems, the teacher might say that the learner can consistently do 75% of the steps in the long division process correctly without help. The student still cannot do long division problems, but the statement reflects progress toward the goal. It also reflects a success-oriented sensitivity on the part of the teacher.

LESSON PLANNING. Once a student's baseline behavior is determined, the task analysis acts as a means of measuring progress or nonprogress toward the goal. Based upon the information obtained each day, the teacher can modify the lesson plan for the subsequent day's instruction. Trend lines can be used to predict where a student should be in a week using three or four days of data. For example, based upon the trend noted in the graph in Figure 2.8 the learner has been mastering about 1.5 new subskills each day (twelve skills in eight days) at the current rate of performance (assuming that all steps in the task analysis are equally difficult) the learner should master all the steps in the task analysis in about six more days of instruction.

Figure 2.8
Hypothetical Projection for Student Skill Acquisition Rate

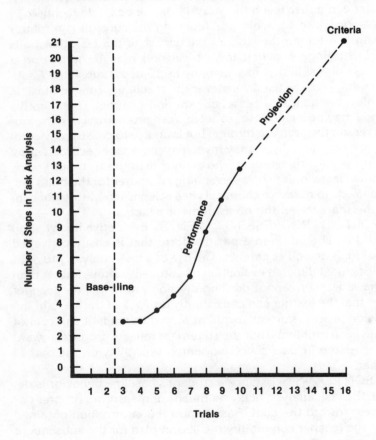

There will be day-to-day variation but overall the rate of learning is predictable. If the student does not meet the projection, a change in the teaching procedure may be in order or a more careful analysis of the steps in the task analysis needs to be made. Also, having done a task analysis, the teacher is aware of the critical steps needed by the student to perform a task correctly. As the student attempts to perform the required behavior, the teacher can interrupt incorrect actions (errors) so that the learner is only required to exhibit correct behaviors.

ENHANCING SKILL ACQUISITION. By breaking a task into its component parts, the achievement of the objective is made easier: "Life is hard by the yard, but a cinch by the inch." Accordingly, an objective may seem unobtainable by a learner who has repeatedly experienced failure, but given small, easily obtainable steps directed toward the goal, the learner may find the task considerably easier to attain. The steps in the task analysis are sequenced in the order they are to be executed. If a student fails to follow one of the steps, the teacher can immediately note the error and intervene to correct it. Analyzing a task into its component parts is a valuable skill that each teacher should possess. Such analysis helps the teacher pinpoint specific observable problems, which can be translated directly into behavioral objectives, and ultimately into a plan for remediation.

WRITING A TA. To write a task analysis the teacher should:
1. Do the task herself
2. Determine if there is more than one way to do a task or determine if there is a preferred way to do the task (i.e., ask experts to observe experts doing the task)
3. Write each step for the method selected
4. Have a second person read the task analysis and do the task according to what is written
5. Observe a person doing the task and follow along via the written task analysis
6. Revise steps as needed

USING A TA. To use a task analysis the teacher should:
1. Request that the student perform the task
2. Provide no hints or prompts
3. Check with a " + " or " – " each step performed correctly or incorrectly

4. Take several trials to establish a reliable measurement
5. Plan instruction based upon the student's performance
Figure 2.9 represents an example of a task analysis. Additional examples can be found in Chapter XII on Teaching Arithmetic and Problem Solving.

Figure 2.9
Task Analysis of Two-Digit Subtraction Problem
with Regrouping (Borrowing)

$$e.g. \quad \begin{array}{r} 52 \\ -\ 37 \\ \hline \end{array}$$

1. Subtracts from right to left.
2. Regroups (borrows) one group of 10 from 5.
3. Subtracts bottom number from top number in unit column.
4. Writes answer beneath line in units column.
5. Subtracts bottom number from top number in tens column.
6. Writes answer beneath line in tens column.

Graphing Behavior

A common method for summarizing data is graphing. We have already shown one advantage of using graphs, which is to project when a student should master a skill. Objectives that have been task analyzed provide data on student progress that can be easily graphed. In addition, information such as the number of problems worked, the percentage of words spelled correctly, or the number of words read per minute can be displayed on a graph.

Visually depicting information on a graph allows the teacher to quickly determine if a behavior is increasing, decreasing, or remaining constant. Figure 2.10 depicts three graphs which clearly illustrate this point. While graphing is generally not a complicated process there are some basic rules which should be followed in creating a graph.

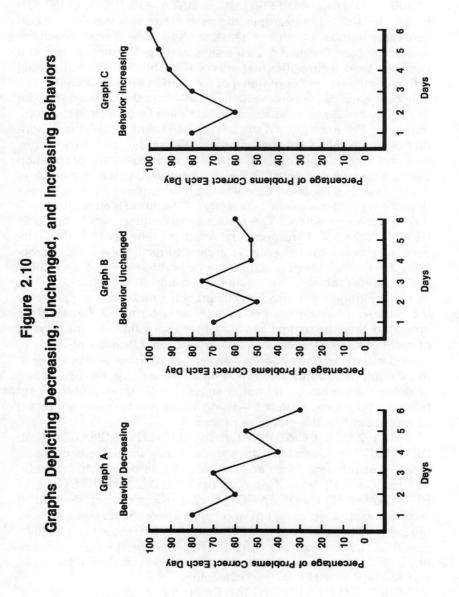

Figure 2.10

Graphs Depicting Decreasing, Unchanged, and Increasing Behaviors

RULE 1. ALL PERFORMANCE DATA ARE IN A COMMON BASE OR UNIT. For example, the percentage of words spelled correctly, the number of steps in a task analysis done correctly, and the number of states named are all examples of performance data in a common base. It simplifies matters considerably if tests are prepared with a common number of items or a common time limit so that the data base each day is consistent. In cases where the base differs from day to day or session to session, the data must be converted to a common base. For example, if a student is given twenty problems to work on Monday, eight on Tuesday, twelve on Wednesday, and ten on Thursday, and each day he solves five problems correctly, the information cannot be graphed before the data are converted to a common base. In this case, the common base would be determined by dividing the number of problems worked correctly by the number attempted each day to get a percentage. The resultant percentages would be 25%, 62%, 41%, and 50%, respectively. Another example of this data conversion process is the following: A student correctly solved fifteen problems in a five-minute period; twenty-one problems in a seven-minute period; thirty problems in a ten-minute period; and forty-five problems in a fifteen-minute period. Correctly graphing these data requires that the number of problems per minute be determined, because the amount of time the student had available to her influenced the number of problems she did each session—which could lead the observer to conclude that her performance was increasing. However, by converting the information to a common base, we see that her actual rate of doing the problems did not change; she did three problems per minute. Understanding Rule 1—using a common base—is important to understanding the graphing process.

RULE 2. THE HORIZONTAL AXIS SHOULD DESIGNATE A TIME DIMENSION (e.g., sessions, days, trials). There should be equal spacing between the markings and the axis should be clearly labeled.

RULE 3. THE VERTICAL AXIS SHOULD DESIGNATE STUDENT PERFORMANCE INFORMATION (e.g., percent correct, number of steps completed, words typed per minute). There should be equal spacing between the markings and the measure represented in equal units (e.g., 10, 20, 30, 40 *not* 10, 30, 35, 50, 60). The lowest level of performance, "0," should *not* meet the horizontal line but should be raised just above it to make for easier reading.

RULE 4. PUT THE STUDENT'S NAME AND CLASS ON THE

GRAPH AND TITLE IT SUITABLY. A graph should convey information efficiently. There should be little if any need for written text to accompany it as an explanation.

RULE 5. LABEL THE BASELINE AND TRAINING PHASES AND SEPARATE EACH WITH A DOTTED VERTICAL (PHASE) LINE. The convention of using a broken vertical line to separate phases quickly transmits to the reader the student's performance level before intervention and immediately after intervention. The phase line should be *between* the markings on the horizontal axis. Figure 2.11 shows a graph with all components done correctly.

Figure 2.11
Sample Graph

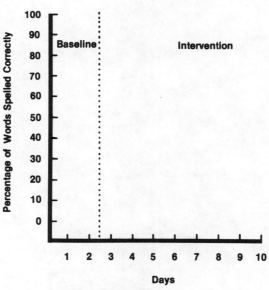

Summary

This chapter focuses on the process of informal assessment with emphasis on Murphy's Law which states, "Anything that can go wrong will go wrong." It happens that one of the challenges of education is the attempt to discern exactly what is going wrong for an individual student. Education of EMH students will consider all of the following in the informal assessment process: criterion-referenced tests, error analysis, analysis of behavior versus content, task analysis, and graphing. The end result should be an on-going assessment process which leads directly to more learning for each student.

Remember this . . .

1. Telling a student what he is expected to achieve will facilitate the acquisition of that skill.

2. You need approximately 50% as much practice or study time after you master some material as it took you to reach mastery in order to remember the material.

3. Several short practice sessions will help students remember material better than one long practice session.

4. Mnemonics and other mediational strategies will help students remember what was taught.

5. Organizing material in small steps in a sequential order from easy to difficult will increase the efficiency of teaching.

6. Some things that pass for teaching in a classroom really do not affect student achievement or behavior change.

CHAPTER III

Principles of Instruction

Strategies for delivering instruction are the educator's basic tools. As the experienced cook will have favorite pans and measuring cups and know when to add "a pinch of that," so will the classroom teacher learn to take the basic instructional strategies and blend them to create a learning environment. This section is intended to lay the groundwork for teachers wishing to be "chefs." Principles of instruction will be discussed and then an explanation of learning versus achievement will be offered. Finally, instructional strategies will be described under three basic elements of learning: acquisition, retention, and transfer.

The best way to enhance the social and academic performance levels of educable mentally retarded learners is by *teaching* them. Such advice to the novice teacher would seem to be neither necessary nor helpful, but a great many things can and do take place in a classroom. There are some activities which on the surface pass for teaching, but in reality fail to demonstrate learning or achievement. A teacher who has said that in the classroom each student works at his own level, independently, and progresses at his own rate would sound admirable and appear to satisfy the requirements of individualized instruction. A critical question, however, is "what is the teacher doing while the students are progressing at their own rate?" The following is a list of things that the teacher should be doing during that time:

1. Moving from student to student quickly, spot checking their work, and giving encouragement
2. When locating a student with a "problem," send the student to the chalkboard to begin working the problem. Provide instruction and correction.
3. Be sure to see the work of as many students each day as possible. To insure that this happens, do not sit at each stu-

dent's desk but walk briskly from student to student, stoop or stand, check work, and proceed to the next student.

4. Start "rounds" with the student left off from the previous day.
5. Before the next day, check work of all students not seen.
6. Look for error patterns in student work even if only one or two items are incorrect. What made those problems different from the next? If you suspect an error pattern, create a parallel problem and have the student work it immediately.
7. Work with the student or small groups who are having some problems for a portion of the period.
8. If you have an aide, be sure that the aide is checking students' work at their desks during this time. (Read the section in Chapter IV on aide usage.)
9. Periodically survey class to see if all students are working.

The authors have observed teachers in action where very few of these things were taking place. What did they do wrong? Here is a partial list:

1. Failed to see more than 10% of the class's work
2. *Sat* by each student's desk
3. Failed to correct student's work for over a week
4. Started each day's round with the same student
5. Failed to survey classroom and had five students doing no work
6. Failed to monitor the activities of the aide who decided to cut out letters for a bulletin board
7. Failed to respond to raised hands

A teacher whose class is characterized by these preceding seven statements did very little teaching and also violated all of the tenets of the "individualized instruction" program which supposedly was being followed. We mention the preceding points so that you have some ideas regarding how you should structure your use of time if you do run a "self-paced" curriculum in some subject areas. Instructional materials are not the key to achievement and learning, but rather the behavior of the teacher. Materials do not teach, only teachers do.

Learning Versus Achievement

When the terms "learning" or "achievement" are used as *nouns*, most individuals would find little difference in their meanings, but when the terms or their derivations are used as *verbs* there is a significant difference in how the words are interpreted. Teachers need to be concerned with "learning" as a verb and not solely as another word for achievement. According to Carroll (1963), learning involves a decrease in the number of trials (or amount of time) needed to acquire new information. It is a measure of rate. Achievement is a measure of mastery of a particular task or skills. In the interests of making efficient use of time, previously mastered skills need to be the building blocks for new skills. It is not enough to increase the achievement levels of learners but to structure the environment and the task such that a student "learns how to learn." There are a variety of strategies which a teacher can use to decrease the amount of time which it takes a student to learn a new skill. Much of this has to do with the scope and sequencing of skills or materials to be taught. In the educational psychology literature these would be listed as strategies dealing with *transfer*.

Instruction needs to stress when stimuli in the old and new tasks are similar and also the similarity of the responses. It also needs to address the similarity of tasks within a new set.

Examine the two arrangements of the list words in Figure 3.1. Which arrangement do you believe a student would learn to spell faster? Remember, both lists cover the same words but the *arrange-*

Figure 3.1
Sample Word Lists Organized Systematically or Randomly

ARRANGEMENT A

Week 1		Week 2		Week 3		Week 4	
went	lent	drink	bed	sing	fling	bend	band
sent	tent	sink	fed	wing	king	send	sand
bent	vent	mink	led	thing	sting	lend	land
dent		link		ring		mend	

ARRANGEMENT B

Week 1		Week 2		Week 3		Week 4	
went	fed	sent	led	bent	sing	dent	wing
lent	thing	tent	ring	vent	fling	link	king
drink	sting	sink	bend	mink	send	bed	lend
mend		band		sand		land	

ment of the words differ. We believe that list A probably would be learned faster because the words have been *grouped* according to one or two common variables. In list B the arrangement of the words is random with little similarity between words which are to be learned in the same week. Not only should the arrangement of material for a given lesson be organized according to some relevant dimensions, but the arrangement of lessons should be organized to capitalize on between lesson transfer. Teaching root words one week followed in subsequent weeks with suffixes or prefixes (e.g., -ed, -ing, -s, -es) which build on these root words would once again decrease instructional time and maximize the transfer of previously learned material to the acquisition of new material.

Instructional Strategies

The term "instructional strategies" is a term which encompasses a variety of methods, materials, and/or procedures which a teacher may use to help a student achieve an instructional objective. Many of these strategies grew out of research on the application of learning principles to functional academic subjects. In the planning and delivery of instruction, the teacher needs to consider many of these principles and, depending upon the responses from the learner, "shift" from the use of one strategy to another. All strategies do not work equally well with all learners but the teacher must analyze the responses of the learner and determine if the strategy is effective or if some aspect needs to be changed.

There are three elements of learning with which a teacher needs to be concerned: acquisition, retention, and transfer. Each of these are important in the teaching-learning process and there are specific strategies which a teacher can use to enhance each.

Acquisition

Acquisition refers to the learning of a new skill, concept, or body of information. There are two critical tasks which a teacher must adhere to when teaching for acquisition. The first is the presentation of the information to the learner, and the second is providing the learner with practice sessions to initially learn the material.

Retention

Special education teachers need to be concerned with not only the initial acquisition of a skill or concept but also the retention of it over time. The words that the student spelled correctly on Friday's test need to be remembered into adulthood. The extent to which this occurs is the basis for determining how well we have structured the instructional situation to facilitate retention. We all forget. The role of the teacher in retention is to slow down the rate of "forgetting" and to keep it at a level where a brief review will bring a learner back up to criterion level. There are a variety of strategies which a teacher can follow in structuring the environment and lessons which will enhance retention. Several of these will be discussed in this chapter.

Transfer

When information or skills which have been learned influence the acquisition of new skills or concepts which are closely related to the previously learned material, the process is referred to as *positive transfer*. If the previously learned material interferes with the acquisition of new material it is referred to as *negative transfer*. Special education teachers need to be aware of factors which influence transfer because these affect the manner in which the teacher will organize the scope and sequence of lessons and objectives as well as particular teaching strategies. The use of transfer strategies will also increase the rate at which new concepts and skills can be learned.

Strategies for Acquisition

INSTRUCTIONS. An efficient means for developing a new skill is through the use of *verbal instructions, pictures, reading,* or *demonstrations* (modeling). By no means are these procedures necessarily used in isolation from each other except in basic research studies. There are two propositions associated with these procedures which the teacher should follow. These are:
1. Getting the student's attention
2. Telling or showing the student the objective of the lesson (i.e., what the student will be expected to do at the end)

ATTENTION. There are a variety of things which a teacher can do to secure and maintain attention of students. For one, the teacher can use students' names (e.g., Bill, Tom, Mary, today we are going to . . .) *before* giving instructions. A second strategy is to *maintain eye contact* with students during a lesson and to stop the lesson if student's attention seems to wander. A third strategy is *interspersing questions* and asking students to respond throughout the lesson. A fourth strategy is teaching in *close proximity* to the students rather than at a distance. Being in close proximity can also help in the maintenance of control within the room. Recognition of which students are not attending is easier, and bringing learners back into the lesson without disrupting the flow is simpler.

REVELATION OF OBJECTIVES. Behavioral objectives are written for the purpose of determining precisely what we want a learner to demonstrate at the conclusion of a lesson or series of lessons. Popham (1971) has indicated that telling a student what he is expected to perform before teaching the lesson enhances his acquisition of the skill. If we tell a student that we want him to be able to correctly spell a specific set of twenty words or to learn the states and their capitals, we increase the probability that the student will demonstrate mastery of each objective. Students should not be kept in the dark regarding what the expectations or objectives are for a particular subject. Knowing the objectives enables them to better focus their attention on the relevant dimensions of the task. This phenomenon was made quite clear to the authors one day when their seven-year old son brought home his first spelling test with over half of the words marked wrong. He explained to us that he had done all the activities in the book and had written each word ten times just as the teacher instructed him. He didn't realize that he was supposed to memorize how to spell the words. The problem was readily rectified when we explained that doing those other activities was *supposed* to help him remember how to spell the words but if they didn't work very well that he should practice spelling the words aloud and try to write each from memory and then checking to see if he was correct. There are two lessons which can be learned from this example. The first is that the teacher needs to tell the student what they are expected to do. The second is that the teacher needs to develop practice activities which have a *direct* relationship to the expected outcome. This second point will be discussed more fully under the section on *appropriate practice*.

PRACTICE. Another factor which influences acquisition of skills and concepts is *practice*. Questions which must be answered by the teacher involving practice include:

1. How often to practice
2. How much practice
3. What kind of practice should take place

Should a student practice or study intensely for a prolonged but concentrated period of time or should the practice be in short time segments over an extended period of time? The best "rule of thumb" that the research can offer us on this question is that short practice sessions which are distributed over time in general are superior to intensive periods of practice (McGeoch and Irion, 1952). The exception to this statement is in specific trial-and-error learning and problem-solving situations. Some factors which the teacher should consider when determining the length of a practice session are:

1. Is it a skill that needs a *warm-up*?
2. Does student interest or attention wane quickly?
3. Does the task create fatigue?

The teacher should examine the characteristics of the task to be learned and the *characteristics* of the student to determine optimal lengths of practice time and the distribution of each practice. Use of other strategies such as reinforcement, feedback, peer tutoring, and use of audiovisual aids may also influence the scheduled length of time for practice.

The development of many skills requires repeated practice in order to achieve mastery. Educable mentally retarded students generally need more practice time to reach mastery on a task than nonretarded youngsters. Students will generally show an initial spurt in performance in the early practice trials followed by a period of nongrowth and then another period of improvement up to the criterion level. The teacher needs to schedule time and activities which focus on the practice needed to master specific skills. A note of caution regarding practice needs to be mentioned. The repetitive use of the same materials used in the same way each day becomes boring not only for the student but the teacher as well. Materials and activities need to be varied for practice sessions while still maintaining a reasonable level of interest.

Basic skills which require repeated practice include spelling, math facts (addition, subtraction, division, and multiplication), fraction/decimal equivalencies, sight words, abbreviations, and states and their capitals. There are many others. To take the boredom out of the practice, teachers should organize games and activities which are aimed *initially at accuracy* such as untimed worksheets, self-correctional materials, untimed flash cards with recording of performance (percent correct), and/or peer practice. After students have demonstrated a consistent and high level of accuracy, games and activities which focus on *speed* should be used for practice. One or two minute time test sheets, student races, and beat-the-clock games are activities which can be used to develop speed. Remember, first develop accuracy and then focus on speed.

We have already established that practice is an important component of skill acquisition but the type of practice and the appropriateness of the practice are two final factors which must be considered by the teacher. Should the practice be done orally, in cursive writing, in manuscript writing, by typing, or by selecting the correct answer? Should the material be practiced with the correct response in view or from memory? Part of the answer can be secured by reviewing the nature of the objective. If the objective is, "Given twenty spelling words orally by the teacher, the student will write in cursive and from memory the correct spelling of these words with 100% accuracy," the series of activities which should be undertaken to meet that objective should be obvious. Related activities such as putting the twenty words into alphabetical order, writing a sentence with each word, drawing a picture with each word, or finding the correctly spelled word from among four closely related misspellings, while worthwhile and valuable activities, probably would contribute little to the fulfillment of this specific objective (they may be contributing to the fulfillment of other objectives, however, which unfortunately are neither stated nor evaluated). You should devise practice activities which closely approximate the manner in which the performance variable will be measured.

Much of what passes for practice in the schools is busy work, designed for the purpose of keeping students quiet and out of trouble rather than being planned activities designed for the acquisition of specific skills. On the other hand, appropriate practice focuses on the development and acquisition of specific skills. Such practice enhances the learning process.

ORGANIZATION OF LESSONS/MATERIALS. The manner in which the material is organized influences how quickly or easily new skills or information will be acquired. Factors related to the organization of lessons or materials include the following:

1. Sequencing of objectives and information
2. Size of teaching steps

3. Principle of minimal change and dimension control
4. Use of advanced organizers and related strategies

SEQUENCING OF OBJECTIVES AND INFORMATION. In general, information or skills which are taught in a logical order are acquired more easily than information or skills which are taught in a random order. The basis of programmed instruction is founded upon a logical ordering of information for presentation. The concepts and procedures of task analysis also apply here. Objectives, information, or skills should be divided into the smallest component parts and ordered logically, empirically, or developmentally. The research on programmed instruction with the mentally retarded supports the principle of sequencing of objectives and information.

SIZE OF TEACHING STEPS. Related to the sequencing of objectives or materials is the question of how much material should be taught at any one time. The general rule of thumb is that teaching in very small steps is most effective. Depending upon the learner characteristics, however, larger teaching steps can be accommodated without a significant loss in achievement (Cartwright, 1962). Blake (1975) found that as material is added, the task gets proportionately harder. In most instances the teacher controls the amount of material presented at a given time. Some authors (Faas, 1980) write of "information overload" in regard to the presentation of too much information which interferes with skill acquisition. In order to determine the optimal size of the teaching steps the teacher will probably need to follow a trial-and-error process and monitor student performance. When in doubt, think small.

MINIMAL CHANGE AND DIMENSION CONTROL. Retarded children learn best when the changes between different steps of a program are small and similarly related. Learning to read the words "mat," "rat," and "sat" should be easier after learning to read the words "map," "rap," and "sap." The principle of minimal change and dimension control requires that new material be related to previously learned material. Dimension control, which was covered in some detail in Chapter II, requires that the order of material be organized such that each segment can be explicitly differentiated and that the teacher is aware of the differentiation of each segment. One example of the use of dimension control is given by Blake (1974) for teaching lower case manuscript letter formation. In her grouping the letters of the alphabet were divided into eight categories based upon their formation.

ADVANCED ORGANIZERS AND RELATED STRATEGIES. Ausubel (1978) proposed the use of an advanced organizer which is used in written material to provide structure for the reader to comprehend the material which will follow. Ausubel's use of the term "advanced organizer" is very explicit and narrowly defined. Some authors (e.g., Wehman and McLaughlin, 1981) have extended the meaning of the advanced organizer concept to include overviews, preview outlines, introductory statements, and teaching rules. The basis of their use is to relate previously learned material (i.e., information in a student's cognitive structure) to new information which will be presented.

TEACHING STRATEGIES. Rounding out our list of instructional strategies are seven strategies which a teacher can use to enhance the acquisition of skills. Among these are:

1. Levels of questions
2. Knowledge of results
3. Cuing, cluing, prompts
4. Manipulatives and/or worksheets
5. Reinforcement
6. Positive and negative instances
7. Mnemonics

QUESTIONING. Bloom's taxonomy of educational objectives lists six levels of questions (knowledge, comprehension, application, analysis, synthesis, evaluation) which can be assessed in regard to cognitive objectives. Research has demonstrated that students learn to respond to higher levels of questions if they have had the opportunity. The levels of questions which a teacher uses will limit or greatly enhance the learning opportunities of the students being taught. Some characteristics of the mentally retarded are a reflection of their education rather than being a function of their retardation. Once in a general methods class in special education, the course instructor asked the students to read a story found in a fourth-grade basal reading book. He then asked the students to write questions about the story which they might ask a mentally retarded student, a normal student, and a gifted student. The questions written by the students fell neatly into Bloom's six levels with the questions for the mentally retarded student being categorized at the two lowest levels, the normal student being asked questions ranging from Level 1 to Level 4, and the gifted students being asked questions only in Levels 4 to 6. The sad part of the exercise is that these future teachers would have restricted the learning opportunities for the mentally retarded students in terms of the level of questions they would have asked. Mentally retarded students do not generally learn what we haven't taught them.

Questions comprise a high percentage of most teachers' instruction (Hunkins, 1967). Studies of teachers' questioning behavior have revealed the following:

1. Ten primary grade teachers asked an *average* of 348 questions each during a school day (Floyd, 1960).
2. Fourteen fifth-grade teachers asked an average of sixty-four questions each in a thirty minute social studies lesson (Schreiber, 1967).
3. Twelve elementary school teachers asked an average of 180 questions each in a science lesson (Moyer, 1966).
4. Pupils in classrooms where high level questions are used by the teacher are more likely to employ such questions themselves when they engage in class discussions and class work (Hunkins, 1967).
5. Higher level questions stimulate higher levels of achievement (Hunkins, 1967).
6. Teachers who are considered "effective" normally ask recall or factual questions 40 to 60% of the time, questions which are analytical or of higher order 20 to 30% of the time, and procedural questions about 20% of the time (Floyd, 1960; Guszak, 1967; Schreiber, 1967).

The conclusion one can reach from this research is that students benefit from the frequency and incisiveness of good questioning. Therefore, teachers need to practice asking good questions and to question students often. Points to consider when questioning include all of the following:

What to avoid in questioning

1. Yes/no questions
2. Ambiguous questions
3. Spoon-feeding questions (too obvious)
4. Questions which are confusing because they contain too many factors to deal with at once

Approaches to use when questioning

1. Vary the use of narrow and broad questions
2. Pause to give students time to think
3. Ask questions that can be directed to more than one person
4. Distribute questions equally among class members

Characteristics of good questions
1. Make them clear
2. Use sensible word order and phrasing
3. Use correct grammar
4. Relate to student experience
5. Relate to instructional goals
6. Allow for reflection and critical thinking
7. Include stable guidelines for responses
8. Provide students with new ways of dealing with important areas

Remember who, what, where, which, and when are key words.
Divergent Questioning Model
1. Quantity: How many ways, how many ideas?
2. Viewpoint or involvement: What would this look like to a person ten feet tall?
3. Conscious self-deceit: How would you solve this if you had all the money in the world?
4. Forced association: How is a tiger like a basketball?
5. Reorganization: What kind of pet would you have if you were three inches tall?

KNOWLEDGE OF RESULTS . Feedback can take many forms. The teacher can place a gold star on a paper, circle or "X" incorrect responses, indicate the percent correct, write comments on papers, ask the student to talk with the teacher, or any one of a hundred other responses. Research has demonstrated that feedback in the form of knowledge of results is important in the acquisition phase of instruction. The form which this feedback takes and the immediacy with which it is delivered are also important. Page (1968) found that written comments and a grade on student's work corresponded to a subsequent improvement in their written work as compared to a grade alone. Feedback should give students information about what they have mastered, what they are doing wrong, and how they can correct their errors. Another principle of using feedback is to provide it as soon as possible after a student has completed a task. When students have done written work, that work should be checked as soon as possible. The teacher needs to also be sure that the student has reviewed the feedback given by the teacher and corrected the errors. If papers are corrected but the student does not review the feedback, the instructional importance of feedback would be lost.

CUES, CLUES, AND PROMPTS . Closely related to feedback and knowledge of results are the devices a teacher uses with students to identify, correct, or prevent their own errors. These aids include verbal instructions, or reminders like "remember to dot your 'i's' and cross your 't's'," "there is one wrong in that first row, see if you can find it," or a demonstration by a teacher (modeling) of how to do a particular exercise or skill. Cues and prompts are generally used to minimize the probability that the learner will make an error. They set the conditions for a successful experience for the learner and prevent errors. Some teachers have students use graph paper to keep numbers in computational problems properly aligned so as not to make errors in computation. In teaching handwriting, teachers can place a dot at a certain position on the line as a reminder to the student on where the letter formation should start. Teachers can color code with highlighter root words or suffixes in new spelling words to call attention to these dimensions of the task for the learner. Physically guiding a student through a task is another form of prompting. Physical guidance involves the actual act of manipulating the learners' hands in the completion of a task. Sometimes this is referred to as "hand-over-hand" instruction. Each of these examples demonstrates how cues or prompts are used to make a task easier for a learner. Cues are used primarily to encourage success.

Once success has been demonstrated with these aids, the teacher must then begin *fading* their use. Failure to fade leads to dependence on the cue in order to perform the task correctly. Trial and error is the recommended procedure for determining when to fade a prompt. The teacher needs to closely monitor student performance while fading a prompt and to maintain a consistent schedule of reinforcement during this period.

REINFORCEMENT. Positive reinforcement of academic and social behavior is a critical element in the instructional process. In order to be effective, the delivery of the reward must

1. Be immediate
2. Be perceived by the learner as being related to a particular behavior

Teachers need to identify the reward preferences of different learners. Knowledge of results may or may not be reinforcing for a learner. Generally for the mentally retarded learner, tangible and social rewards are more reinforcing than the satisfaction of completing a task correctly. The events and conditions which learners find reinforcing are a function of their personal/social histories. Chapter IV explains more about the procedures to follow for determining reward preferences.

POSITIVE AND NEGATIVE EXAMPLES. The development of concept learning is particularly enhanced by the use of positive and negative examples. Instruction identifies for the learner not only many examples of a concept but also contrasts this with examples of related concepts and points out the differences. For example, if the teacher wanted a student to identify "nouns," she would define that a noun was the name of a person, place, or thing and then cite examples of nouns. She would make a similar list of non-nouns (e.g., action words, function words, adjectives). Figure 3.2 presents some positive and negative instances of concepts. It is important to make these contrasts; otherwise, a student could generate a rule based upon only an incomplete understanding of the concept. The teacher should verbalize to the student "This is a _____, this is not a _____." The teacher would then point out the distinctive features of the examples of the concept that differentiate it from non-examples. In using these positive and negative instances, it is important to give a wide variety of examples.

MNEMONICS. The word *mnemonic* means "aiding the memory." A mnemonic technique therefore is a procedure which aids the learner in remembering specific events, words, or facts, which will need to be retrieved at a future time. There are a variety of mnemonic techniques which are in use. The use of stories, rhymes, acronyms, verbal mediators, and visual imagery are all strategies used in mnemonics. A basic rule is: "You can remember any new piece of information if it is associated to something you already know or remember." Small aids like these enable a student to remember facts more easily. You the teacher need to help the learner build these links or associations. Some examples of task-specific mnemonics are presented in Figure 3.3.

The keyword method (Atkinson, 1975) is a mnemonic strategy which has been used in teaching elementary school children to remember the states and their capitals (Levin, Shriberg, Miller, McCormick, and Levin, 1980) and word meanings (Levin, McCormick, Miller, Berry, and Pressley, 1982).

To use the keyword method to remember states and their capitals there are three steps to follow:

1.   The learner should form a stable association between the name of the state and a keyword for that state.

Figure 3.2
Positive and Negative Instances of Concepts

Concept	Positive	Negative
3		
Rectangle		
Noun	tree dog house man park city	the could big a and
Hot	fire boiling water sun coffee pot toaster oven	ice cube freezer snow moon drinking water rain

Figure 3.3
Examples of Mnemonics

Topic	Mnemonic
A. Social Studies:	
Huron, Ontario, Michigan, Erie, and Superior	HOMES
B. Spelling:	
principle and principal	The school princi*pal* is your *pal*.
piece	A *pie*ce of *pie*.
arithmetic	*A rat in* Tom's *house may eat* Tom's *ice* cream.
C. Music:	
Lines on the music staff, the treble clef:	
EGBDF	*Every good boy does fine.*
Spaces on the music staff, the treble clef	FACE
D. Math:	
1. Name of the top and bottom numbers in a fraction	*denominator—down* Little numbers eat big numbers.
2. Meaning of the symbols < and >	The symbol < is an open mouth; anything to the narrow end is smaller than at the wide or open end.
3. Rule of 9	Any number from 1 to 9 added to 9 will be less than the number itself in the one's place (e.g., 9 + 7 = 16; one less than seven is six, the sum is *six*teen).
E. Science:	
Colors of the rainbow or a prism: red, orange, yellow, green, blue, indigo, violet	ROY G. BIV
F. Time:	
1. To remember which way to turn the clock when changing from Standard	When going anywhere you "spring forward" and "fall backward." Set the clock an hour "for-

Figure 3.3 (Con't)

Topic	Mnemonic
time to Daylight time and vice versa	ward" in the spring and an hour "back" in the fall.
2. Number of days in the months of the year	*Rhyme*: 30 days hath September, April, June, and November; all the rest have 31 except February with 29 when leap year comes.
	Knuckles: Starting on your left hand from left to right say the months of the year. January is a knuckle, February is in a hollow, March is on a knuckle, April is in a hollow, May is a knuckle, June is a hollow, July is a knuckle. On the right hand continue: August is a knuckle, September is a hollow, October is a knuckle, November is a hollow, December is a knuckle. All the knuckle months have 31 days.
G. Functional:	
"Port" means left" while "starboard" signifies "right." A red light is on the port side and a green light is on the starboard side.	Put short words in one group— the long words in another: left—port—red right—starboard—green

2. Using a different keyword, the learner forms a stable association for the capital city.
3. The keywords are linked together by a visual image (a line drawing in which the two keyword referents are related to one another).

For example, "marry" sounds like part of the state of Maryland and "apple" is part of Annapolis. A visual image of a minister marrying two apples would link the association of the words.

The applicability of mnemonics beyond the laboratory is demonstrated by the wide range of people who have found such techniques useful. It has been used effectively with mentally retarded children (Campione and Brown, 1977), young children (Levin, 1976), the elderly (Robertson-Tschabo, Hausman, and Arenberg, 1976), and brain-injured patients (Lewinsohn, Danaker, and Kikel, 1977). Spontaneous use of mnemonics has not been demonstrated as yet with mentally retarded children (Campione and Brown, 1977).

STRATEGIES FOR RETENTION. There are fewer strategies which can be followed for the retention of information and skills than for the acquisition. The major conditions which a teacher can use to maintain acquired skills are:

1. Overlearning/mastery learning
2. Reminiscence
3. Spaced review

MASTERY LEARNING/OVERLEARNING. The terms mastery learning and overlearning are closely allied. In mastery learning, the criterion level for performance is specified in advance of instruction. Student achievement of that performance objective is referred to as mastery. Overlearning refers to practice beyond the point of mastery. Failure to follow a mastery-based instructional program and failure to plan for overlearning activities are two reasons for depressed achievement scores of mentally retarded learners.

Students enter all learning situations at different levels of performance. For example, on Monday, Student A can spell 80% of the new words, Student B can spell 50%, and Student C can spell 20%. If all youngsters are expected to learn their spelling words in five days, Student A has a definite advantage both for acquisition and retention. Figure 3.4 shows the theoretical learning rates for each of these students over the course of the week. Student A achieved mastery on Day 2, Student B achieved mastery on Day 4, and Student C never reached mastery. On a retention test six weeks later Student A got 100%, Student B got 90%, and Student C got 60%. Why? One explanation could be that Student A had three days of overlearning, Student B only one day, and Student C none at all. The student who had the most days of overlearning remembered the words best.

In order to "break" this very predictable ordering of student performance, the teacher needs to adopt a mastery teaching model that allows all learners the opportunity to master the spelling words and to overlearn the words following mastery. According to Blake (1974), students need about 50% as many trials of overlearning following mastery as it took to achieve mastery. This means if it took twenty

Figure 3.4

Theoretical Learning Rate and Retention of Spelling Words for Three Students

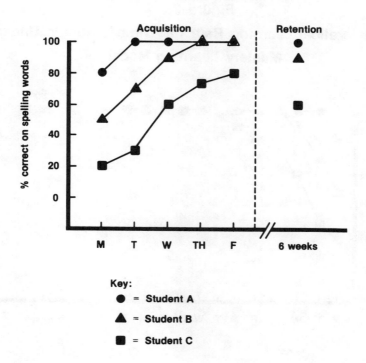

Key:
● = Student A
▲ = Student B
■ = Student C

trials to reach mastery, then the optimal trials for overlearning would be an additional ten. In our example found in Figure 3.4, Subject A probably had more opportunity for overlearning than he needed and Subject B needed at least one more day of practice. For Subject C we don't know how many trials of overlearning he needed because at the end of five days he still had not reached mastery. If each of these students would have been permitted to achieve mastery and to overlearn the material according to their need for overlearning, then the results of a retention test following termination of instruction for each student would have been the *same* for each student. In Figure 3.5 let's extend the example of the three students under a mastery learning mode.

Figure 3.5
Theoretical Learning Rate for Three Students Under Mastery Learning Model

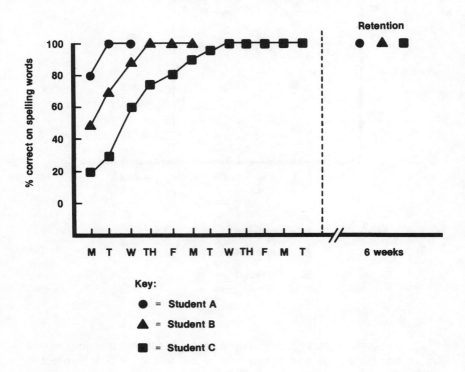

Key:

● = Student A

▲ = Student B

■ = Student C

As you can see in Figure 3.5, the mastery learning model does not make one learner achieve faster than another (There are strategies dealing with organizing materials which can decrease learning time). The actual length of instruction, mastery, and overlearning time for Subject A would be three days, for Subject B six days, and Subject C twelve days. The final result, however, would be that on a retention test six weeks after instruction, each student's performance would be the same *on that set of words*. The difference between performance in Figure 3.4 and Figure 3.5 is that in Figure 3.4 Subject C always fails. The purpose of special education is to structure successful learning experiences for students. This mastery learning model allows the failure set to be interrupted and to change a learners attitude toward new tasks.

REMINISCENCE. A period of rest following an extended practice session appears to increase performance. This period of rest is referred to as "reminiscence." A student practices a skill, rests (or changes activities), and then resumes the original task. The student now remembers more than he did at the end of the initial practice session. The strategy of reminiscence has been demonstrated effective with both handicapped and nonhandicapped learners (Ellis, Pryer, and Barnett, 1960; Wright and Willis, 1969). Teachers need to plan activities so that, following long periods of practice, rest or a less strenuous period of activities are undertaken.

SPACED REVIEW. Any acquired skill which is not practiced by a learner will eventually decrease or be forgotten. In the same way that intermittent reinforcement helps in the maintenance of a skill or behavior, spaced review helps a learner maintain a high level of performance. Students need periodic review and practice in order to maintain a skill. The teacher whose students have spent a month on multiplication facts and problems will probably note a slight decline in their performance in subtraction. A once-a-week review of addition and subtraction work would probably be sufficient to bring their skills back to an optimal level of performance.

TRANSFER AND GENERALIZATION STRATEGIES. Transfer and generalization refer to learning that takes place in one situation which influences (facilitates) learning in a second situation. Transfer and generalization do not occur spontaneously for the mentally retarded but must be planned for and taught. Two principles of learning that influence transfer are:

1. Intertask similarity
2. Specific instructions for transfer

INTERTASK SIMILARITY. Organizing objectives or content in an orderly way to emphasize the relationship between the different levels of material can decrease the time it takes to learn the new set of content. By the careful sequencing of content a teacher can save time and enhance learning. The teacher needs to examine the distinctive features or dimensions of the total task to be learned and then organize it to include a sequenced number of changes between each teaching segment.

SPECIFIC INSTRUCTION FOR TRANSFER. Many skills are taught in school which are thought to be important for independent functioning outside of school and into adulthood. The teacher needs to periodically plan simulations to provide practice for a skill which is to be performed in an out-of-school environment. For example, making change should not simply involve practice through paper-and-pencil exercises but rather through actual manipulation of money. Spelling words in isolation may not transfer into writing these same words in sentences or paragraphs without some practice of this specific skill. Solving word problems in a book needs to be practiced through "real-life" examples with problems related to shopping, measurement in woodshop, or computing miles per gallon problems in drivers education. For the mentally retarded learner there is a need to meld classroom activities with out-of-school situations. One method for doing this is through the development of a home-managed program. Cooperative parents can be a valuable asset to a classroom teacher. You can guide them into working on the application of school-achieved skills with their son or daughter in real-life situations which occur at home. Chapter IV deals more extensively with the development of home-managed programs.

Summary

This chapter has highlighted a variety of principles which a teacher can follow to enhance the acquisition, retention, and transfer of skills in the mentally retarded learner. The set of principles discussed does not constitute the universal set of skills needed by the teacher to enhance achievement.

In planning instruction for her students it is important for the teacher to incorporate these principles into the day-to-day activities in a cohesive manner.

Remember this . . .

1. You must plan students' "free time".

2. The most important indicator of outstanding teachers is amount of time they spend teaching.

3. Lack of consistency destroys the effectiveness of management programs more than any other component.

4. It is fair to have individual students doing different quantities of work.

5. Duties for paraprofessionals should be prioritized.

CHAPTER IV

Structuring Classroom Environments

Physical Arrangements

"Room assignment for Ms. Miller: North School, Room #13." Such a notice may appear in your mailbox any bright August day and send you off to investigate your new territory. A class list notifies you that your year will begin with sixteen students while a quick look at your room informs you that you possess twelve desks and thirteen small chairs. Custodian, principal, and supervisor may all scratch their heads and express the hope that "something might turn up" but you dare not build your room on such dreams. Accept your role as a professional and:

1. Introduce yourself to every teacher in the building, ask them for help, and specify the problem. Do not hesitate to trade! You may have thirty spelling workbooks so you can deal!
2. Introduce yourself to the school secretary and by your sincere and concerned manner induce her to unlock any storage room so that you may seek your own solutions.
3. Accept reality. You are responsible for the physical arrangement of your classroom and that responsibility begins immediately, not when more or better furniture and equipment arrives. Be flexible; be inventive; be positive.

Planning the Layout

The physical layout of your classroom should be carefully planned so as to deliver, reinforce, and maintain the educational/social goals

77

of your room. However, the fact that something is planned does not mean that it is static. Furniture may need to be moved at different times of the day or week to accommodate such activities as art, television, story reading, small groups or punishment. Room arrangement may be changed at times within the school year due to curriculum changes, arrival of new students, or management plans.

Figures 4.1 and 4.2 show sample classrooms at the start of a school day and for a reading class. The teacher (and aide) should be able to visually monitor the entire classroom from any location but the learners should have limited visual contact with others in the room. Individual, small group, and reinforcement areas are all provided for. When doing initial planning, remember that the "noise" of the group should be physically separate from the work area of the individual. Bookshelves, files, fabric, screen, pegboard, masking tape, and study carrels can all be used to designate performance areas in the classroom.

Areas for individual work should be comfortable, quiet, and well lit. If individual learning centers are a component of the room, it will be necessary to teach targeted students how to use the centers. Learning centers must have specific plans, objectives, and means of evaluation so that at each center a plan should be posted containing the following:

1. Skill
2. Objective
3. Material
4. Directions
5. Evaluation

Group areas should have adequate seating in a section of the room removed from individual study but still allowing the teacher to monitor the entire room. Reinforcement areas can be planned only after the modes of reinforcement have been determined. *Please plan your reinforcers.* Reinforcement is not and should not be "fun" that takes place outside of the educational/social curriculum. An activity can be pleasurable and still promote learning of appropriate social behavior. A puzzle can teach planning, visual discrimination (shapes and colors), cooperation, as well as the states in the Union. Games, when thoughtfully selected, can promote growth in math, spelling, reading, social interaction, and organization. Plan your reinforcers and then locate them in the most suitable area in your classroom.

Figure 4.1

Classroom Arrangement A

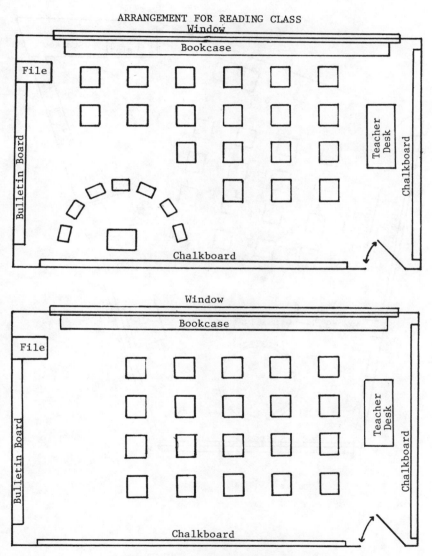

ARRANGEMENT FOR READING CLASS

NORMAL LARGE GROUP ARRANGEMENT

Figure 4.2

Classroom Arrangement B

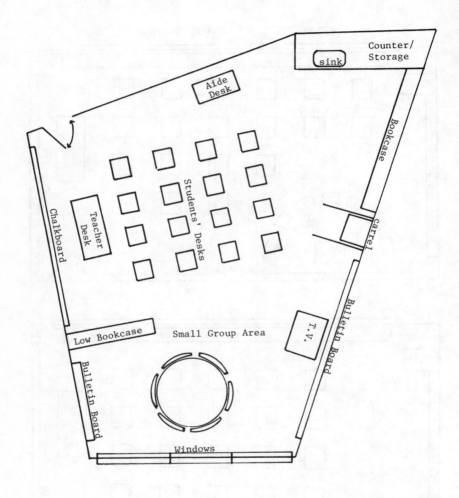

Instructional Time

Classroom and individual schedules can be developed when the teacher knows:
1. The curriculum
2. Length of the school day
3. Times for lunch, PE, and any other standard classes that will take the students out of the room
4. Times for subjects into which targeted students have been mainstreamed
5. When an aide or volunteer will be working in the classroom
6. Length of time needed for each activity

Schedules must be specific and detailed in order to maximize the use of instructional time. A study by Fredericks, Anderson, Baldwin, Grove, Moore, and Beaird (1978) found that the most important competency indicator of outstanding teachers was the number of minutes of instruction provided each day. In fact, there is substantial documented evidence to indicate a functional relationship between the amount of instructional time and academic achievement (Black and Burns, 1975; David, 1974; Fisher, Filby, and Marliave, 1977). Quite simply, more teaching equals more learning, and both are the result of the well-organized school day.

Figure 4.3 is an example of a teacher's master schedule and Figure 4.4 shows an individual student's schedule. Please remember that when "free time" is a component of your schedule as a means of delivering reinforcement, it should still be carefully planned (appearing spontaneous) instructional time.

If you have an aide or volunteer help in your classroom, these individuals also need a schedule. In other words, every minute of the day must be planned for every person in the classroom.

Lesson Plans

After the schedule is developed, the daily lesson plan is the next step in providing effective instruction to meet individual needs. Lesson plan formats are variable but each includes answers to the questions what, why, and how:

WHAT? — — Behavioral objective with the behavior described, measured, and evaluated

WHY? — — Determined through formal or informal assessment

HOW? — — Techniques for presentation

Figure 4.3 Master Schedule

Monday	Tuesday	Wednesday	Thursday	Friday
8:30 - 8:55 P.E. 9:00 - 9:25 Mark Fleming - Reading Glendal - 9:15 Henshaw Sean - Math Regina - Math Chris - Math Tommy - Reading & Math	8:30 - 8:55 P.E. 8:30 Glendal - Math 9:00 - 9:25 See Monday Tommy - Math & Reading	8:30 - 8:55 P.E. 9:00 - 9:25 See Monday Tommy - Math & Reading	8:30 - 8:55 P.E. 9:00 - 9:25 See Monday Tommy - Math & Reading	8:30 - 8:55 P.E. 9:00 - 9:25 See Monday Tommy - Math & Reading
9:25 - 9:50 Reading - Regina, Chris Phonics - Sean	9:25 - 9:50 Reading - Regina, Chris Phonics - Sean Glendal - Math	9:25 - 9:50 Reading - Regina, Chris Phonics - Sean	9:25 - 9:50 Reading - Regina, Chris Phonics - Sean Glendal	9:25 - 9:50 Reading - Regina, Chris Phonics - Sean
9:50 - 10:20 Sean - folder Chris - Sedlak Mark - Reading 10:00 - 10:25 Music - Regina, Glendal, and Tommy 10:30 - 10:55 Sean, Chris 10:20 - 10:55 Recess	9:50 - 10:20 Sean - folder Chris - Skill booster/ Math drill Mark - Skill Booster Glendal - Reading 10:10 - 10:55 Art - Regina 10:20 - 10:55 Recess	9:50 - 10:20 Regina - Plus/SRA Mark - Weekly Reader Glendal - Reading Nicky - Weekly Reader 10:00 - 10:25 Music- Chris, Sean 10:30 - 10:55 Music - Regina, Glendal, Tommy 10:20 - 10:55 Recess	9:50 - 10:20 Sean - folder Regina - Plus/SRA Chris - Plus/Math drill Mark - Skill Booster Glendal - Reading 10:20 - 10:55 Recess	9:50 - 10:20 Sean - folder Regina - work from Ms. Sedlak Mark - American History 10:10 - 10:55 Art - Chris, Tommy and Glendal 10:30 - 10:55 Recess
11:00 - 11:25 Library	10:55 - 11:20 Glendal - Phonics Mark - Math drill Chris - Phonics Regina - Phonics Sean - Plus/Jenn	10:55 - 11:20 Glendal - Phonics Mark - Math drill Chris - folder Regina - folder Sean - folder	10:55 - 11:20 Glendal - Phonics Mark - Math drill Chris - Phonics Regina - Phonics Sean - Plus/Jenn	10:55 - 11:20 Glendal - Reading Chris - folder Regina - Phonics Sean - Handwriting 11:00 - 11:45 Art - Mark

Figure 4.3 Master Schedule (Con't)

Monday	Tuesday	Wednesday	Thursday	Friday
11:30 - 11:55 Sean, Regina - Spelling Chris - folder Mark - Sedlak work Glendal - folder	11:20 - 11:55 Sean, Regina - Spelling Chris - folder Mark - Handwriting/folder Glendal - folder	11:20 - 11:55 Sean, Regina - Spelling Chris - Plus/SRA Mark - folder Glendal - folder	11:20 - 11:55 Sean, Regina - Spelling Chris - folder Mark - Handwriting/folder Glendal - folder	11:20 - 11:55 Sean, Regina - Spelling Chris - Phonics Glendal - folder
11:55 - 12:30 Group	11:55 - 12:30 Group	11:55 - 12:30 Group	11:55 - 12:30 Group	11:55 - 12:30 Group
12:30 - 1:10 Lunch	12:30 - 1:10 Lunch	12:30 - 1:10 Lunch	12:30 - 1:10 Lunch	12:30 - 1:10 Lunch
1:10 - 1:40 Regina - Parker Chris - Phonics Glendal - Spelling Sean - Reading Tommy - Handwriting	1:10 - 1:40 Regina - Puzzle Chris - Jenn/room art Mark - Math Glendal - Spelling Tommy - Handwriting	1:10 - 1:40 Regina - work from Ms. Sedlak Chris - Phonics Mark - Math Glendal - Spelling Sean - Reading Tommy - Handwriting	1:10 - 1:40 Regina - work from Ms. Sedlak Chris - work from Ms. Sedlak Mark - Math Glendal - Spelling Sean - Reading Tommy - Handwriting	1:10 - 1:40 Regina - folder Chris - Jenn Mark - Math Glendal - Spelling Sean - Art 1:15 - 2:00 Tommy Handwriting
1:40 - 2:10 Sean - Skill booster Chris, Mark - Spelling Glendal - Reading Regina - Parker	1:40 - 2:10 Sean - work from Ms. Sedlak Chris, Mark - Spelling Glendal - work from Ms. Sedlak Regina - folder	1:40 - 2:10 Sean - Sedlak work Chris, Mark - Spelling Glendal - Jenn Regina - folder	1:40 - 2:10 Sean - Sedlak work Chris, Mark - Spelling Glendal - work from Ms. Sedlak Regina - Phonics	1:40 - 2:10 Chris, Mark - Spelling Glendal - Sedlak work Regina - Jenn/green book 2:00 Sean - Reading
2:10 - 2:30 Handwriting TV - 2:15 Wordsmith	2:10 - 2:30 Handwriting TV 2:15 Slim Goodbody 2:15 - Music - Mark	2:10 - 2:30 Handwriting TV - 2:00 Other Families Other Friends	2:10 - 2:30 Handwriting TV - 2:15 Discovering 2:15 - Music - Mark	2:10 - 2:30 Handwriting TV - 2:30 Short Story or Recess
Free time and work completion	Free time and work completion	Free time and work completion	Free time and work completion	Free time and work completion

Figure 4.4 Sample Student Schedule

NAME: _____ Sean _____

Monday	Tuesday	Wednesday	Thursday	Friday
8:30 - 9:00 P.E.	P.E.	P.E.	P.E.	P.E.
9:00 - 9:25 Math	Math	Math	Math	Math
9:25 - 9:50 Phonics	Phonics	Phonics	Phonics	Phonics
9:50 - 10:30 Folder (5)	Folder (5)	10:00 - 10:25 Music	9:50 - 10:30 Folder (5)	Folder (5)
10:30 - 10:55 Music	10:30 - 10:55 Recess, Work Completion, Discussion	10:30 - 10:55 Recess, Work Completion, Discussion	10:30 - 10:55 Recess, Work Completion, Discussion	10:30 - 10:55 Recess, Work Completion, Discussion
11:00 - 11:25 Library	10:55 - 11:20 Plus (6) Jenn (5)	Folder (5)	Plus (6)/Jenn (2)	Handwriting
11:30 - 11:55 Spelling	10:20 - 11:55 Spelling	Spelling	Spelling	Spelling
11:55 - 12:30 Group	Group	Group	Group	Group
1:55 - 1:40 Reading	Reading	Reading	Reading	1:15 Art
1:40 - 2:10 Skill-booster	Work from Mrs. Sedlak	Work from Mrs. Sedlak	Work from Mrs. Sedlak	Reading
2:10 - 2:30 Hand-writing/TV	Handwriting/TV	Handwriting/TV	Handwriting/TV	
2:30 - 3:00 Work Completion or free time	2:30 - 3:00 Work Completion or free time	2:30 - 3:00 Work Completion or free time	2:30 - 3:00 Work Completion or free time	2:30 - 3:00 Work Completion or free time

The following is a sample lesson plan. You will note that it is not elaborate and does not contain great detail, but it does give sufficient detail for a trained teacher. Beginning teachers should have lesson plans with greater detail.

Sample Lesson Plan

Students	— Regina, Sean, Paul
Objective	— Students will be able to correctly write the response to a set of random multiplication problems from tables one through five 90% of the time.
Materials	— Drill sheets, written tables, flash cards, blank paper, tests
Preassessment	— Regina, 40%; Sean, 70%; Paul, 65%
Presentation	— Written practice with multiplication tables available, flash card drill, discussion of patterns in the tables, prompting, overlearning through writing each table two to three times

Accountability, individual needs and IEP goals, grading, communication with staff, and management plans will all be enhanced by the skillful development of lesson plans. Skillfully prepared lesson plans will denote the use of many sound instructional strategies (see Chapter III) and serve as a means of assessing the use of such strategies.

Management Planning

The law of reinforcement states that when a behavior results in a pleasant event or reward, it is likely that the frequency of the behavior will increase. Another way of saying this is the "Premack Principle" which suggests that when a low probability behavior is followed by a high probability behavior, the likelihood of the low probability behavior occurring again in the future is increased, or as Grandma said, "Eat your spinach and you may have some pie." Teachers want their classrooms to be places where positive behaviors are consistently exhibited and so teachers must plan the pairing of pleasant events with appropriate behavior. A learner who is in a good mood, who is involved in meaningful activities and pleasant interactions, is a learner who has a teacher skilled in classroom management. This skillful teacher has, of course, carefully planned the school day, set goals, limits, rules, and consequences. But above all, this skillful manager is consistent (i.e., at all times, in all places, in procedures, rewards, and punishment). Lack of consistency destroys the effectiveness of management programs more than any other component. This teacher also delivers immediate consequences for behavior. For example, when Josh completes his work, he immediately receives a check on his daily schedule. This makes Josh feel good about completing his work and ties the pleasant event to the behavior of completing work. The less skillful teacher may delay the reinforcement, in this case the check mark, with the following results:

1. Josh loses the good feeling attached to completing his work.
2. When the reinforcer is given later, he does not associate the reinforcer with the behavior of work completion.
3. If Josh has engaged in inappropriate behavior after he has completed the work, but before he received the reinforcer, he may associate the reinforcer with the inappropriate behavior.

Our skillful teacher is also patient and knows that students will "test" programming so that inappropriate behavior tends to increase at the start of most programs. She is not afraid to give the program a chance and knows that different students will develop positive behavior at various rates.

Before a teacher can be truly skillful in the realm of classroom management, certain basic procedures must be understood and practiced. Measurement of behavior, methods of identifying reinforcers, and specific management techniques will be discussed in the following section.

Measuring Behavior

Observational measurement systems serve several purposes:

1. To determine what factors may be influencing behavior.
2. To determine whether a behavior is truly excessive or deficit.
3. To procure initial measurements for comparison with later ones as a means of evaluation.
4. To determine priorities in respect to the need for several behavior changes.

Figure 4.5 defines the basic recording methods used to measure behavior in a variety of settings. Two of these which may need additional explanation are interval recording and frequency recording.

Figure 4.5
Observational Recording Methods

Recording	Description	Example
Continuous	A written account of everything that occurs in a certain time period. This is analyzed to see what occurs before the behavior (antecedents), the behavior, and what occurs afterward (consequences)	A written account of a typical school day for Jack
Permanent Product	Tangibles which can be observed and counted	Problems correct on a worksheet
Frequency	Record of the number of times a behavior occurs in a specified period of time	Number of times student is out of seat
Duration	Record of total time period the behavior lasts	Length of tantrums
Interval	A period of time is divided into equal parts and it is recorded whether the behavior occurs during the interval	During ten 10-minute intervals, hitting occurred during 6 intervals
Time-Sampling	At specific intervals the observer records occurrence or nonoccurrence of a specific behavior	Every 5 minutes, student is checked for on-task behavior

Example A shows a sample of interval recording. This data was recorded over a two-hour period during the school day. The aide recorded, during every ten-minute interval, whether the student demonstrated out-of-seat behavior. Since the student was out-of-seat during seven of twelve intervals, it was estimated that out-of-seat behavior occurred 58% of the time.

Example A: Interval Recording
Behavior: Out-of-Seat (+ = out of seat)
Interval =
10 minutes   10 10 10 10 10 10   10 10 10 10 10 10

| + | + | − | − | + | − | | + | + | + | − | + | − |

This frequency data was taken by a teacher concerned with a student's aggressive behavior toward peers. He recorded the number of times the student hit, kicked, or threw an object at another student during the school day. As you can see, the data is merely hash marks, with each mark indicating an incident. Without some measurement of behavior, the teacher may be correct in assessing that a student has a problem but incorrect in specifying the precise problem behavior. The professional who consistently measures behavior will always have data to support classroom management objectives.

Example B: Frequency Recording
Behavior: Number of times _____ hit, kicked, or threw
               an object at a student.
Date: _____

$$||||\ \ ||||\ \ |||$$

Identifying Reinforcers

As previously stated, the law of reinforcement states that when a behavior results in a pleasant event or reward, it is likely that the frequency of the behavior will increase. Reinforcers are different for each individual (see figure 4.6). A trip to the zoo may seem like a pleasureable event, but if the student once had a frightening experience at the zoo, such a trip may be a punishment. Reinforcers may be disguised and hard to identify. A student reprimanded for misbehavior may continue to misbehave because adult attention of any sort is reinforcing to that individual. On the other hand, a teacher may know that a student is reinforced by a particular activity but the availability of the activity does not produce an increase in the target behavior. In such a situation it is quite possible that not engaging in the target behavior produces a greater reinforcer. For example, one of your students likes to help you grade papers. He has problems completing his work so you develop a program in which he receives the opportunity to help grade papers when his work is completed. This does not work when he develops a strong liking for the girl sitting next to him. Finishing his work would mean moving away from her.

Identification and evaluation of reinforcers is a necessary process and an ongoing one as reinforcers do change. There are several ways of determining reinforcers:

Figure 4.6
Possible Reinforcers

food	stickers	puzzles	pat on the back
TV time	balloons	adult attention	playing outside
crayons	gold stars	pet	participating in a game
markers	certificates	posters	hug
pencils	free time	library time	"good work" note to parents
ticket to a sporting event	reward party	tokens	extra PE
movie	game	praise	daily report card
ticket to a concert	recess	baseball cards	crossing guard
make-up	toys	field trips	hall monitor
comb	magazine	listening to the radio	decorate room
jewelry	paper	smiles	lunch with aide or teacher
record	folders	helping the teacher	home visit
book	tape	eraser	trip to the park

1. Observe what the student likes
2. Ask the student
3. Allow the student to sample several potential items or activities and observe which he wants more of (reinforcer sampling)

Basic Management Techniques

The following discussion defines and describes basic techniques for classroom management. Although teachers will employ a combination of methods, for the purpose of explanation they will be described separately as teacher attention, positive reinforcement, negative reinforcement, behavioral self-control, punishment, extinction, time-out, modeling, response cost, and differential reinforcement of other behaviors.

POSITIVE REINFORCEMENT. Appropriate behavior is followed by a reinforcing event to increase the strength of that behavior.

Description: 1. Identify the behavior to be strengthened.
                2. Identify reinforcers.
                3. When the behavior occurs, immediately deliver the reinforcer.

TEACHER ATTENTION. Interpersonal interaction employed to increase the strength of a behavior.

Description: 1. Identify behavior to be strengthened.
                2. Identify type of teacher attention, i.e., praise, labeling, facial expression, physical contact, other gestures and words of approval.
                3. Verbally label process and product behavior. For example: "Jill, I like the way you wrote your name (process), and it is easy to read (product)."
                4. Deliver social reinforcers frequently and enthusiastically.

NEGATIVE REINFORCEMENT. Appropriate behavior is followed by removal of an aversive event to increase the strength of that behavior.

Description: 1. Identify the behavior to be strengthened.
                2. Identify aversive events (frown, criticism, poor grades).
                3. When the target behavior occurs, immediately remove the aversive event.

BEHAVIORAL SELF-CONTROL. Student controls his behavior through the recognition and control of events affecting personal behavior.

Description: 1. Student identifies the behavior to be changed.
                2. Student identifies events associated with the behavior.
                3. Student decides how to alter these events.

PUNISHMENT. Inappropriate behavior is followed by an aversive event to decrease the strength of that behavior.

Description: 1. Identify the behavior to be decreased.
                2. Identify an aversive event.
                3. When the behavior occurs, immediately produce the punishment (aversive event).

EXTINCTION. All reinforcement is eliminated when an inappropriate behavior occurs to decrease the strength of that behavior.

Description:
1. Identify the behavior to be decreased.
2. Identify all reinforcing consequences of the behavior.
3. Remove all reinforcement when the behavior occurs. Be aware that a higher rate of maladaptive behavior generally occurs upon initiation of an extinction program so that abandoning the program prematurely may serve to reinforce the higher rate of response.

TIME-OUT. To impose a period of time during which reinforcers are not available as the consequence of inappropriate behavior.

Description:
1. Identify the behavior to be increased.
2. Identify a physical area or a means of making reinforcers unavailable.
3. When the behavior is exhibited, immediately enforce the no-reinforcement period.

MODELING. Arrangement of the environment so that a student learns new behavior or strengthens existing behavior through the observation of another individual.

Description:
1. Identify the behavior to be influenced.
2. Arrange situations so that the student observes others engaging in the target behavior.
3. Label the target behavior using the person's name ("You are dressed so neatly today, Mark").

RESPONSE COST. Inappropriate behavior results in the removal of a reinforcer to decrease the strength of that behavior.

Description:
1. Identify the behavior.
2. Identify the reinforcers which will be removed.
3. Remove the reinforcer immediately after behavior occurs. Be aware that response cost may result in negative emotional reactions and must be judiciously applied.

DIFFERENTIAL REINFORCEMENT OF OTHER BEHAVIORS (DRO). Reduce the strength of inappropriate behavior by reinforcing all appropriate behavior.

Description:
1. Identify inappropriate behavior.
2. Provide reinforcement for all responses except the target behavior.

3. Behavior change occurs through the student seeking the positive consequences. For example, the student would be complimented for working at her desk and ignored for being out of her seat.

Combining Techniques

Many of the basic management techniques can be combined to result in more effective strategies and some combinations are specific programs. Techniques can be combined in a variety of ways to meet the needs of the learner. For example, positive reinforcement, modeling, and extinction can be combined. While the students are being reinforced for appropriate behavior, the target student may begin to model more appropriate behavior at the same time that off-task behavior is being ignored. Again, the combination that you select will depend on the needs of the student and the situation. It should be noted that any effort to decrease behavior should be combined with techniques to increase appropriate behavior.

Contracts and token systems are two types of programs that are a combination of techniques. Contracts are an agreement between the teacher or parent and the learner (see Figure 4.7). All parties must agree to the program and the contract must be clear in terms of behavioral expectations and consequences.

Token systems use items such as chips, stars, check marking, and money which can be exchanged for back-up reinforcers, that is activities or objects given at a later time. Tokens are awarded as reinforcers for appropriate behavior or deducted as in the response-cost technique for inappropriate responses. Token systems must be carefully planned so that:

1. The student does not lose all opportunities to earn reinforcers before the day is over. If a student has lost all chances of earning a reinforcer, he will have no incentive to engage in appropriate behaviors the rest of the day.
2. Reinforcers are not attained too easily.
3. Consequences can be easily imposed so as to assure consistency.
4. A transition can be made. The program must be faded so that the student does not become dependent on the tokens.

Figure 4.7
Sample Behavioral Contract

I agree to do all of my math, reading, reading workbook, and hand-writing assignments. I further agree to attend PE, music, art, library, and TV and to behave according to class rules both in the room and out. In exchange, I will be given reading and/or library time after my work is completed.

_____

Student's signature

I agree to give Tommy time for reading and/or library use after he has completed the work listed above. If Tommy is not working, he will be kept in at recess. For 2 days of incomplete work Tommy may be paddled.

_____

Teacher's signature

This contract is valid from January 18 through January 29.

_____

Witness' signature

Structuring the Events to Prevent Problems

The highly structured classroom sets the stage for the avoidance of inappropriate behavior. When the learner knows what is expected, he can feel secure and comfortable knowing that his day is organized, his academic goals are set, and rewards and consequences for specific behaviors are in place. In the structured classroom:

1. Detailed student schedules are posted.
2. Students are knowledgeable as to the quality and quantity of work expected.
3. Students are frequently identified by name, especially when engaging in appropriate behavior.
4. Students receive teacher attention frequently.
5. Student work is graded immediately when possible.

6. Students receive frequent and specific feedback on behavior and academic work.
7. Students are knowledgeable as to the specific rewards and reinforcers available to them and when such may be obtained.
8. Students are knowledgeable as to the specific behavior which will achieve a reward or reinforcer for them.
9. Students are knowledgeable as to the consequences of specific inappropriate behaviors, when such consequences will be delivered, and any additional ramifications of such consequences.
10. Students have opportunities for individual and group work.

To further clarify the difference between the structured and the unstructured classroom the following list has been developed. These situations are not observed in the structured classroom:

1. Students wandering about the room
2. Students asking "How much of this do I have to do?"
3. Students whose raised hands are being ignored
4. Students whose appropriate behaviors are being ignored
5. Students whose inappropriate behaviors are being ignored
6. Students who say that they don't have anything to do
7. Students producing a series of incorrect responses on their written work
8. Teacher or aide sitting alone at desk for any length of time
9. Teacher or aide out of room for any length of time
10. No schedules, rules, or other notices posted

Pulling It All Together

Another legitimate heading for this section would be *There's No Substitute for Time and Effort*. Successful classroom management takes a great deal of thought and planning, especially after hours. Management is an on-going process in which new goals and new techniques are constantly challenging the teacher. As stated previously, the teacher (and other significant adults or peers) must be consistent, every day, every hour. A second difficulty or challenge revolves around the cry "but it's not fair," "Why should Bill have only thirty math problems?" "Why should Melissa not have science?" — these and other questions seem to make many teachers unnecessarily uncomfortable. Different students will be doing various amounts of work, will be involved in different subject areas, and will have different management plans. There is nothing unfair about this, especially when the teacher can document that each student is receiving an education, appropriate and individualized to meet his needs.

Parents and the Classroom Structure

All too often parents are ignored as a potential force in the educational development of children. Parents are most often the educator's natural ally, but there are parents whose background, behavior, or attitude work against the goals of education. In all cases, the teacher can develop or foster, by careful planning, a cooperative attitude that will in turn be reflected by the learner in the classroom in terms of greater academic achievement and/or an increase in appropriate behavior. Reporting individual progress to parents is a technique which can be used to "mold" the relationship between parents, child, school, and educator. The following components of progress reporting have been used successfully by thoughtful classroom teachers.

Report Cards

In most schools a standard report card is in use and even if the teachers are allowed input as to the design of the card, individual preferences will still exist. Report cards are accepted by the majority of parents as significant. Often, a teacher will be aware that various rewards have been attached to the achievement of certain "grades" on the report. But does the parent understand the report? Possibly not and almost certainly not in accordance with the teacher's criteria. Consequently, we advise that you add to or alter your "card" so that it reflects the objective criteria used to grade the student. If A, B, C's are used, it may be necessary to indicate that A = 90 to 100%, B = 80 to 89%, and so on. It may also be advisable to state the grade level at which the child was working when that degree of success or failure was reached. If Satisfactory, Pass, Fail are used, it would benefit student and parent (and certainly allow the teacher to feel that some real communication was taking place) if percentages, grade level, and even a " + " or " − " system were included.

Report cards often have Behavior and Personal sections included. Anecdotal records and frequency counting may help the teacher to be more objective when it is time to fill out these sections but parents still will not know the standard or the range of deviation from the standard that you allow unless you tell them. If space on the card does not permit this type of information, write it, reproduce it, and explain it at your first conference (before report cards go out) and include it in the report card envelope.

If you do these things, parents will know that out-of-seat behavior is unacceptable in your room, that Harry is doing B work (80 to 89%) at the third grade level in math, and that a Pass in personal grooming means that Sue came to school with clean hands 50% of the time. When a parent knows specifically what their child is achieving in school: (a) more reasonable goals may be set; (b) progress or deterioration is more easily spotted; (c) cooperative attitude toward a home-school management program may develop; and (d) supervision of the child may increase. All of these things help to reinforce the goals of education.

Notes

Many teachers quickly discover the power of the note but often it is only used on special occasions. While any special success or particular problem should result in some correspondence with parents, notes may also be a part of the daily or weekly schedule. Notes bring parents into closer contact with the school and with their own child, reinforcing the work done by the educator at conferences and report card time. Avoid using notes only in times of unpleasant crises — "Good news notes," "Helper notes," "Brag notes" are all ways of demonstrating to the student and parent what good things this learner has accomplished.

Home-School Management

Polls of parents and educators list discipline among the top issues confronting the public schools (Horacek, 1979). Discipline problems at school can be greatly reduced through the use of a home-school management plan. Such plans obviously require continuous communication between school and home. Studies using daily report cards and home-based contingencies have reported a significant reduction in disruptive classroom behavior with a corresponding improvement in academic performance for elementary and secondary aged children

(Schumaker, Hovell, and Sherman, 1977; Todd, Scott, Bostow, and Alexander, 1976). The teacher could develop a report card and assess student social behaviors and academic performance on a daily basis. Parents then are informed of the student's performance via the report card and reward positive behavior and academic performance by granting privileges such as increased television time or release from a household chore. Parents may also withhold television, telephone, or radio privileges as punishment for inappropriate behavior or performance. All rewards and punishments must be designated and approved by teacher and parents before the plan goes into operation.

Contingency contracting, which is a written agreement that lists specific behaviors and resulting consequences and has the goal of exchanging reinforcers between two or more people, can be used in a home-school management system. Truancy problems lend themselves particularly well to such a plan, with privileges given or withheld according to the learner's attendance record. An example of such a contingency contract is displayed in Figure 4.8.

Paraprofessionals

The prefix "para" means "with" and therefore the term paraprofessional refers to individuals who work with but under the supervision of a professional. In this case the term can refer to teacher's aides, educational assistants, volunteers, or parent helpers. In most cases, however, it refers to a paid employee of the school district, generally a teacher's aide or assistant.

This individual can play a key role in the total instructional program and therefore the careful selection and training of this individual is of great importance.

Interview and Selection

As a professional educator you may be asked to help with the selection of paraprofessionals or to give suggestions concerning the job descriptions of these individuals. The following section offers a framework for the interview and selection process (Boomer, 1980).

Questions at the interview should seek to determine the applicant's ability to do the job. Previous work experience should be explored so that useful "hidden" skills can be determined (sewing fac-

Figure 4.8
Sample Contingency Contract for Home and School

I, *Susan Salt*, agree to attend school 8:15 AM to 3:00 PM for two weeks beginning April 16 through April 27. In return I will receive one ticket to the May 1 Beach Boys Concert. If I am truant I will lose all use of the TV and radio for a 7-day period.

_____
Signature

I, *Harry Salt*, agree to give Susan one ticket to the May 1 Beach Boys Concert after she attends school 8:15 AM to 3:00 PM for two weeks April 16 through April 27. If she is truant I will withhold all use of TV and radio for a 7-day period.

_____
Signature

I, *Barbara Pinardi* (teacher), agree to inform Mr. Salt immediately if Susan is truant.

_____
Signature

tory, typist, handyman). Questions about hobbies and other interests will bring forth information about skills that can later be used in the classroom. For example, interest centers or academic units may be developed or enhanced by the paraprofessional with an interest in woodworking, music, or automobile mechanics. Previous experience with children would be a valuable asset for the individual securing this position so the interviewer should seek data on work history, 4-H, Scouting, Sunday School, and coaching. Our classrooms need staff with a positive attitude toward schools and teaching, so inquiry about the applicant's attitudes toward school would be appropriate. A key question would be "Why do you want to be a special education paraprofessional?" Positive answers would include "I like children," "I want to be a teacher," or "I've done similar volunteer work and enjoyed it" while negative feelings would be found in "I don't have anything else to do," "The hours aren't bad," and "I can't find anything else."

Also, at the interview the general operation of the classroom should be discussed including the type of disability served, the number of children, their ages, and whether the room is self-contained, resource, or specific subject. The major duties of the paraprofessional should be explained as well as the pay schedule, sick leave, vacation, starting time, and length of the school day. Finally, the applicant should be given a chance to ask questions.

In the Classroom

The paraprofessional in the classroom can maximize instructional time to students, reinforce the teacher's instruction, and provide more one-to-one interaction with students. The paraprofessional or aide must understand his or her role in the management plan in effect in the room and be consistent in implementing those plans. In the first week of school the educator should acquaint the paraprofessional with:

1. Written lists of duties, prioritized, if possible (see Figure 4.9)
2. Specific schedule (see Figure 4.3)
3. Classroom rules and procedures
4. Individual management plans
5. Deadlines
6. Appropriate dress
7. Modes of addressing students and parents
8. Data collection techniques
9. Specific starting and finishing times
10. Importance of confidentiality
11. Importance of regular attendance
12. Procedure for fire and tornado drills

Teachers need to be aware that aides should *not*:

1. Act as substitute teacher
2. Assign grades to students
3. Be used to carry out corporal punishment
4. Take the initiative in communicating with parents
5. Have sole responsibility for writing goals and objectives
6. Always be responsible for the "problem" student(s)
7. Disclose confidential information

Figure 4.9
Classroom Duties and Procedures

1. Respond to all students who have raised their hands.
2. Circulate among the students at frequent intervals, make sure they are not having problems with their work, and compliment them for working.
3. Respond to inappropriate behavior.
   a. Simply calling a student by name, frowning, or shaking your head usually stops the behavior.
   b. It may be necessary to remind the student of the consequences of his behavior and at times student behavior may then be ignored (esp. when not disruptive)
   c. Major "call outs" and only major "call outs" result in a mark on the board next to the student's name. Other inappropriate behaviors receive different punishments:
      a. rules
      b. apologies
      c. loss of recess — work not done
      d. homework — work not done
      e. loss of party or other privilege
      f. extra work, etc.
4. Check student work — always keeping ears open and frequently looking for raised hands.
5. Produce student work — handwriting, math, other worksheets.
6. Keep student folders filled.
7. Work on room order, decorations, etc. as work permits.

NOTE: Different students may have different programs. Be careful not to violate these programs. Ex. — Tommy has a contract which allows him to lose recess for not working and after 2 days of incomplete work he may be paddled. Therefore Tommy would *not* be punished in any other ways for *not working*.

In the past, using aides for basically clerical and "housekeeping" activities was a common practice but today's paraprofessional is expected to contribute much more. Aides *can*:

1. Help students with activities given by the "regular" teachers
2. Arrange field trips and guest speakers
3. Reinforce positive behavior

4. Assist in large and small group instruction
5. Work with individual students
6. Observe and record behavior
7. Prepare bulletin boards
8. Correct student work
9. Develop worksheets and other instructional materials
10. Assist with audiovisual equipment
11. Model appropriate behavior
12. Work with teachers to determine individual needs of students and develop programs to meet those needs
13. Assist students with make-up work
14. Assist with hands-on activities
15. Help students with personal problems
16. Provide guidance to students
17. Work with school personnel and students to promote acceptance of special classes and their students
18. Provide students with help in written or oral communication

As noted earlier, the duties or activities of the paraprofessional in the classroom should be prioritized. With a host of prioritized duties, the aide should be able to meet the requirements of the class and the individual without adding to the stress upon the teacher. A basic prioritized list of duties might look like this:

1. Respond to raised hand
2. Continually survey the room, respond to behaviors (appropriate and inappropriate) as necessary
3. Check student work
4. Check off completed work on student schedule
5. Prepare materials and bulletin boards

Paraprofessionals are, consequently, extremely important to our special education classroom. The professional teacher will have more time to deliver direct instruction when the paraprofessional is skillfully used to deliver appropriate services to students. Competent use of such paraprofessionals may take some planning and thought but the reward of their service in the classroom can be tremendous. Teachers should not hesitate to request inservice training for their paraprofessionals and encourage them to seek to improve their skills in the classroom. Professional teachers will give the paraprofessional credit for work well done and encourage colleagues to respect the service given by the individual (Steppe-Jones, 1981).

Effectiveness of Paraprofessionals

The literature is relatively consistent regarding the effectiveness of paraprofessionals. Paraprofessionals have demonstrated success in providing services to disabled students including the developmentally disabled, emotionally disturbed, learning disabled, preschool aged, and severely/profoundly retarded. Studies by Blessing and Cook (1970), Schortinghuis and Frohman (1974), Sedlak (1982), and others have demonstrated positive results on both academic and behavioral variables. The critical aspect for success was the close supervision and clear delineation of instruction that the paraprofessional was to deliver. It is the teacher's responsibility to develop these instructional plans and to supervise the work of the aide.

Summary

Thoughtful planning followed by consistent teacher behavior creates the structure for a successful classroom environment. When all the components described throughout this chapter (e.g., physical arrangements, schedules, plans, etc.) are in place, the environment for successful learning has been established. Continue planning your move into the arena of instruction.

Remember this . . .

1. The quality of the available software is more important than the price of the hardware in microcomputers.

2. The systematic use of media can enhance learning and save instructional time.

3. If earphones do not fit the jacks in your machine, adapters are available at moderate cost.

4. Various media can be used to circumvent, accommodate, or compensate for a disabling condition.

CHAPTER V

Technology and Instruction

Various machines and media have been used quite successfully in the past with the handicapped for the purpose of circumventing, accommodating, or compensating for the disabling condition. Their systematic use by the classroom teacher of the educable mentally retarded can do much to advance the achievement levels of the learners and to maximize the use of instructional time. In order to be successful the teacher needs to know what technology is available, what types of support devices or programs are needed to use them, and how to systematically plan to use it in a classroom setting. The teacher of the educable mentally retarded should be familiar with the operation and use of calculators, cassette tape recorders, Language Masters®, Speak and Spell/Math/Read®, programmed instruction materials, microcomputers, and video tape recorders and cameras.

Calculators

Calculators provide an acceptable alternative to hand computation in arithmetic. They also function as strong motivational devices for students in special classes. Sedlak, Sun, and Harper (1982) used calculators with elementary age learners in a cross-categorical classroom. As a part of the treatment, the learners "checked" their hand calculations of computation problems and word problems. Students demonstrated an increase in computation skills over a control group. Sedlak et al. also noted that the learners initially needed to be taught how to operate a calculator. Merely giving the students a calculator to work problems did not result in their getting more problems correct primarily because the sequence of skills in manual computation and calculator usage are different. Sample task analyses for using a calculator are found in Chapter XII of this book.

Cassette Tape Recorders

The use of cassette tape recorders represent a reasonable alternative to reading as the primary means of acquiring information in content subject areas, e.g., social studies, science, health. Recorders are relatively inexpensive and have a wide variety of uses. A major drawback to their use is the time required to prepare the tapes. Here is where the teacher needs to be organized and creative. Putting printed material on tape need not be the job of the teacher but can be done by the classroom aide, volunteers, room mothers, "student council members" (as a service project), or other members of the class. Talking Books for the Blind is also a source of taped materials which might be usable with the educable mentally retarded learner. In 1978, Congress changed the definition of who would be eligible for services from the American Printing House for the Blind in terms of their talking books program. Anyone who is unable to read print is eligible for services. These services include the permanent loan of variable speed cassette tape recorders, adapters, and access to a cassette tape library at no cost. Further information on the program can be secured by writing:

American Printing House for
the Blind or Physically Handicapped
Lexington, Kentucky
or contacting your local public library.

Variable-speed tape recorders offer one major advantage over conventional recorders and that is the playback speed feature. The speed of playback can be varied from a rate of fifty words per minute (wpm) up to 250 words per minute, without excessive distortion of the voice. Speeding up the playback on a conventional machine results in a garbled or "Donald Duck" effect. The variable-speed machines minimize this distortion. This speeded-up playback is referred to in the literature as "compressed speech."

Being able to increase the playback speed to 250 wpm means that a student can be taught to listen to material at about the same rate as most people could read that material. The key here again is the emphasis on teaching. Students must be trained to use the machine and also to enhance their listening comprehension skills so as to make maximum use of the machine's capabilities.

Some advantages and suggested uses of cassette tape recorders which are conventional or variable speed include

1. Allows the student to replay all or a segment of a tape for review
2. Allows the student to play a tape at a slow rate or accelerated rate
3. Can be used at a learning station
4. Instructions can be individualized for students
5. Students can record their reading or spelling lesson and self-monitor mistakes
6. Teacher can record large group lectures for individual student review
7. Students can record stories which later can be transcribed for reading lessons
8. Use for room background music
9. Record radio news broadcasts
10. Record TV and radio commercials for discussion

Cassette tapes can be erased and reused. Sometimes they can be erased by accident. By punching out the plastic squares on the edge of the cassette tape, it cannot be accidentally erased by a student. Snap-in plugs can always be purchased to fill in these squares later if you wish to record over the tape.

Language Master®

The Language Master® is an adaptation of a tape recorder with a magnetic tape fastened to the bottom of a stimulus card. When the card is inserted in the machine, whatever is recorded on the tape is played back to the learner. Figure 5.1 illustrates a language master and card. The top portion of the card can contain a picture or words. Commercially prepared cards are available in language arts, speech, math, and science. Blank cards can also be purchased and lessons created by the teacher. Since the student can record, erase, or play back information on the cards, the teacher should not assume that what is printed on the card is the same information that is recorded. It is a good practice to "spot check" the cards before handing them to the students. The machine can be used in the teaching of sight words, alphabet recognition, spelling, numerals, and a variety of other skills. The machines are used quite often with non-English – speaking students as a means of developing a speaking and listening English vocabulary. They have been used in conjunction with microcomputer programs as an inexpensive means to add audio instructions to simple programs. For spelling programs the words are printed on the opposite side of the card so that the student can practice the word and then "check" it by flipping the card over.

Figure 5.1

Language Master®

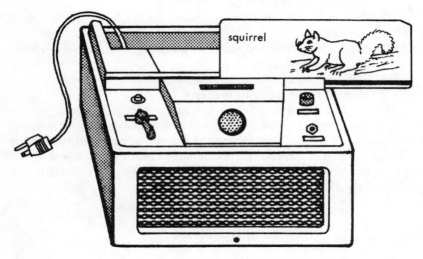

Speak and Spell/Read/Math®

Texas Instruments has made a major breakthrough in educational hardware with the series of machines they produce in spelling, reading, and math. These machines use a touch-sensitive keyboard for responses. Each has several major programs which can be used. Before attempting to use them with students, the teacher needs to become thoroughly familiar with the machine features.

Two features of the Speak and Spell® machine are a drill-and-practice program in which words are organized into ten item sets. In one version a list of ten words is displayed one at a time on the machine and each word is pronounced. The student is then quizzed on the spelling of each word. In a second version, just a quiz is given without the introductory warm-up. In each case the student is given two opportunities to spell the word and is told if it is wrong. After two errors on the same word, the machine spells the word on the display and orally. The machine keeps score of student's success and reports with a visual display and an audio message at the end of ten words. Speak and Spell® also contains a version of "hangman" and has a secret code feature for fun activities. Letter recognition is another feature of the machine, which makes it usable with youngsters in this readiness stage. Speak and Math® has math problems in varying difficulty levels in the four basic operations. Practice is also provided on number patterns and trying to guess what number comes next. Speak and Read ® has features similar to the other machines and has similar operation requirements. Additional plug-in modules are available to expand the offerings.

Earphones and Headphones

A variety of audio devices provide the option for the teacher to have students use earphones or headphones while they are in use. Headphones and earphones offer two advantages over the use of a speaker:

1.   Earphones eliminate background noise and help a student direct his attention to the audio output.
2.   The audio is not distracting to other students in the room. Unfortunately there are many different sized jacks and plugs needed for different audio devices. The most common diameter size for earphone jacks are 1/8 inch and for headphone jacks 1/4 inch. There are different jack sizes and plug lengths and diameters required for different machines. Fortunately most electronics stores carry adapters which allow a teacher to convert any size plug on an earphone or headphone to be compatible with the audio device. The cost of a set of three or four adapters is about $4.00 and should be a part of the "hardware" available in a classroom. These converters slip directly on the shank of an headphone or earphone plug and allow the same earphones to be used with a wide variety of audio devices. Different audio devices which a teacher may find available in a classroom include:

1. Radios
2. Variable speed tape recorders
3. Language masters
4. Cassette and reel-to-reel tape recorders
5. Slide/tape machines
6. Educational electronic games
7. Televisions

Programmed Instruction Materials

There are a variety of programmed instruction (PI) materials available for the special education student. Some of these are in textbook formats, while others are machine operated. The design of all PI materials rely heavily on the same basic principles:
1. Careful analysis of the task
2. Presentation of information in small incremental steps
3. Overt responding by the learner
4. Feedback to the learner
Some programs have branching capabilities while most which are not machine operated are basically linear. Some PI programs can be extremely tedious and slow paced. They are best used for short periods of time (e.g., ten minutes or less) in order to preserve student interest.

Microcomputers

Probably no other technological breakthrough has had such a significant impact upon education as the microcomputer. The refinement of silicone chip technology laid the foundation for the development of these machines. A microcomputer is a typewriter-sized machine capable of reading and executing various commands or storing programmed information in memory for retrieval. Some have devices which permit the machine to synthesize speech or play back prerecorded messages from a tape or chip. Some can respond to oral/spoken commands. The possible uses of these machines with handicapped learners are extensive.

Parts of a Microcomputer

Despite differences among the systems applied by the different microcomputer manufacturers, a microcomputer system (see Figure 5.2) usually includes:

1. A microprocessor
2. A typewriter-style keyboard for entering instructions, data, or for responding to machine queries
3. A monitor, cathode ray tube (crt) or television for displaying information
4. A cassette tape player and cassette tape or disk drive and floppy disk (see Figure 5.3) for the storage and retrieval of information or programs.

In addition to those components, a variety of peripheral equipment can be added to the system as the need arises or the funds become available.

Figure 5.2
Basic Microcomputer System Station

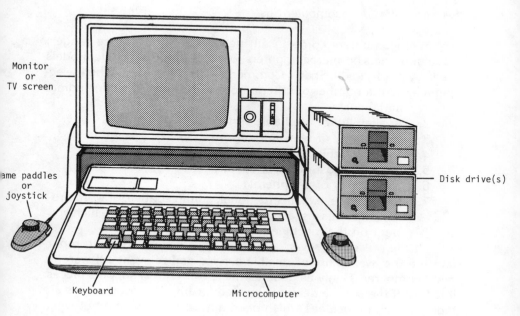

Figure 5.3

Floppy Disk

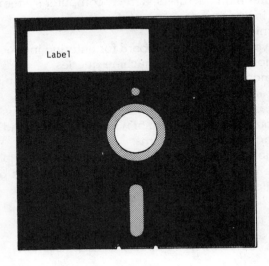

Label

Selection of a Microcomputer System

Microcomputers come in all memory sizes and price ranges. Popular models of microcomputers found in schools include models made by Apple, Radio Shack, Commodore, IBM and Atari. When selecting a system a number of criteria need to be considered including:

1. Initial cost
2. Availability of a reliable service dealer
3. Availability of relevant software
4. Extent of child-proofing
5. Ease and cost of expandability
6. Availability of peripherals
7. Primary use, e.g., instructional, administrative, or word processing. (This last aspect may dictate the features which you want on the machine.)

Of the preceding seven criteria the two which are most important are the availability of reliable service and relevant software. A microcomputer is only as good as these two critical support pieces. It is best if the service dealer is located locally. Microcomputers are highly reliable machines which need almost no servicing but when something goes wrong you feel confident if an expert is available to deal with the problem and perhaps supply you with a "loaner." Actually, repairs are not complex since almost all parts have been modularized. The repair technician merely pulls one set of chips and installs another set. The "diagnostic" work on the system is generally done by a software program that the technician has been trained to use.

Microcomputers are not magic black boxes. They are simply machines which follow instructions. These instructions are referred to as *programs* or *software*. They represent the most important part of the system.

Before selecting a microcomputer examine the software available and determine if it is adequate for your needs. Appendix A has a list of addresses for software distributors and also addresses for periodicals on microcomputers. Your local book store or microcomputer store will also have this information. Do some comparison shopping before making the purchase.

Modes of Instruction

Microcomputers can deliver instruction in a variety of ways. The major instructional modes are drill and practice, tutorial, and simulations. Drill-and-practice programs should be used with previously taught concepts in which the learner needs practice in order to reach a reasonable level of mastery. Short drill-and-practice programs are easy to integrate into an ongoing curriculum and are a good way for special education teachers to use "micros." Commercially available and public domain drill-and-practice courseware are widely available for basic math facts, spelling, fraction/decimal equivalencies, states and their capitals, and parts of speech. Any activity which can be put on flashcards or a worksheet can be put into a drill-and-practice format for a microcomputer. Such a practice is not necessarily advisable. The advantages of using micros for drill and practice over traditional worksheets are:

1. Immediacy of feedback to the learners
2. The novelty effect of using the machine
3. Time savings for the teacher
4. The variety of rewards
5. Active (overt) responding by the learner
6. Endless patience of the machine

A new type of drill-and-practice software for educational application is ARC-ED courseware (Chaffin, Maxwell, and Thompson, 1982).
This type of software has combined the features of video games with
educationally relevant content. Several drill-and-practice programs using this format are available under the trade name of Academic
Skillbuilders and are marketed commercially by DLM, Inc. The authors
had used two of these programs with elementary age behaviorally
disordered students in conjunction with one minute timed tests. Using the microcomputer and the Academic Skillbuilder (AS) materials
was contingent upon improved performance on one minute tests.
Students' performance on both timed tests and the AS materials improved over a baseline condition.

Under the tutorial mode, new concepts are presented to the
learner and then the learner is tested by a series of questions. The program evaluates the learner's responses, provides feedback, and then
continues the instruction, recycles the student through the material
again, or takes the student to a remedial branch in the program. If
the learner is having trouble the branch may be to a sub-program which
explains the concept in another way or in a more simplified fashion.
Students who make few errors move rapidly through the program.
These tutorial programs can be brief supplements to classroom instruction or lengthy in-depth courses.

In this mode the learner is presented with situations requiring decision making. The subsequent chain of events is based upon these
decisions. These simulations imitate real problems. For example, a
simulation on comparison shopping would require a student to make
decisions of the "best" buys. The student would be told that he had
a certain amount of money to purchase items on a shopping list. Too
many poor choices would result in the student not being able to purchase all items. If the student made all the "best" choices he might
end up with money to buy a "treat" or to put into savings. Simulations can be fun and excellent learning experiences particularly
because they require students to make decisions and then suffer the
consequences. Educable mentally handicapped learners have difficulty
making appropriate decisions and selecting the best alternatives.
Simulations can help in this regard.

Selection of Software

The heart of a microcomputer system is the software or program which is stored on a disk or tape and which make the system useful. The machine is quite useless without an adequate supply of programs for use with your students. Locating programs for use on the system can be a fun activity although it can also be quite time consuming. There are several sources of programs which you can explore. These include:

a. Commercial publishers
b. Microcomputer manufacturers
c. Microcomputer journals and magazines
d. Microcomputer clubs
e. Other schools

You can also try writing your own programs, although most teachers will probably choose one of the former sources. Some programs are copyrighted and should not be copied. There are, however, a number of programs which are in the public domain and can be readily copied without legal entanglements. Other schools and microcomputer clubs probably have a library of some programs in the public domain. You will also find these public domain programs for sale by small distributors. Referring to classified ads in microcomputer magazines will allow you to locate these vendors. You are probably wasting money if you buy these programs without first investigating whether they are available locally. Regardless of where you get programs, there are a couple of factors which you should consider in evaluating the courseware. Lathrop (1982) has listed the following 10 reasons for rejecting a program:

1. Audible response to student errors
2. Rewarding failure (e.g., hangman)
3. Uncontrolled sound
4. Technical problems
5. Uncontrolled screen advance
6. Inadequate instructions on how to operate the program
7. Errors in grammar, spelling of content
8. Insults, sarcasm, and derogatory remarks
9. Poor documentation
10. Denial of a back-up copy

Many of the programs available probably could be rejected for at least one of the preceding ten points. The teacher needs to decide if the particular inadequacy is serious enough to negate its use or purchase. In some cases the "problem" can be easily corrected by someone with minimal programming skills. The audible response for student errors can be deleted, spelling and grammar errors corrected, and sarcastic feedback rewritten.

Locating good microcomputer courseware is not easy. You will need to review the courseware before using it to determine if it is "learner-proof." It can be extremely perplexing to a student to get a message on the screen which says "syntax error" or "variable quantity error." These terms do not bother computer buffs but are hardly acceptable to novice users.

Computer Literacy

As a special education teacher you should become computer literate. Figure 5.4 and 5.5 have lists of some commands that are used with an Apple microcomputer. Many of these same commands will

Figure 5.4
Basic Commands for Operating an Apple® Microcomputer

Command	*Meaning*
RUN	Type this and then the program title to make a program appear.
BRUN	Type this and then the program title if a program in the catalog has a B in front of it.
LIST	This command will list all of the lines in your program in order.
TEXT	After running a program in graphics, type this to get back to regular BASIC.
CATALOG	This command tells you the programs that are on the disk.
PR #6	This command will reload the program from the disk.
CTRL C	Stops the execution of a program. Hold down CTRL and C keys at the same time.
SAVE	Type this command and then a program title to save a program on the disk.
NEW	This command will erase any program in the memory of the machine.
CALL 936	This command clears the screen when program is in Integer >.
HOME	This command clears the screen when program is in Applesoft].

Figure 5.4 (Con't)

Command	Meaning
PRINT	This command followed by a message in quotation marks will print the message on the screen (e.g., PRINT "Hi!")
GR	Typing this tells the computer you are going to do graphics.
REM	This command will print explanations in the program that do not show when the program is executed. It can be used to explain what a certain set of commands is doing.

Figure 5.5
Selected Computer Terms and Meanings

Term	Meaning
Command	A single word or phrase that tells the computer to do something with a program.
Control Characters	Special characters generated by holding the CTRL key down while pressing another key (e.g., CTRL C).
Cursor	A symbol that appears on the output screen when the computer is ready for input.
Diskette or Disk	A small, flexible disk used to store information in magnetic form.
I/O	An abbreviation for input/output which is the way a computer communicates with the outside.
Lines	The elements that make up a BASIC program. Every line has a line number followed by a statement.
Line Number	A number that identifies a line in a BASIC program.
Random-Access Memory (RAM)	Memory hardware that temporarily stores the programs and data that is entered into the computer.
Read-Only-Memory (ROM)	Memory hardware that permanently stores built-in programs and data.
Syntax Error	A spelling, punctuation, or grammar mistake in a command or statement.

work with other types of microcomputers. Figures 5.6 and 5.7 contain two programs written by the first author. The first is a spelling program. Words can be added or deleted in lines 700 and 701. The second program is an addition drill-and-practice program. If you have access to a microcomputer, type in one or the other and then run them. If you don't feel like typing much but want to enter a program, type in this one.

```
10  HOME
20  PRINT "SUPER STAR"
30  GOTO 20
```

There is a listing of software companies and publications in Appendix A. Send them a postcard and get on their mailing lists. You can acquire a great deal of information about microcomputers just from the advertisements. It is also a good idea to visit a local computer store and get a free demonstration.

Figure 5.6
Sample Spelling Program

```
220  HOME
225  READ A$
230  HOME : VTAB 10
231  NORMAL
240  PRINT "HIT THE SPACE BAR AND SPELL"
250  HTAB 29
260  VTAB 10
265  INVERSE
280  PRINT A$
290  GET Z$
310  HOME
320  HTAB 17
330  VTAB 10
340  INPUT B$
350  IF B$ < > A$ THEN PRINT "NO": GET Z$: GOTO 230
365  HTAB 10
366  VTAB 10
370  IF B$ = A$ THEN PRINT "GREAT—GREAT—GREAT"
380  GET Z$
505  GOTO 220
700  DATA JANUARY, FEBRUARY, MARCH, APRIL, MAY, JUNE, JULY, AUGUST
701  DATA SEPTEMBER, OCTOBER, NOVEMBER, DECEMBER
```

Figure 5.7
Sample Addition Drill Program

```
10    HOME
20    REM   ADDITION DRILL PROGRAM
30    X = 0
40    Y = 0
50    HTAB 13: VTAB 10
60    PRINT "ADDITION DRILL"
70    HTAB 17: VTAB 12
80    PRINT "LEVEL 1"
90    GET A$: HOME
100   REM   GENERATE RANDOM NUMBERS A% AND B%
110   A% = RND (10) ★ 100
120   B% = RND (10) ★ 100
130   REM   PRINT PROBLEM AND GET ANSWER
140   PRINT
150   HTAB 15: VTAB 10
160   PRINT A%; " + "; B%; " = ";
170   INPUT C%
180   REM   IS ANSWER CORRECT?
190   IF C% = A% + B% THEN 240
200   REM   ANSWER IS NOT CORRECT
210   PRINT "NOPE...TRY..TRY..AGAIN"
220   Y = Y + 1
230   GET A$: HOME: GOTO 150
240   Y = Y + 1
250   X = X + 1
260   PRINT "    RIGHT ON...GOOD WORK"
270   GET A$: HOME
280   IF Y = 10 THEN GOTO 300
290   GOTO 100
300   PRINT "YOU GOT ";X;" RIGHT OUT OF";Y
310   END
```

Do's and Don'ts

1. Don't use the computer *exclusively* for the playing of video games.
2. Do keep work sessions at the microcomputer relatively short.
3. Do look for software variations which allow the student to practice the same set of skills.
4. Do make a contract with students on proper behavior when

using the microcomputer, and be consistent in delivering consequences.

5. Do have students chart or record performance data after each session.
6. Do review student performance data regularly and change the level of program if necessary.
7. Don't use the computer as a substitute for direct instruction.
8. Don't use the computer as "busy work" just to keep students occupied.
9. Do teach the students the proper care of the equipment, names for the devices, and how to properly handle disks.
10. Do use the computer with pairs or small groups of students in cooperative team activities and not just one-on-one instruction.

Video Tape Recorders and Cameras

Video cassette recorders and cameras have a variety of applications in a classroom for the mentally retarded. Many schools use the systems to tape evening television programs for viewing the next day. Schools often write for special permission to be allowed the privilege to tape these shows for one time only use. Your school or district librarian would be best informed on the copyright fair use laws in regard to the duplication and use of commercially broadcast programs. The types of shows which can be taped and might be useful in a class for the mildly retarded include documentaries and news broadcasts.

Another use for a videotape system is in the areas of social skills development and oral communication. Videotaping simulated job interviews and job activities provides a feedback mechanism for both the teacher and the student to critique. The system can also be used by the teacher to improve her skills or that of her aide by taping and then replaying and reviewing segments of the school day.

Summary

The technology options described in this chapter were presented to stimulate your thinking on options for presenting information to your students. They were also presented to allow you to consider how their use could circumvent or accommodate a disabling condition within the learner. None of these devices will be effective unless they are used as an integrated and planned part of a learner's instructional program by the teacher. The options presented here do not constitute the universal set of available technologies for use by the teacher and the learner. Each year new options have become available. The special education teacher should be alert to nontraditional uses of these new products.

Appendix A: Microcomputer Publications and Software Sources

Publications

Softside
P.O. Box 68
Milford, NH 03055

The Book
14013 Old Harbor Land Suite 312
Marina Del Rey, CA 90291

Technological Horizons in
    Education
P.O. Box 992
Acton, MA 01720

On Computing
P.O. Box 307
Martinsville, NJ 08836

Byte
70 Main Street
Petersborough, NH 03458

Educational Technology
140 Sylvan Avenue
Englewood Cliffs, NJ 07631

Personal Computing
1050 Commonwealth Ave.
Boston, MA 02215

Media and Methods
1511 Walnut Street
Philadelphia, PA 19102

Software Sources

The Software Exchange
6 South Street
Milford, NH 03055

Synergistic Software
5221 120th Ave SE
Bellvue, WA 98006

Edu-ware Services, Inc.
2222 Shermon Way #102
Canoga Park, CA 91303

Microlab
811 Stonegate
Highland Park, IL 60035

On-line Systems
36575 Mudge Ranch Rd.
Coasegold, CA 93614

Rainbow Computing, Inc.
Garden Plaza Shopping Center
9719 Reseda Blvd.
Northridge, CA 91324

MUSE Software
330 N. Charles St.
Baltimore, MD 21201

Southwestern Data Systems
P.O. Box 582-5
Sontee, CA 92072

Continental Software
30448 Via Victoria
Rancho Palos Verdes, CA 90274

Remember this . . .

1. Worksheets are probably the most abused type of educational materials used in a classroom.

2. Instructional television can be an effective and efficient means to teach social studies, science, and health.

3. The chalkboard is generally the most heavily used piece of instructional media in a classroom.

4. There are correct and incorrect ways to design worksheets.

CHAPTER VI

Instructional Media and Materials

There are no magic black boxes or instructional materials which guarantee success. Even "validated" or "field-tested" materials have limitations. Each must be used properly by a trained professional. There is no substitute for being thoroughly familiar with the instructional materials you will be using, the content you will be teaching, or the machinery you will be operating. This chapter will deal with a variety of media and materials which the teacher of the mentally retarded will find useful. Materials catalogs and even some journal articles attempt to perpetuate the myth of "foolproof" materials. What this chapter will highlight is the fact that teachers need to make intelligent decisions regarding the media and materials which they use. The media and materials do not teach, only teachers (and paraprofessionals) can teach.

The media or materials are the means a teacher uses to present information, practice skills, or reinforce related experiences, but it is the teacher who organizes the instruction and directs the learner's activities. Teachers use a variety of media and materials for the following reasons:

1. Changing materials minimizes boredom on the part of the learner.
2. Presentation of the same information in a different format facilitates transfer and generalization of a skill.
3. Use of different materials and examples facilitates concept formation.

4. The use of different materials maintains the learner's interest and helps focus attention.
5. Different materials provide alternatives for extended practice which is necessary for skill development in basic academic areas, e.g., computation or sight-word vocabulary. (See Figure 6.1 for a list of free and inexpensive material.)

Figure 6.1
Free and Inexpensive Materials for Teachers

1. The Children's Zoo, Eli Lilly & Co. Public Relations Services, 307 E. McCarthy St., Indianapolis, IN 46285 (1970, 12 pp; free)
2. Coloring Books, Animal Welfare Institute, P.O. Box 3650, Washington, D.C. 20007. Single copy free to teachers: 20¢ each to others.
3. Animal Friends, Animal Rescue League of Boston, P.O. Box 265, Boston, MA 02117. Bi-monthly: 4 pp, $2.00 annual subscription for 6 issues.
4. Card Aids, Teachers Exchange of San Francisco, 600 35th Avenue, San Francisco, CA 94121. Add 50 cents to prices for shipping:
    More Time to Draw (cursive) $1.95
    More Time to Draw (Manuscript) $1.95
    Time to Draw $1.95
5. Exploring the World of Arts (SC-4306) World Book-Childcraft International, Inc., Merchandise Mart Plaza, Chicago, IL 60654; 1978 20 cents.
6. Resource Handbooks. Instructor Publications, Inc., P.O. Box 6177 Duluth, MN 55806; 48 pp each $2.95 each.
7. Suggestions for Your Art Education Program. Consumer Relations Manager. Binney Smith, Inc., 110 Church Lane, P.O. Box 431, Easton, PA 18042.
8. The Overhead Projector in Mathematics Classroom. National Council of Teachers in Mathematics. 1906 Association Drive, Reston, VA 20091, 1974, 32 pp; $2.00.
9. Pin It, Tack It, Hang It: The Big Book of Kid's Bulletin Board Ideas. Workman Publishing Co., Inc., 1 West 39th Street, New York, NY 10018, 1975, 288 pp, $14.95.
10. Posters and Prints; Giant Photos, Box 406 Rockford, IL 61105, A large assortment of color posters and pictures are available for 25 cents to $1.50; send for free brochure.

Figure 6.1 (Con't)

11. Posters for Teachers and Librarians: A Sourcebook of Free and Inexpensive Items. Dale E. Shaffer, Library Consultant, 437 Jennings Avenue, Salem, OH 44460, 1978, 31 pp, $3.50.

12. Visual Aids Posters, Hayes School Publishing Co., Inc., 321 Pennwood Avenue, Wilkinsburg, PA 15221, $2.00 each.

13. Famous People: Historical, Biographical Book of Birthdays. Louis F. Mlecka, Publisher, P.O. Box 908, Brookville, FL 33512, 1973, 300 pp, $1.95.

14. A Special Kind of Courage. Bantam Books, 666 Fifth Avenue, New York, NY 10103, 1976, 274 pp, $1.75.

15. Books and Articles about the Sea. Miami Seaquarium, Public Information Office, 4400 Rickenbacker Cswy., Miami, FL 33149, Rev., 1976, 38 pages, 50¢.

16. Edible Wild Plants. Scarfo Productions, 1114 Osborne Rd., Dowenington, PA 19335, 1973, $3.50.

17. Man's Habitat in the City (#79061) $1.50 G4-9 National Wildlife Federation, 1412 16th St., N.W., Washington, D.C. 20036.

18. How to Care for Living Things in the Classroom. National Science Teachers Association, 1742 Connecticut Avenue, N.W., Washington, D.C. 20009, 1978, 20 pp, $1.00.

19. Nature by the Month, The Interstate Printers and Publishers, Inc., 19-27 Jackson St., Danville, IL 61832, 1976, 80 pp, $2.95.

20. Exploring the World of Work (SC-4307) World Book—Childcraft International, Inc., Merchandise Mart Plaza, Chicago, IL 60654, 1978, 8 page fold-out, 20¢.

21. Federal Job Information Centers, U.S. Civil Service Commission, Washington, D.C. 20415, 1978, 11 pp, free.

22. Exploring Careers (BLS Bulletin 2001) a set of 15 booklets, 1978, 28 to 50 pp each, $2.00, U.S. Department of Labor, Bureau of Labor Statistics, 230 South Dearborn St., Chicago, IL 60604.

23. How to get and keep the right job. Carnation Co., Public Relations, 5045 Wilshire Blvd., Los Angeles, CA 90036, free.

24. After High School—What? C5506, 1973, 15 pp, $1.50, Channing L. Bete Company, 200 State Rd., South Deerfield, MA 01373.

25. Seven Careers (FIL049) American Foundation for the Blind, 15 W. 16th Street, New York, NY 10011, Rev. 1973, 12 pp, free.

26. Be Informed on News Media. New Readers Press, Box 131, Syracuse, NY 13210, 1976, 40 pp, $1.20.

Figure 6.1 (Con't)

27. Debate Material. The Foundation of Economic Education, Inc., 30 S. Broadway, Irvington-on-Hudson, NY 10533, one package free.

28. Newspaper Workshop: Understanding Your Newspaper. Globe Book Co., Inc. 50 W. 23rd St., New York, NY 10010, 1978, 152 pp, $4.28.

29. Woodsy Owl Environmental Education Teacher's Kit. Woodsy Owl Forest Service. USDA, P.O. Box 1963, Washington, DC 20013. Free single copy.

30. Forms in Your Future. Globe Book Co., 50 W. 23rd St., New York, NY 10010, Rev. 1980, 112 pp., $3.48.

31. Your Right to Write. Clorox Co. Consumer Services, P.O. Box 24305, Oakland, CA 94623, 10 pp., up to 25 copies free.

32. ADA Instructional Aids. American Dental Assoc., Bureau of Health Education and Audiovisual Service, 211 E. Chicago, IL 60611, free brochure.

33. Yes You Can Teach Dental Health (#244-25902). American Alliance for Health, Physical Education, Recreation and Dance, Publications Sales, P.O. Box 870, Lanham, MD 20801, 46 pp., $2.10.

34. Early Childhood Education Activity Books. Milken Publishing Co., 1100 Research Blvd., St. Louis, MO 63132 (at economical prices).

35. DLM's 101 Ways to Beat the Clock for $5.00 or Less. Developmental Learning Materials, 7440 Natchez Ave., Niles, IL 60648, 1980, 38 pp., free.

36. Golden Readiness Books. Western Publishing Co., School and Library Div., Dept. FC, P.O. Box 708, Racine, WI 53401, most under $1.00, request free brochure.

37. Through Their Looking Glass (#84-6). Incentive Publications Inc., 2400 Crestmoor Rd., Nashville, TN 37215, 1979, 104 pp., $5.00.

38. The World Around You: Environmental Education Packet. The Garden Club of America, 598 Madison Ave., New York, NY 10022, one packet free to teachers each add $2.00.

39. Amoco Teaching Aids, Amoco Educational Services, Public Affairs—MC 3705, P.O. Box 5910-A, Chicago, IL 60680, 7 pp., free.

40. Journey Through a Stock Exchange. American Stock Exchange, Publications Dept., 86 Trinity Pl., New York, NY 10016, 1974, 24 pp., single copy 50¢.

41. Audiovisual Aids and Materials for Teaching Economics (#288), 3rd ed., 1980, 176 pp., $3.50.

42. Kid's Stuff Teacher's Plan Book (#60-9). Incentive Publications, Inc., 2400 Crestmoor Rd., Nashville, TN 37215, 1978, 56 pp., $3.95.

Figure 6.1 (Con't)

43. NAEP Materials. National Assessment of Educational Progress, 700 Lincoln Tower, 1860 Lincoln St., Denver, CO 80295.

44. Toward a Contact Curriculum (G480). Anti-Defamation League of B'nai B'rith, 823 United Nations Plaza, New York, NY 10017, 1974, 54 pp., 95¢.

45. Basic English Review. South Western Pub. Co., 5101 Madison Rd., Cincinnati, OH 45227, 1977, 220 pp., $3.95.

46. The Development of Language Arts: From Birth Through Elementary School. Professional Educators Publications, Inc., Box 80728, Lincoln, NE 68501, 1973, 79 pp., $1.75.

47. Fonetic English Spelling. Fonetic English Spelling Ass., 1418 Lake St., Evanston, IL 60204, 1966, 50 pp., $1.00.

48. Language Patterns and Usage, 1979, 6 books, 1 per grade, 72 pages, each 94¢. The Continental Press Inc., Elizabethtown, PA 17022.

49. Reading for Fun: How to Establish a Motivational Reading Program for Children. Children's Reading Program, Div. of Continuing Education, Univ. of Kansas, 645 New Hampshire, Lawrence, KS 66044, 1980, 21 pp., $2.00.

50. Spelling: A Mnemonics Approach. South-Western Pub. Co., 5101 Madison Rd., Cincinnati, OH 45227, 1977, 239 pp., $3.66.

51. Hooked on Books: Program and Proof. Berkley Pub. Co., 200 Madison Ave., New York, NY 10016, 1966, 236 pp., $2.50.

Compiled by Janice Harper

Worksheets

By far the most commonly used form of instructional material used by the classroom teacher is the "worksheet." Not only is it the most commonly used but also it is probably the most commonly "misused" type of instructional material. In many classrooms the worksheet is the substitute for a good management system or good instruction. In the 1970s teachers were introduced to "self-paced" instructional programs which were "individualized" according to student performance data. Many of these self-paced materials were teacher independent and heavily based upon paper-and-pencil worksheets or workbooks. Students were grouped into "instructional modules" based upon their criterion-referenced test performance. Like many educational innovations, the system was abused. Some teachers saw the materials as a substitute for teacher-directed lessons, and students made contact with the teacher only when they needed help. The slow learner may not know when he needs help and, therefore, gets very little. Worksheets are an essential component of the instructional process, but the teacher must be aware of their limitations and possible misuses.

Limitations and Misuses

Sternberg and Sedlak (1981) have delineated a number of misuses of worksheets, which include:
1. Being used for classroom control
2. Producing instructional isolation
3. Being a substitute for instruction
4. Providing permanent products of failure
5. Allowing students to practice their errors
6. Masking processing errors

Some teachers use worksheets as a substitute for a classroom management plan. Their rationale is that students need to be kept busy so as not to cause problems. As long as there are available worksheets students will keep quiet. There are other instructionally valid ways to keep students busy, for example, working on a project in pairs or small groups. Unfortunately, such an activity requires that a classroom management plan be in effect and that students understand the rules. Teachers without such a plan rely on worksheets and isolation as their means of management. A teacher who is ill-prepared to teach a lesson or who is not comfortable with the content of the subject matter will substitute worksheets for the instruction (Sternberg and Sedlak, 1981). Being able to explain math or science concepts requires that the teacher understands the concepts. Worksheets don't require a great deal of understanding.

The fact that worksheets provide a permanent product of a learner's work has both pros and cons. A worksheet covered in red with "X's" speaks clearly to the learner. He has failed. The mentally retarded have a history of failure. Failure (and permanent products of failure) will do little to decrease a learner's failure expectancy. Worksheets which are completed by the learner must be corrected as soon as possible. In fact, it is a good idea to spot check sheets while a student is working so that he is not allowed to practice his errors.

The authors have seen far too many examples of student's work where more than 50% of the items were incorrect.

Finally, if a student is only given an opportunity to demonstrate his understanding of skills and concepts on worksheets, he may be getting correct answers for the wrong reasons. Chapter III provides some examples of this failing. Because worksheets allow limited behavioral interaction, a student only practices a skill in one way—through writing. Reading, for example, is an auditory process and yet some reading programs rely heavily on paper-and-pencil "instruction." The learners develop silent reading skills measured by paper and pencil tests but perform less adequately in oral reading and phonetic word-attack skills. Appropriate practice is an essential component to remember when selecting a piece of media for instructional purposes.

Proper Design and Use of Worksheets

It is important to minimize the reading requirements of the worksheet for the mentally retarded. The worksheet should be uncluttered and present no more than two different activities (see Figures 6.2 and 6.3). It is preferable that the worksheet have only one activity. The number of problems or items on a sheet needs to be determined by the teacher in accordance with the level of functioning of the learner. Successful completion of a worksheet can have a highly reinforcing effect on a learner. With one learner a worksheet might only have five or six items while for another learner it might have 100. A worksheet should provide a student sufficient work to be completed within ten minutes. If the task looks too foreboding the learner will give up. Some rules for the design and use of worksheets include:

1. Minimize unnecessary reading requirements.
2. Maintain an uncluttered appearance.
3. Number of items should not exceed what a student can do in ten minutes.
4. Only skills or information which were previously taught should appear on the sheet.
5. Items should be organized by dimensions for easy error analysis.
6. Do the first item or two with the learner to be sure he understands the directions.
7. Teacher should examine work for systematic errors.

8. Sheets should be corrected promptly by the teacher and returned to the learner.
9. The learner should correct all errors.
10. Write comments on learner's paper (e.g., "good work," "keep trying," etc.).

Reusable Worksheets

Worksheets can be covered with clear contact paper or laminated. You won't do this with most worksheets except those which might be used for drill purposes. Worksheets on addition, subtraction, multiplication, division facts, states and their capitals, states and their ab-

Figure 6.2
Examples of Poorly Designed Worksheets

NAME		
54	53	47
− 17	+ 26	× 3
5 7 9 4 9		
+6 −2 +3 +7 +1		
3√27	9√42	12√38

Directions:
Underline all of the nouns, circle the verbs, and X-out the adjectives.
1. Bill and Mary had a picnic lunch.
2. The fat clown fell on his face.
3. The large balloon drifted over the mountains and across the tranquil plain.

Problems

1. Different numbers of items on each line.
2. Cluttered appearance.
3. Not organized by dimensions.
4. Wide difficulty range.

Problems

1. Not organized by dimensions.
2. Directions too complex — student could make errors because of directions and not because he doesn't know a noun, verb, or adjective.
3. No place for "name."
4. Vocabulary in sentences is probably too difficult.
5. Cluttered appearance.

Figure 6.3
Well Designed Worksheets

NAME _____ DATE_____

Directions: Add

25	36	15	14	53
+ 17	+ 18	+ 36	+ 17	+ 29

26	24	32	22	16
+ 13	+ 25	+ 17	+ 75	+ 31

Directions: Subtract

42	54	51	31	82
− 17	− 18	− 36	− 17	− 29

39	49	49	97	47
− 13	− 25	− 17	− 75	− 31

NAME _____ DATE_____

Directions: Circle (○) the *nouns*.

1. The cat ran across the busy street.
2. The fat dog chased the rabbit.
3. Bill and Tom had a picnic lunch.
4. Springfield is the capital of Illinois.

Directions: Put an "X" on the *verbs*.

5. The cat ran across the busy street.
6. The fat dog chased the rabbit.
7. Bill and Tom had a picnic lunch.
8. Springfield is the capital of Illinois.

breviations, presidents, antonyms, and colors, are some which you might wish to use more than once. Students can write on the sheets in crayon, grease pencil, or overhead projector pen and then wipe off with a cloth or tissue.

Manipulatives

The use of manipulatives offers the learner as well as the teacher instructional options not present in worksheet-oriented programs. These options can best be described by the factors that are inherent in the use of manipulatives.

First, the use of manipulatives helps to provide individualization of instruction. Although one might assume that using manipulatives would mandate one-to-one instruction, this is not necessarily the case. For example, knowing the mathematics concept level of each learner, small group instruction can be pursued with the teacher meeting each learner's needs with the same manipulatives. In that the teacher controls the questions being asked of each learner, individualization of instruction can be realized.

Second, the use of manipulatives allows the teacher to provide instruction in a given area while partialing out reading as a requirement for problem solving. For example, in that verbal problem solving represents an important aspect of applied mathematics, it is necessary to provide instruction in the area even though poor reading skills are evident. By using manipulatives, verbal problems can be presented and used to insure that the learner is attending to the language of the problem and not just the numerals.

Third, the use of manipulatives maximizes behavioral interactions. When the teacher employs objects or pictures in instruction, she typically must be close to the learners. The learner may interact with the teacher in a number of different ways. The learner may build, identify, write, or state the correct answer.

Fourth, the use of manipulatives provides instant feedback. By using manipulatives effectively, the teacher can demonstrate not only the correct answer but also the correct process or procedure to follow. Learners who cannot tolerate delay in feedback can be given manipulatives to prove the accuracy of their responses as well as to reinforce the use of a correct process.

The use of manipulatives allows students to work together cooperatively. Students may work to solve a common problem, and at the same time, realize that problems can be solved in many different ways. Diagnosis on the basis of observable behavior is another advantage of the use of manipulatives. When a teacher asks a learner to demonstrate with manipulatives the procedure or process used to solve a problem, any difficulties that the learner experiences can be observed and analyzed.

Finally, the use of manipulatives masks failure to the learner. When the teacher presents a problem to the learner which requires the learner to demonstrate understanding of a process or answer, incorrect responses can be removed, and the teacher can present concepts to which the learner can respond successfully. The result being that no permanent product of failure remains and the learner is exposed to continuous success.

All of the following materials can be manipulatives:

flannel boards	paper letters
felt boards	play money
magnet boards	clocks
globes	puzzles
telegraph key	puppets
stencils	clay
patterns	flash cards
blocks	road maps
logs	dolls
abacus	measuring devices
mock-ups and cutaways from commercial and industrial firms	looms

Instructional Games

All games can be instructional and used to promote growth in math, spelling, reading, social interaction, and organization. Students are usually motivated by games so that the teacher who consistently uses games in the classroom should see an increase in appropriate behavior as well as in learning, transference, and maintenance of skills. Although there are many excellent games commercially available, some game material will have to be developed in the classroom. Game construction requires certain designing in order to produce the required results. The designer must give the game a title which is descriptive and motivating. Sources of ideas for games can be explored and include teachers' journals, idea books, TV game adaptations, and students themselves. The purpose of the game must be defined as well as the number of participants, and sequenced directions.

According to Salend (1979) teacher-constructed games can be evaluated on the following:

1. Are the rules understandable and complete?
2. Have prerequisite skills been identified and taken into account?
3. Are the format and content appropriate to the participants?
4. Is the game free of biases, gender, or ethnic?
5. Can the game be played without supervision?
6. Is the game motivating?
7. Does the game promote social interaction?
8. How much time is needed to play the game?
9. How many participants does the game require?
10. Is the vocabulary level appropriate?
11. Are the objectives specified and does the content reinforce the objectives?
12. Is the mode of response suitable?

Basic classroom games are:

Crossword Puzzles	Rebus	Truth or
20 Questions	Anagrams	Consequences
Bingo	Bees	Seven Up
Hidden Words	Scrambled Word	Concentration
Hangman	Sentences	Puzzles
		Checkers

Many of these basic games can be developed for use in more than one subject area. We may have traditional Bingo, or construct a bingo of places, people, and events that deal with history, geography, reading plus current events. Bingo can be used to teach synonyms, antonyms, and homonyms. We may hold spelling bees, addition or multiplication bees, or current-event bees. A puzzle of the U.S. could develop fine-motor skills and a knowledge of U.S. geography. Then the teacher might say, "Now come to the desk and try to list twenty states" or "Now let's time you and see if you can get that puzzle completed in five minutes or less."

Other easily constructed games are Word Checkers and Month Identification. Word Checkers is played exactly like regular checkers except that words have been taped to the squares with masking tape and the player must be able to read the word or words on the square if he is to complete a move. If he misses, he is told the correct answer but cannot move until his next turn. Month Identification calls for a picture suitable for each month with the numbers one to twelve under each picture in random order. The player is given an answer sheet with a list of the months in order. Then the pictures are held up and the player places the number of the picture next to the name of the month it illustrates. This type of game can have only one player and the other participant can be a student aide, or teacher or can be played by the entire class.

Keep in mind that instructional games should be easy to make and use. Do not use time needed for planning and instruction to create elaborate games. Encourage student help for the actual construction and don't forget to trade games with other teachers and the school library.

Bulletin Boards

Bulletin boards should be a teaching tool, should contribute to the tone of the classroom, and should not require a considerable amount of time to prepare. Do not hesitate to use free poster-type materials that come to you in the mail or are made available by the government or various industries. Students can be responsible for keeping the room supplied with cut paper letters. Students can often be involved in the actual construction of bulletin boards so that they benefit from the work and planning that such a project involves. For example, if you want to teach the idea of a pattern (math, art, music) students could be given materials and directions for pattern construction and encouraged to develop their own for bulletin board use. The result is a bright and interesting display, providing the teacher with an opportunity to introduce the idea of pattern, while allowing the student to develop that idea. Use bulletin boards as interest-rousing as well as instructional devices. Do not overlook the bulletin board as a means of showing sample work, announcing activities, teaching current events, presenting problems, and testing (see Figures 6.4, 6.5, and 6.6).

Figure 6.4
Bulletin Board A

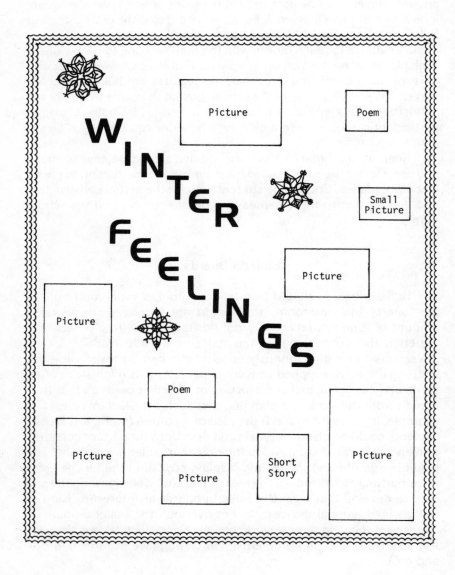

Figure 6.5
Bulletin Board B

Charleroi Calendar

February

Sun	Mon	Tues	Wed	Thur	Fri	Sat
				1	2	3
4	Winter Carnival	6	7	8	Basketball Game	10
11	Lincoln's Birthday	13	Valentine Party	15	16	17
Home Show	19	20	21	Washington's Birthday	23	24
25	School Musical	27	28			

Figure 6.6
Bulletin Board C

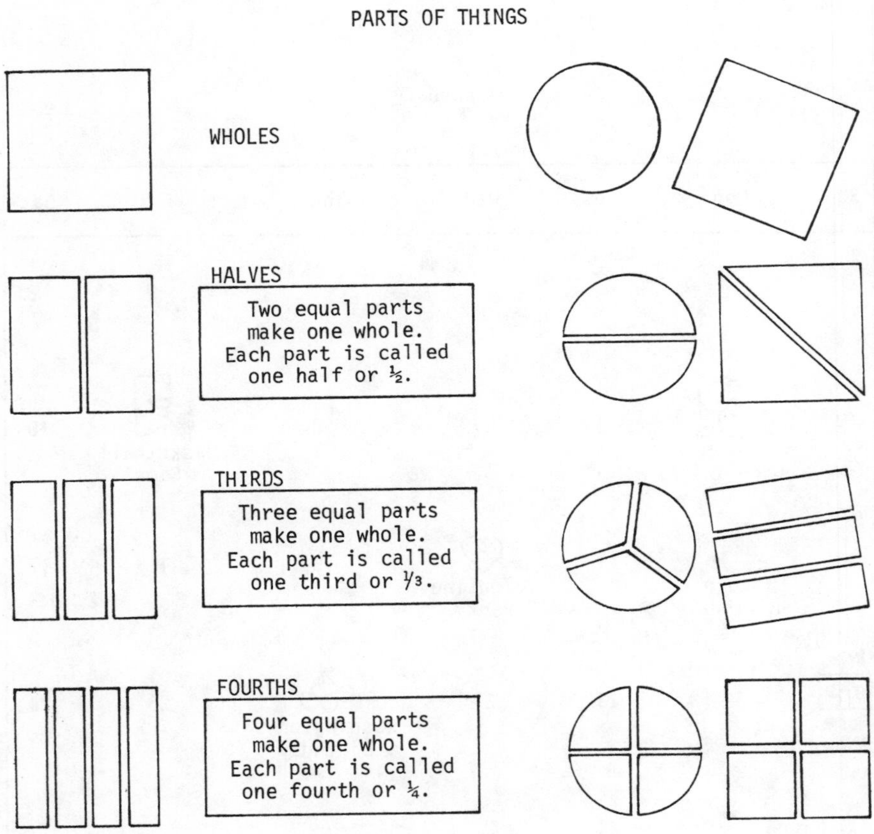

PARTS OF THINGS

WHOLES

HALVES

> Two equal parts
> make one whole.
> Each part is called
> one half or ½.

THIRDS

> Three equal parts
> make one whole.
> Each part is called
> one third or ⅓.

FOURTHS

> Four equal parts
> make one whole.
> Each part is called
> one fourth or ¼.

When designing a bulletin board consider:
1. Balance
2. Unity
3. Movement
4. Clarity
5. Simplicity
6. Space
7. Line
8. Shape
9. Size
10. Texture
11. Color

Self-Correcting Materials

Instructional materials which have a self-correcting feature are available from commercial publishers or can be easily constructed by the classroom teacher, aide, volunteer, or even students (see Figure 6.7). Mercer and Mercer (1978) indicate that self-correcting materials are useful with learners who have a history of failure because they minimize the public occurrence of a mistake when practicing. The learner also receives immediate corrected feedback so that he does not practice his errors. Students approach them from the perspective of the task being a game. Mercer and Mercer (1978) have identified ten different formats which can be used for the construction of self-correcting materials. These include the use of a flap, slot, matching cards, puzzle, balance scales, tab, pocket, electricity, and magnetism.

Conventional Instructional Equipment

The chalkboard remains the most frequently used type of instructional equipment. As with most types of equipment it holds high motivational promise. Students like to write and draw on a chalkboard.

A student, "stuck" on a math problem at his seat, can be brought to the board for a brief math lesson. The change, from seatwork to boardwork, often gets the student back on track. Drill and practice, games, quick examples, and individual work may all take advantage

Figure 6.7
Samples of Self-Correctional Devices

Flap

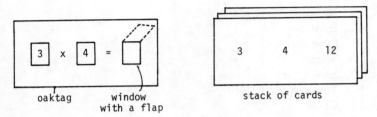

oaktag   window   stack of cards
           with a flap

Directions: The oaktag sheet is placed on top of the stack
             of cards with the flap closed. After the learner
             responds he checks his answer by raising the flap.

Tab

	Pull up		Pull up
1. The opposite of black is	_____		1. white
2. The opposite of slow is	_____		2. fast
3. The opposite of go is	_____		3. stop
4. The opposite of run is	_____		4. walk
5. The opposite of win is	_____		5. lose

Pocket

Directions: Glue or staple to the back of a question sheet an envelope with the answer key.

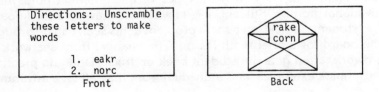

Front   Back

Figure 6.7 (Con't)

<u>Magnet</u>

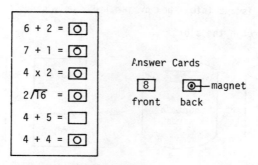

Answer Cards

8   ⊙—magnet

front   back

Paper clip is hidden behind a piece
of paper following each equation.
The answer card will stick to each
equation which is "8."

<u>Puzzles</u>

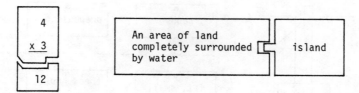

<u>Meeting Cards</u>

Cards have question or problem on front and answer on back.

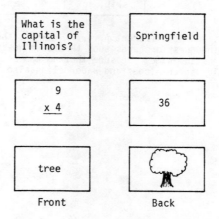

Front   Back

Figure 6.7 (Con't)

Slot

A slot is cut into a box or jar lid. Only cards of "correct" size will fit through the slot.

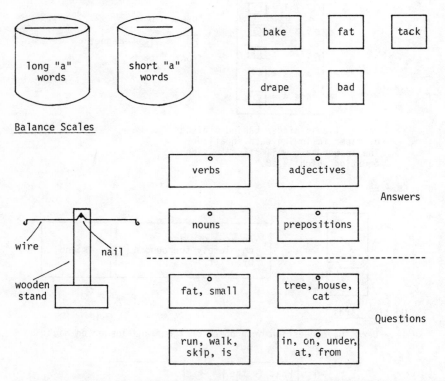

Balance Scales

Directions: Glue different numbers of cards to the backs of the answer and corresponding question cards such that each question and corresponding answer weighs the same. Be sure that no two answer cards weigh the same. You could use envelopes and paper clips also for this activity.

Figure 6.7 (Con't)

Electricity

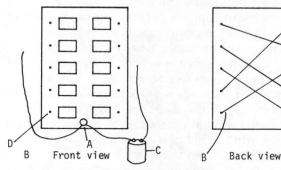

Front view   Back view

A. light, buzzer, or bell

B. wire

C. dry cell

D. metal tab

of the availability of the chalkboard. Notices to students about coming events, changes in the daily schedule and behavior may also be written on the chalkboard and remind the teacher as well as the student of fluctuating situations. Teachers should not overlook the chalkboard in their mastery of media.

Projectors — Overhead and Opaque

Overhead and opaque projectors are valuable and versatile pieces of equipment. They have both instructional and motivational value in teaching the retarded.

An overhead projector can be used to project an image from a transparency onto a screen, wall, or chalkboard. Transparencies can be made ahead of time by the teacher (or purchased from a commercial publisher). When the lesson is taught the teacher needs merely to put each transparency on the overhead as needed. The pace of a lesson can be regulated by blocking out segments of the transparency and then gradually revealing each section. Instructional time is maximized in the presentation of the lesson because rather than spending time writing the information on the chalkboard the teacher can be giving additional information. Transparencies can be prepared in a variety of background and print colors. Specific segments of information on the transparency can be highlighted by preparing it in a different color. Use of the projector allows a teacher to face the students while teaching (unlike teaching from a chalkboard) and to continuously monitor for lapses of attention. Students enjoy writing on transparencies or directly upon the glass top of the overhead projector.

Paper-based teaching material can easily be transformed into a transparency with the aid of a thermofax machine. Menus, employment forms, checks, and job announcements can all be easily duplicated onto a transparency and then projected with the overhead. Students or teacher can then complete them.

An opaque projector can be used to project printed material or three-dimensional objects. It is not as convenient to use as an overhead but has the advantage that most any type of material can be projected with no advance preparation. One "fun" activity with an opaque is to project images onto the chalkboard or large sheets of paper (or bulletin boards) and then trace them. If you are not a particularly gifted artist, the opaque projector is one device that can help tremendously when you want to "draw" a complex figure for a chart or bulletin board.

Instructional Television

Public television stations offer an excellent array of programs in social studies, health, science, mental health and language arts. The regular and judicious use of these programs can be a highly beneficial component of the curriculum. The typical program is only fifteen minutes in length and is well developed and highly organized. The shows can be taped to be shown later if the regularly scheduled times are not convenient. Schools can subscribe to the local educational network and get study guides and program listings which can help teachers plan and guide instruction.

It is stimulating for the student and provides a change of pace from seatwork and regular classroom activities. It is also an activity which emphasizes listening skills. Brief programs prevent or reduce attention span difficulties as does the fast pace. Most teachers could rarely deliver as much content in so brief a span of time or as dramatically as these instructional programs.

For example, the amount of time which it would take a teacher in a classroom to set up an experiment, prepare the students for what is to take place, carry it out, explain the results, and clean up would far exceed the amount of time which it would take to view such a lesson on educational TV. The nature of the medium allows several camera angles and close ups of important exerpts of the experiment. Used on a regular planned basis educational television programs can make a significant contribution to the total curriculum.

Summary

Instructional media and materials exist in quantity but must be used intelligently. We have attempted to discuss many of the common instructional media and materials, to point out pitfalls and to imagine appropriate, and even creative, use of the above. These media and materials exist to support the curriculum and the effort of the classroom professional, not to supplant them. Use these instructional aids correctly and they will work for you and your student.

Remember this . . .

1. Behavioral objectives are precisely defined statements which focus on student outcome behaviors.

2. The teacher's major role in the IEP process is the development of measurable behavioral objectives.

3. The requirements of PL 94-142 are not always adhered to by school districts.

4. It may help to have a conference with parents before the official IEP meeting.

CHAPTER VII

IEP's, Objectives, and Curriculum

A learner's IEP with its explicit goals and behavioral objectives must be as tied to curriculum as curriculum is intertwined with individual goals and objectives. This symbiotic relationship creates a situation which demands that a discussion of one necessitates a discussion of the others. This chapter attempts to guide the teacher through that relationship by explaining curriculum development through environmental analysis, explaining behavioral objectives as they should be written, and taking a brief look at IEP development.

While "methods" and "instructional strategies" constitute the variables under the heading "how to teach," "curriculum" defines the parameters of "what to teach." Discussion of curriculum can be a relatively "dry" subject albeit an important one.

Historical Overview

When asking the question "what to teach?" the teacher of the mentally retarded can be overwhelmed by the sheer volume of information which would be considered important for a student to learn. The teacher must therefore establish priorities regarding what in this vast array of knowledge is critical to successful functioning presently and in adulthood. To this end then the decisions must be driven by a philosophy. In the history of special education the philosophy which has shaped curriculum has changed and, consequently, so has the focus of the curriculum.

In the 1940s and 1950s the curriculum emphasis was on the "applied arts." Teacher training programs required courses in "arts and crafts" for the mentally handicapped, and there were few special education classrooms without a rug loom or planned periods of study which dealt with sewing, knitting, and potholder making. During this same period, the curriculum focused on the development of "self-concept." Academics were downplayed since these were the areas where the student was unsuccessful. Less instruction in content areas took place. Students were meant to be successful, and in order to accommodate success, academic subjects were not emphasized.

In the late 1950s and early 1960s Simches and Bohn (1963) found that the prevailing philosophy was to teach a "watered down" version of the regular curriculum. During this period in our history, students were not taught subjects different from the regular classes but just less of each. In the late 1960s and early 1970s the federal government took an active role in curriculum development and funded curriculum development projects for the mentally retarded in science, math, social learning, and physical education. The focus of these curriculum efforts was driven by a number of tenets:

1. Special education teachers were ill-trained to select relevant components of the curriculum.
2. The "method" of instruction was critical for the effective teaching of the mentally handicapped, and this method needed to be interwoven into the fabric of the curriculum.
3. Curriculum materials with multiple options of presentation and student response needed to be developed to meet the behavioral needs of the learners.
4. Students in special education classes were suffering from a "content deficit" in these learning environments. A resurgence of a content-based curriculum was needed.
5. Finally, the "process" of the curriculum needed to have a problem-oriented basis. Rather than focusing on isolated facts, the integration of lessons in these new curricula needed to focus on problem solving skills so that the learner could apply these skills to situations encountered in everyday living.

In the 1970s and 1980s the focus of curriculum has been refined still further with a philosophy toward the development of skills which an individual needs to function independently in specific environments in society and to be able to secure and maintain a job. The catch words which describe the focus of contemporary curriculum development efforts are "functional" and "chronologically age appropriate." The philosophy of functional and chronological age–appropriate objectives was proposed by Lou Brown and his associates at the University of Wisconsin at Madison. While Brown's focus has been on curriculum for the moderately and severely handicapped learners, the utility of the model is such that many of the principles are equally applicable to the more mildly handicapped, particularly those aspects which deal with environmental analysis and community-based training.

Curriculum and the Mentally Retarded

The dimensions of a curriculum for the educable mentally retarded should encompass many of the same content and subject areas taught to the regular student. The curriculum should focus not only on the "3 R's" but also on science, social studies, health, and vocational/career education. Information in these areas can be integrated into the math and language arts curriculum through examples provided by the teacher. The focus of the curriculum should be upon the development of functional vocationally oriented skills and those skills needed for independent living. In the primary grades, the emphasis on these skills can be peripheral to the development of basic academic and social skills; at the secondary level, the program should emphasize vocational skills and procedures for accommodating or compensating for academic and social skills deficits. Academic skills development is not ignored at the secondary level, but the curriculum needs to focus on the adult world of work and functional independent living skills. One measure which a teacher could use to gauge this change could be the amount of time spent each day in different areas of instruction. Figure 7.1 depicts this relationship.

While the subject matter will parallel that taught to the regular student, the manner in which the information is presented, the rate at which material is covered, and the emphasis upon individual needs should differentiate it from the instructional practices in the regular grades. Priorities regarding what to teach in terms of specific content in a skill area can be determined through an environmental analysis of the community. This environmental analysis will enable the teacher to identify specifically the spelling words to be taught, the functional reading skills needed, and the general information base needed by a retarded learner.

Figure 7.1

Relationship of Curriculum Emphasis and Age of Student

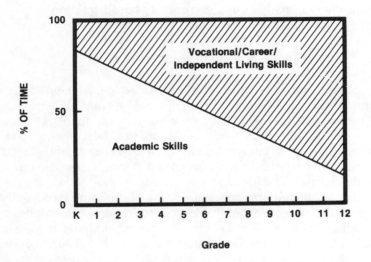

Environmental Analysis

The environmental analysis model (Brown, Branston, Baumgart, Vincent, Falvey, and Schroeder, 1979) relies upon the environment in which a student will be living as the source of curriculum goals and objectives. The model provides an analysis of the academic, social, and psychomotor skills needed to function successfully in an identified environment or subenvironment based upon an activity which would be conducted within that environment. Figure 7.2 provides a graphic display of the analysis of the environments and subenvironments to the point where identified skills are depicted. Figure 7.3 lists a series of questions which should be asked to determine the academic, social, motor, decision making, and related cognitive skills necessary for functioning in the targeted environment. An analysis of these related academic and cognitive skills is critical because they help form the basis of the content of school subjects such as spelling, reading, math, geography, etc.

For example, the spelling words used are based upon the words one needs to spell in particular environments and circumstances. The sight-word vocabulary is based upon functionally useful sight words. The model does not replace the traditional scope and sequence of content found in most texts but highlights the functional and essential content needed in particular environments. Some texts and workbooks may overlook or place insufficient emphasis on this content, in which case the teacher can substitute more relevant and functional content from that which is traditionally presented.

The model is particularly useful for teachers at the secondary level in their vocational training programs. To use this model effectively to prepare students for both current and subsequent environments requires that the teacher be knowledgeable of these environments and has done an analysis of these environments. The end result of that process is functional and defensible goals, objectives, and teaching activities.

Goals and Behavioral Objectives

Goals are broad-based statements which are stated implicitly rather than explicitly. Behavioral objectives are precisely defined statements which focus on the outcome behavior of a student. Most authorities agree that a well stated objective has four components: condition, behavior, content, and criteria.

Condition refers to the circumstances under which the learner will be able to exhibit all phases of the objective. These conditions are the "givens" or prerequisites. For example, the *condition* portion of an objective might state, "Given prior instruction in bowling . . . ," "Given a blank sheet of paper . . . ," or "Given a list of words . . ."

Behavior specifies observable acts. Examples of behaviors include the following:

To state	To compute	To demonstrate
To write	To recite	To draw
To match	To identify	To construct

Figure 7.2

Sample Environmental Analysis Model

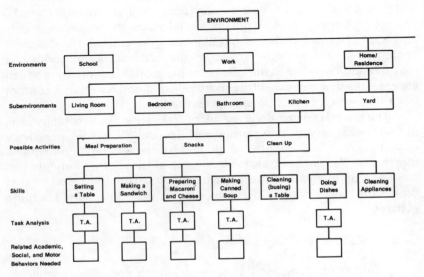

(See Figure 7.3 For Specific Questions To Ask)

To select	To discuss	To compare
To fasten	To cut	To connect

Content deals with the subject matter to be taught or evaluated. Sample content includes:

Single digit numbers
States and their capitals
Personal information (e.g., name, address, social security number)
Wood, metal, plastic
List of words

Sample Environmental Analysis Model (Cont.)

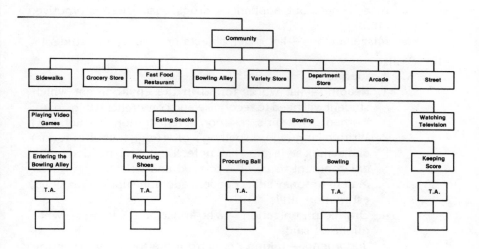

Criteria specify the level of competence which a student must exhibit in order to be successful in the achievement of the objective. These criteria are normally stated as percentages.

Writing Short-term Objectives for IEP's

Well written behavioral objectives are a necessary condition for an appropriate Individualized Educational Program. In addition, the objectives must constitute an integrated program rather than emphasize separate, isolated skills. One aspect of this plan which will need to be formulated is the sequencing of the objectives. Objectives in the

Figure 7.3

Outline for Academic, Social, and Motor Behaviors Needed in Subenvironments

I. Functional Objective Use or Environment Organization
    A. Equipment—list equipment needed in the environment (e.g., shipping cost, produce scale, light switch, doors, etc.)
    B. Departments—list departments needed (e.g., produce, meats, check out, appliances, drugs, cosmetics, automotive, etc.)
    C. Miscellaneous—list other objects needed by the student

II. Skills
    A. Academic
        1. Reading—list words found in the environment which student will need to recognize and comprehend (e.g., men, women, boys, girls, restrooms, registration, cashier, etc.)
        2. Written language—spelling words (e.g., names of foods) and syntax style (e.g., list, note, letter, etc.) needed in the environment to be able to read and write
        3. Match—money skills needed, addition/subtraction skills, estimation skills
        4. Oral communication—Who must be spoken to? What might be said?
        5. Judgments—taking items from the top rather than the middle
    B. Sensory motor
        1. Physical movement
        2. Visual movement
        3. Auditory
    C. Social skills—waiting turns, sharing, taking reasonable amount of time to complete task, asking for assistance

III. Prior Information Needed
    A. What to buy
    B. How long to stay
    C. Estimated cost or budget allowance
    D. Travel needs

same curriculum domain need to be ordered either from easy-to-difficult or on the basis of needed prerequisite skills such as in a task analysis. Another aspect of the sequencing problem is to list the objectives in terms of their importance and interrelationships.

Pitfalls in Writing Objectives

The teacher's major role in the IEP process is the development of functional and measurable behavioral objectives. Teachers approach this task with some trepidation. Tymitz (1980) found the most problematic area for teachers was developing statements which were logically and sequentially related. Tymitz-Wolf (1982) identified three major pitfalls in the development of IEP objectives which should be avoided:

1. Restating a goal as an objective by only changing the criteria
2. Stating a specific activity as a short-term objective
3. Writing incomplete, ambiguous, or nonmeasurable objectives

Taking a more positive approach to the development of functional and measurable behavioral objectives leads to three rules which offer considerable direction to the teacher.

RULE 1: SUBSKILL MASTERY CAN LEAD TO GOAL ACHIEVEMENT MORE READILY THAN MANIPULATING THE STANDARD OF PERFORMANCE. The teacher should task analyze the skill into its component parts and write these as short-term objectives rather than use the short-term objectives as successive approximations of the target behavior. For example, if the goal is "to increase ability to hit a baseball with a bat," the short-term objective *should not* be "Given a bat and a ball thrown across the home plate at moderate speed, the learner will hit the ball 30% of the time, 40% of the time, 50% of the time . . ." It would be far better to have a series of short-term objectives such as the following:

1. Given a bat, the learner will grip the bat within two inches from the slender end with both hands 100% of the time.
2. Given a bat, the learner will swing the bat in a smooth, level motion with arms extended 100% of the time.
3. Given a bat and a home plate, the learner will stand at the home plate with the bat properly gripped over the appropriate shoulder 100% of the time.

4.   Given a bat and a home plate, the learner will stand parallel
     to the home plate with feet square to the shoulders 100%
     of the time.

RULE 2: SHORT-TERM OBJECTIVES ON IEP'S SHOULD
DESCRIBE FUNCTIONAL SKILLS WHICH CAN BE TAUGHT
THROUGH A VARIETY OF ACTIVITIES. While there are some exceptions to this rule, the teacher should be wary of short-term objectives
which are overly limiting. A specific activity generally should not be
stated as a short-term objective on an IEP. For example, if the overall
goal is "to increase expressive language skills," an appropriate short-
term objective might be "Given pictorial stimuli or real objects of common nouns, the learner will identify these nouns by naming spontaneously 100% of the time." A less appropriate objective would be
"Given a worksheet with pictures of toys, the learner will name the
toys." The teacher should list the categories of nouns which might be
involved in the short-term objective to make it more useful (e.g., toys,
foods, transportation, clothing, environment).

RULE 3: SHORT-TERM OBJECTIVES SHOULD BE WRITTEN
SUCH THAT A SECOND PERSON COULD READ THE OBJECTIVE
AND BE ABLE TO ASSESS THE STUDENT AND DEVELOP A SET
OF ACTIVITIES WHICH REFLECT THE INTENT. It is not an easy task
to write clear behavioral objectives which are also functionally relevant. Teachers often find that the most important objectives are also
the most difficult to phrase. The end result, unfortunately, can be that
only the most mundane (but easily observable) behaviors are written
as short-term objectives in the IEP. The authors believe that no matter how difficult an objective is to phrase, the teacher should make
an attempt to write it even if Rule 3 is violated.

IEP Requirements

Federal law requires an IEP—approved in writing by parents or
guardians—for every child in a special education program. Parents
and guardians have the right to not approve the testing, placement,
or the special program for their child. Further, they have the right to
an impartial due process hearing if they and the school district cannot reach an agreement.

The IEP is a vital part of PL 94-142 and includes the following
components:

1. A statement of the present levels of educational performance of the child
2. A statement of annual goals, including short-term objectives
3. A statement of the specific educational services to be provided and the extent to which the student will be able to participate in regular educational programs
4. The projected date for initiation and anticipated duration of such services
5. Objective criteria and evaluation procedures for determining on an annual basis whether instructional objectives are being achieved

The IEP Meeting

Before the IEP meeting, review all student records and update formal and informal testing. Go to the IEP meeting with student records, all of your data (behavioral observations, grades, test scores, examples of student work), and any district forms completed. It may help to have a conference with the parents in the month before the official meeting to prepare them and give them time to think about their child's education. Districts often (and inappropriately) put time limits on IEP meetings so that a parent conference prior to the official meeting may be a great service to the student.

IEP meetings are run differently in every district so there are no specifics we can offer on precisely what to expect or what the teacher's role will be during the meeting. After the conference, it is almost certain that the teacher would write all short-term objectives if they were not developed at that conference.

Most students reading this text have studied PL 94-142 and understand its intent. Reality, however, does not always accurately represent the intent of the law. The following situations are actual case studies encountered by the authors which reflect less than optimal compliance with the law in regard to IEP development. We have offered some possible solutions to some, but for others even we are at a loss to solve. Be wary of these "danger zones," and do not be naive enough to think that they do not exist.

IEP Danger Zones

1. The student's IEP cannot be located. It is possible to begin a teaching position and discover that none of the IEP's that you were promised can be found. (Some might suspect that they do not exist.) The scenario goes approximately like this: "Yes, Mrs. Ramicone, Ms. Schuetz will have left IEP's for all twenty students in her file cabinet. Since school begins tomorrow, I suggest you go to the classroom and work out the students' schedules, mainstreaming where indicated. All other needed materials were ordered by Ms. Schuetz and will be on the worktable." Unfortunately, Mrs. Ramicone finds no IEP's or material but does meet twenty students the next day.

This situation occurs frequently, and the pressure to develop and produce the IEP's will be tremendous. Begin by thoroughly reading each student's record and then proceed to whatever formal and informal assessments are appropriate. Follow up any indications that students have been successfully mainstreamed in past years, accept this situation as one which is now your problem, and use your evenings and weekends in a professional fashion.

2. Your district has an individual in the main office who generates goals and objectives by going through each unit in the reading, spelling, and math series in use in the special education classroom. You, then, are told to write the student's name on the list of goals and objectives which match the book the student currently uses and file the list in your file drawer. What happened to individualization and learner characteristics? Expediency took their places. Attempt to use what is written by doing some editing, but remember that an appropriate IEP is your responsibility, and if you must write your own to fulfill that obligation then go directly to work.

3. The IEP's previously developed in your district do not include vocational goals, and such goals are not encouraged by the others on the IEP team. The district offers no vocational program for EMH students (work/study, machine shop, office machines, etc.), and such students are routinely denied admission into existing vocational programs. You have students who need to begin developing employment skills now or their chances for an independent life style will be severely hampered.

We believe that you have an obligation to do your very best to obtain an appropriate education for your students. We also believe that you may be putting your job in jeopardy by acting as an advocate against the decisions of your district. As we have no absolute answer to this dilemma, we can only offer possible approaches. Contact the advocacy agency or group in your area to see if it will work on this problem; contact parents who might be willing to take up the fight; attempt to develop a program such as a work/study or work/release type that you can take charge of or that volunteer parents can help supervise. If you are a nontenured teacher, you will have to weigh the possibility of job loss against the knowledge that you have students who need services that are not provided.

4. You are an itinerant secondary EMH teacher who spends no more than ninety minutes with any group of students. Students are mainstreamed the remainder of the school day. The district has no classes for students with behavior problems and no self-contained special education classes. You have an EMH student who has a history of behavior problems, and for the last six months his behavior has been most unacceptable with many violent episodes. As part of your normal record keeping, you have been collecting data on these episodes. Your supervisor has told you that under no circumstances are behavioral goals to be written for this student as the district wishes to avoid any possibility of the label "behavior disordered" being attached to this student because they have no wish to provide such services. While seated in the IEP conference room, you look up and see this student's parents arriving with a professional advocate and a lawyer. They want behavioral goals written on their son's IEP and a program worked out to establish control of his behavior. The district supervisor explains that their son has no behavior disorder and has no history of behavior problems, but rather he is an EMH delinquent-type and they need to do more with him at home. This response is unacceptable to the parents and their representative, but the supervisor refuses to compromise. The parents ask for your opinion . . .

Not only do we have the old dilemma of employment versus conscience but also there is an additional component of which you should be made aware. This situation is headed directly for a due process hearing in which all your research will be part of the case and you will, in fact, be the star witness. Two lawyers and a hearing officer will be questioning you at length and in detail. The "heat" will be on the EMH teacher, not on the district supervisor or any other teacher or administrator. We have seen teachers in tears at due process hearings when responsibility for all action fell on their shoulders and they could not defend their actions (i.e., IEP, record keeping, curriculum). Think about it.

Summary

The classroom teacher's major role in the IEP process is the development of measurable behavioral objectives. The ability to develop such objectives comes in part from a knowledge of functional curriculum goals as well as an understanding of how to incorporate the needs of individual students into the total curriculum. The behavioral objectives in the IEP are tied to the curriculum, and the wise professional will approach them as a unit and not as separate, unrelated entities.

Remember this . . .

1. Students need to be directly taught how to study.

2. The EMR learner often requires instruction in areas educators take for granted.

3. Students may need to be taught how to deliver a compliment.

4. EMR adults exhibit a low rate of voting behavior.

5. EMR learners must be directed into decision-making situations.

CHAPTER VIII

Study and Survival Skills

Students spend a great portion of school time attempting to learn content, often without possessing the skills to master that content. Students with learning problems often require special direct instruction in the area of study skills. With some special learners this may mean that the information must be presented at a slower rate, while with other learners it may mean that much extra practice is needed for skill mastery. Some students with learning problems need to have a skill broken down into many small steps while others can deal with skills only if presented in a certain sequence. Always take learner characteristics into consideration when teaching the following skills: paying attention, following directions, listening, applying alphabetical order and sequence, and using maps, charts, and graphs.

Paying Attention

Until a student learns to pay attention to instructional tasks, other study skills cannot be learned. Removing distractions, breaking instruction into small steps, rewarding on-task behavior, and using stimulating, age-appropriate materials may all help focus the student's attention on the task.

Following Directions

After a student learns to attend to instructional tasks, he or she must learn to follow written and oral directions. Make sure that your students understand the vocabulary used in task directions. At the beginning of the school year, go through the student's book and make a list of all directions (i.e., underline, circle, cross out) and then teach the student how to respond to these directions. Make a reminder poster which lists the most common directions and show a proper response to them.

Listening

Students must learn to listen not only for directions but for main ideas and details. There are many commercially available tapes that students can use to learn to listen for content. Oral reading of interesting and challenging works of fiction will motivate their desire to listen skillfully and therefore increase their ability to do so. Students who exhibit real difficulty in developing listening skills may benefit from a very sequenced, structured technique which has them listen to simple short paragraphs and respond to questions about content and gradually move to works with longer or more difficult paragraphs and questions about main ideas or specific details.

Applying Alphabetical Order and Sequence

Students have not mastered the alphabet until they can enter it at any point. Mastery of alphabetical order goes hand in hand with dictionary skills. Students must learn to estimate where to enter the dictionary in order to find certain words and must also learn to determine if the word they want will be found by turning forward or backward in the book. Students also need to learn how to use the index in a variety of books. Many teacher's guides include suggestions for teaching these skills but never hesitate to modify these or develop your own techniques to meet the needs of the learners in your classroom.

Using Maps, Charts, and Graphs

Simple maps, charts, and graphs should be introduced at the elementary level as part of math, social studies, and classroom management (i.e., stars for work completion, and for attendance). The authors feel that the ability to read a road map is a very important skill. Not only will the proper use of road maps get you where you are going and help you plan trips, but exploring with maps can be a delightful at-home leisure-time activity. Maps can be used as part of the classroom decoration and thus serve a double function. Students may draw their own maps of the classroom, the school, or the community as work with such familiar locales may be a necessary step in the process of learning map-reading skills.

Study Methods

Secondary students need to learn how to study. The EMH learner may not intuitively develop an appropriate study method but rather may need to be exposed to certain known methods in an attempt to find the one most suited to the individual's needs. Sabatino and Lanning-Ventura (1982) presented an overview of the following methods:

1.   P-A-T — Preview-Attacking-Testing
     Students using this method begin by skimming the assignment, paying attention to headings, pictures, and the first sentence of each paragraph. Then the student reads the first and last paragraphs of the assignment paying close attention to topic sentences. Then the student reads any questions attached to the assignment. Next the student reads while actively doing something to fix the material in his mind (i.e., outlining, underlining). Finally, the student works through a testing procedure asking questions that might be similar to test questions, answering questions in the text, getting together with other students who take turns questioning each other, and finally rereading parts of the assignment that testing has shown they have not learned.

2.   Survey Q 3 R
     Students begin by surveying the major points that need to be learned, then turn these major points into questions. The student then reads the material looking for answers to the questions; recites the material to themselves or to another and checks the responses to the questions; reviews the process (i.e., resurvey, requestion, reread, and recite).

3.   Study-Rest-Study-Rest
     This approach is most useful when a long period of study is required. Although individual students set their own times, a typical schedule under this approach would be a forty-five minute study period and a fifteen minute rest period. The

idea is that the rest period allows time for the information to be absorbed. Rest periods may include listening to music, exercising, reading other material, or relaxing. The rest period should become a reinforcement for a successful study period.

4. Question and Answer
    The student or teacher generates a series of questions covering the study material and each question is written on a 3" x 5" card with the answer on the reverse side of the card. The student reviews the question and turns the card over to determine if her response was accurate and complete.

5. Outlines
    Students outline assigned material and study their outlines. Key words from the outline receive special attention.

6. Five-Step Study Plan
    The student begins by previewing the assignment, reading topic sentences and summary paragraphs. Then the student tries to respond to Who?, What?, Where?, Why?, and How? Next the student reads the assignment trying to concentrate on remembering what the author is saying. Then the student thinks about the lesson and talks it over with another student. Finally, before any formal testing takes place, the student tries to recall the main concepts and ideas of the material and supporting details.

Remember, you—the teacher—are responsible for helping each student find an appropriate study method. This may take some time but is crucial for the secondary EMH learner who is mainstreamed into regular academic subjects.

Survival Skills

Survival skills mean different things to different educators. For the purposes of this chapter, survival skills are those basic skills necessary to the EMH learner so that an independent life style can be maintained. Career-education skills, although a component of independent living, are excluded as they will be discussed in Chapter XIV. The EMH learner often requires specific instruction in areas that educators frequently take for granted. Remember, you as a special educator are required to think about the skills your students need to acquire and then to provide them with the means for such acquisition. The thoughtful EMH educator will plan to include specific age-appropriate survival skills in the curriculum. Consider Figure 8.1 which represents a loosely structured survival-skill curriculum in place for grades one-twelve. A closer look at the specific skills which can make up this curriculum should serve as a guide for their inclusion into your curriculum.

Figure 8.1
Survival Skill Curriculum

Grade Ranges	Skill
1–9	Safety signs
1–12	Social skills
1–12	Grooming and hygiene
1–12	Verbal skills
1–12	Nutrition
3–12	Food buying and preparation
3–12	Clothing selection and maintenance
4–12	Use of leisure time
4–12	Decision making
5–12	Citizenship responsibilities
6–12	Personal finance
6–12	Child rearing
7–12	Home maintenance

Safety Signs

Signs are a fact of life and no child or adult can successfully survive without a basic knowledge of specific safety signs. Beginning in the first grade and continuing through high school, educators must make students aware of safety signs and their significance. The signs in Figures 8.2 and 8.3 would necessarily be included in this process.

Social Skills

We "sink or swim" according to our social skills. This is almost alarmingly true. The pleasant, cheerful individual with a fund of small talk frequently has an advantage over the most capable, sincere, and

Figure 8.2
Home and Community Safety Signs

MR. YUK/POISON   FLAMMABLE   NO SMOKING

NO FIRES   NO DRINKING   NO ENTRY

HIGH VOLTAGE   FIRE EXTINGUISHER   FIRST AID

AMBULANCE   DANGER   FIRE ALARM
                 Radiation

FALLOUT SHELTER
(Civil Defense)

Figure 8.3
Driving Safety Signs

hard-working child or adult. Consequently, Mary with an IQ of 85, whose social skills consist of grunts, putting her face directly in the face of another, screaming when criticized, and asking every adult "How much do you weigh?", will be perceived as more mentally handicapped than Marie, with an IQ of 60, who talks pleasantly about the weather, TV, and good restaurants, who apologizes when necessary, and responds to questions in an appropriate manner. As educators, we must not leave the development of social skills to the media or other influences but rather we must take a direct hand in fostering appropriate practices among our students.

Teach your student:

1. How to greet others. "Hi, Babe" may be fine for a peer but an adult may prefer the use of Miss, Mr., Mrs., Dr., or Ms. Appropriate greetings include not only appropriate words but appropriate tone of voice, facial set, and body movement. Strangers may be greeted with "hello," "good morning," or a simple nod.

2. The art of small talk. This may be developed and fostered when you take the time to have simple, informal "chats" with individual students. Such occasions demonstrate to the student the art of small talk and provide them with a good model. This does not mean that direct instruction can be skipped. Do not hesitate to label a student's conversation inappropriate and then provide some more suitable topics of conversation. Have students develop lists of conversational gambits suitable for their age and initiate role-playing practice sessions so that small talk becomes a part of their social repertoire.

3. How to respond to questions. This covers many situations from "would you like more potatoes?" to "honey, would you like a good time?" Basic responses include "yes, please"; "no, thank you"; "I don't know"; "I'm sorry, but I can't"; and "I don't understand." Students can be taught to handle questions politely as well as to decide when questions are inappropriate. For example, if a stranger asks for your address, a stalling or defensive technique is preferred to honesty.

4. Means of handling criticism. While no one enjoys being criticized, few are able to lead lives that are not open to criticism. Some, but not all, criticism is instructive, but our reactions to it greatly influence how we are perceived by

others. Role playing can be used to afford students the opportunity to respond appropriately to criticism. Responses
such as "I'm sorry," "let's talk it over," "I didn't mean to hurt
you," "I'm sorry you feel that way," and "that's a good sug-
gestion" may all be appropriate in different situations. You
may wish to write down some brief descriptions of situations
where criticism justly and unjustly occurs and have students
respond to them. A follow-up session will provide time for
students' questions as well as an opportunity for discussion
on how criticism makes them feel.

5. The apology. Many children and adults never learn to
apologize even though they may feel regret for their
behavior. Some feel that they are demeaned by the act of
apologizing while others simply do not have the words for
an apology in their repertoire. Therefore, the instructor has
a twofold responsibility: The first is to communicate to the
learner why people apologize and the results of being able
to do so; the second is to provide the learner with the means
of apologizing in a variety of situations (see Means of handling criticism for key phrases).

6. How to compliment. Trite but true, the neatly delivered compliment is "music to my ears." Students can be "compliment
deficient" because they have rarely been the recipients of
compliments and/or have given little thought to the practice of complimenting others. Of course, you deliver compliments to your students on a regular basis. Not a day goes
by in your classroom that your students don't hear, "Mark,
I like that belt"; "Sean, your new haircut is neat"; or "this
is great, Chris; you really wrote neatly." Being a good model
can have excellent effects but may not be sufficient. Students
may need practice in delivering compliments. One of the
authors used the technique of holding intermittent compliment sessions in the classroom where every student was
charged with the task of delivering a compliment to anyone
else in the room. Not only did the students enjoy and learn
from the session but the teacher was the recipient of a great
deal of information concerning what students noticed or
perceived as positive.

7. Respect for personal space. Put succinctly, keep your body
at an appropriate distance from others. Have students pair

up and practice "small talk" as they stand at different distances from each other so that they can establish appropriate body-placement practices.

8. Verbal communication encompasses more than the use of words. As students develop and mature from grade 1 through grade 12, they receive instruction which enables them to increase their vocabulary and their ability to express themselves orally. Aside from these academic skills, students must learn to use an acceptable tone when speaking to peers and adults. Students using an unacceptable tone of voice should be stopped and asked to repeat themselves in a more acceptable tone. The instructor may need to model the tone for them. Class discussion on reaction to different voice tones should emphasize the desirability of communicating successfully with peers and adults. It may also be necessary to discuss vulgar and obscene language so that learners come to understand why such a mode of communicating may be counterproductive.

Grooming and Hygiene

Most people want to be attractive to others but such a desire, frequently unexpressed, does not necessarily translate into action. The following observational checklist can be used in the classroom to help you determine what specific areas of grooming and hygiene need to be acted upon.

1. Hair is clean.
2. Hair is combed.
3. Hair is appropriate length.
4. Teeth are clean.
5. Breath is not offensive.
6. Hands and face are clean.
7. Fingernails are clean.
8. Fingernails are trimmed.
9. Clothes are clean.
10. Body odor absent.
11. Clothes are not torn.
12. Make-up is appropriate.
13. Ears are clean.
14. Clothes fit properly.

15. Clothes are modest.
16. Male facial hair shaved regularly or beard nicely trimmed. There are frequent educational television shows devoted to these concerns and class observation of such programs followed by teacher comments and class questions is one way to include this in a curriculum. Be careful that specific students are not singled out as examples as this is a very sensitive area. Private counseling by the educator, the school nurse, or significant others in the school environment is acceptable and often desirable. Educational films and filmstrips also help to deliver information in this area. Individual, small-group, or single-sex viewing with opportunity for discussion may overcome initial student embarrassment and be more effective than large-group, mixed-sex viewing.

Nutrition

This increasingly important area will most likely be dealt with in the framework of a health curriculum. However, the opportunity to discuss nutrition or present material on the subject should always be seized. Students are increasingly exposed to advertisements for "fast foods" and "junk foods" so that they must have an understanding of basic nutritional needs and how such needs are or are not met. Remember, your students are not only responsible for their own health but will likely be responsible for the health of their own children in the near future. Young students may explore nutrition through books, films, posters, etc., while older students may take an active part in menu planning and evaluation of "fast-food" options.

Food Buying and Preparation

Early skills in this realm would include comparison shopping, suitable quantities of certain items, nutritional values of related items (whole, skim, non-fat dry milk), menu planning, as well as preparation of simple foods including cereal, sandwiches, fruit, and beverages. More mature students would be expected to master concepts and skills such as unit pricing, product dating, food storage, and the preparation of basic breakfast, lunch, and dinner menus. When possible, do take students to the grocery store. Actual experience in coping with grocery shopping will enhance related classroom activities, demonstrate transfer of skills, and reinforce learning. Certainly meal planning, cooking, and eating with students should occur in your EMH classroom. By actually performing these tasks, not only is learning reinforced, but proper social and safety skills are practiced (this looks like a bonus to the uninitiated but you had this objective in sight all along).

Clothing Selection and Maintenance

This is an extremely sensitive area and needs to be handled with great skill. Children today tend to be fashion-conscious, adopting certain modes of dress and labeling anyone whose dress falls outside this mode as "weird." Therefore, a classroom teacher must be careful not to embarrass students who have neither the financial means nor the family life to support a stylish mode of dress while, at the same time, informing the entire class about clothing selection and maintenance. Please do not think that we are making too much of this point. Both authors have been classroom teachers and can support their views on how sensitive an area appropriate or inappropriate dress can be.

Younger students can discuss value for cost, frequency of wear or need, basic wardrobe items, handwashing, folding, and hanging of clothes. Older students may need to discuss fabric types and durability, use of washing machine and dryer, frequency of washing, dry cleaning versus washing, sewing buttons, tears, and hems, and how to shop for bargains.

Use of Leisure Time

We teach use of leisure time not only by discussing options but by giving students "free" or leisure time and then directing their use of such time by the options available. Television viewing is a frequent leisure-time activity and one that can fulfill many needs. Students do need direction in television viewing so that they can be more critical users. Discuss programs seen at home as well as those viewed by the class. Focus on entertainment value, information gains, and sensitivity with which characters were portrayed. Guide students to see prejudice and propaganda in certain television programs. Leisure-time activities include much more than the television, therefore many other sources of relaxation should be explored. Games are good individual, group, and family activities as are various sports. Computer games are certainly a part of our society and students should be aware of and comfortable with the operation of these games (see Chapter V). Do expose your students to many of these activities. Reading is such a satisfying way of using leisure time that exploration on this activity can only benefit your students. Encourage them to discuss what they have read but also actively direct them to material that is appropriate for them (both in degree of difficulty and interest level). Work with the school and public librarians. Teach students to use these libraries to meet their own leisure needs. Have your students use libraries frequently so that they become comfortable with them and feel accepted there. Additionally, listening to music, sewing, building, carving, painting, drawing, and gardening are all excellent leisure activities that teachers may wish to explore with their students.

Decision Making

"Learn by doing" may be the key to appropriate teaching of decision-making skills. The "Women's Movement" has made most of us aware of the danger of allowing one member of the family to take total responsibility for financial planning. If this person leaves the family, either by death or choice, others must cope with the loss of leadership whether they are prepared to do so or not. The EMH learner must be forced into decision-making situations rather than protected from the possibility of making a less than perfect choice. Develop your decision-making program so that students learn how to approach the decision-making process, gain experience in decision making, and have an opportunity to observe and discuss the results of certain decisions. Role playing and simulations may be the best techniques to use with your students. Different environments will offer different decision-making situations. The following are probable situations that should be the basis of a decision-making skill curriculum:
At Home
> Situation #1 — You have been offered a good job in a town fifteen miles away but you don't own a car. You have very little money saved but enough for a down payment on a used car. The day you plan to purchase the car, your TV blows up. You can't have the car and a TV with your savings. What will you do?
> Situation #2 — You earn money babysitting but it is not "regular" work. It is October 16 and you know that you will be needing money for Christmas gifts for your family. Also, you would like to go to the movies with your friend, to a basketball game, and

play arcade games after school. You often treat yourself to a candy bar and you want new gym shoes. How will you cover all these expenses?

At Work

Situation #1 — Your boss "hassles" you. She doesn't like it when you are late, doesn't like your funny t-shirts, and thinks you take too many coffee breaks. She may be considering firing you. What would you do?

Situation #2 — The people you work with are lazy. You accomplish three times as much work as they do but you all get the same pay. You begin to wonder if it's worth it and your best friend says "relax, you are too serious, cut your production." What will you do?

Situation #3 — Your company offers a payroll savings plan where they take a portion of your pay and automatically deposit it in a savings account for you. But if you let them do that, you'll have less money for the things you need now. What will you do?

In the Community

Situation #1 — The Super Market in town is very new and quite attractive. Produce is beautifully arranged and everything looks so good. There is another store which is smaller, older, and you have to put your groceries in boxes yourself. The older store offers "off" brands which are less expensive but the Super Market is so attractive and even has music playing while you shop. Where will you shop?

Situation #2 — Local, state, and federal elections are coming up and you are not registered to vote. Today is the last day to register but something has come up (a, b, or c).

a.   Your car won't start, it's raining, you would have to walk.
b.   You want to go to the ball game.
c.   You don't feel very well and your favorite TV shows are on today. What will you do?

At School

Situation #1 — At lunch time a group of your friends usually sit together. One or two of them has been bringing liquor and passing it around. It is against the rules to drink while at school and you aren't old enough to legally purchase liquor. But all your friends are drinking and it does relax you. What will you do?

Situation #2 — You brought a very special pen to school. Your aunt and uncle gave it to you for your birthday and it was expensive. You saw John standing around your desk after lunch and now the pen is gone. You believe that he took it. What will you do?

Guide discussions of these situations so that the ramifications of any possible decisions are discussed so that students will learn to look at the consequences, present and future, of their decisions. Students may wish to develop their own decision-making situations for class use or to role play the different personalities in given situations.

Citizenship Responsibilities

Exercising the right to vote is the hallmark of a good citizen. But a review of the literature by McAfee and Mann (1982) on the participation of the EMH adult in the voting process revealed that such individuals exhibit a low rate of voting behavior and that voting behavior is directly related to educational attainment. EMH students must be taught how to cope with the process of voting as well as how to decide their vote on candidates and issues. The following strategies can be used:

1. Read the daily paper with your students and discuss issues.
2. Watch news programs on TV or listen to news on the radio in class or as homework and discuss issues and personalities.
3. Hold classroom elections so that students can experience the election process firsthand.
4. Make sure that your students participate in all school elections. (Don't be surprised if they have traditionally been restricted from doing so.)
5. Arrange field trips to polling places and to locations where adults register to vote.
6. Familiarize your students with the voting vocabulary as well as any forms included in the voting process.
7. Serve as a good model.

Personal Finance

McAfee and Mann (1982) reviewed the literature on the income of the mentally handicapped. This review indicated that the EMH adult had an income considerably lower than the average citizen. Income did increase with age and length of time spent in the community. Therefore, EMH students have no reason to expect above average financial resources and must learn to budget their income for survival. Planning a budget then might be a major personal finance skill. Check writing, balancing a checkbook, maintaining a savings account, and coping with bills and charge cards are also important skills. Personal finance can be a part of the math curriculum and Friday could be finance day. Assign each student a weekly or monthly income as well as a "home situation" which includes number in family and mortgage or rent payment. Have them develop a budget and work on all budgets until they are relatively reasonable. Then have a "situation jar" with financial situations, both positive and negative, written on small slips of paper and placed in the jar. Situations may include "you have received a $50 bonus," "your roof leaks," "your daughter needs boots," "your refrigerator died," "you inherited $2,000," "you need an operation costing $2,500." Each week your students will select a paper from the "situation jar" and make financial decisions and arrangements based on their selection. Class discussion should follow.

Summary

Students with learning problems require direct instruction in order to master study and survival skills. Your total curriculum should reflect this need and offer the student opportunities for such skill development. Learner characteristics will dictate the method of instruction as well as individual needs. A student who has learned to study and who is prepared to maintain an independent life-style will be the reward for your planning effort.

Remember this . . .

1. No single reading approach has proven to be equally effective with all learners.

2. Reading activities for the mentally retarded should be functional and of high interest.

3. Reading miscues made by variant-English speakers may be either conceptual or dialectical.

4. The *teacher's reaction* to the language of a variant-English speaker in reading is related to the possible problems that the student will encounter in learning to read.

5. The nature of the reading miscues are generally more important diagnostically than the number of the miscues.

CHAPTER IX

Teaching of Reading

The foundation of special education is the principle of individual differences. Two learners with WISC IQ's of 60 and reading levels of 2-0 may not need to be taught reading in the same way. There is no single approach to the teaching of reading which can accommodate all individual differences (Bond and Dykstra, 1967; Stauffer, 1967). The teacher must therefore possess a knowledge of the reading process and the skills needed to be successful. The teacher also must be knowledgeable about different ways to teach these skills and to be able to determine the best method for each learner. Although standardized reading tests will not provide the answer for the teacher, a strategy of "test-teach-test," including the systematic analysis of student performance, will allow a teacher to find an effective strategy or combination of strategies for teaching the individual learner. The teacher should not be caught in the readiness trap, the reason for nonprogress of a learner in reading. The reading process is composed of individual skills, all of which are teachable. The dilemma facing the teacher is to initiate the best strategy.

Reading Characteristics

The elementary aged educable mentally retarded child reads less than others of the same chronological age and usually prefers materials which are immature for his chronological age. Reasons as to "why" they read less often are varied, and for an individual learner some, all, or none of these reasons might be the underlying sources of the problem. Among the reasons offered are: lack of appropriate reading material in the home; lack of adult models in the home who read; early and prolonged failure in the "learning-to-read process"; and current deficits in reading skills resulting in avoidance of reading activities. At the secondary level, the reading interests are the same as those for the normal child (Gates, 1930; Norwell, 1950). Books within the learner's reading level and also on topics related to his interests are difficult to find, however, high-interest, low-vocabulary books offer some relief.

In terms of reading skills, most mentally retarded youngsters do not read up to the predicted level of their mental ages. Whether this finding is the result of the instruction they received, the mental retardation, or just a poor prediction remains to be determined. They have been found to be deficient in oral and silent reading, the use of context clues, sound omissions, locating and recognizing factual details, recognizing main ideas, and drawing specific conclusions (Bleismer, 1969; Dunn, 1954). Word meaning, word recognition, and reading rate are generally on a par with mental-age peers (Bleismer, 1969). In terms of prognosis, with excellent instruction a sixteen-year-old student with an IQ of around 70 should be able to read at a fifth grade level, which is the level at which most newspapers and popular reading materials are written (Bruekner and Bond, 1955).

Essential Reading Goals

According to Gillespie and Johnson (1974) the educable mentally retarded will need to be able to use reading for the successful completion of functional activities related to:
1.   Job applications
2.   Newspaper
3.   Street signs
4.   Telephone directories
5.   Public notices
6.   Signs
7.   Labels on clothing and food products

This is just a partial listing of the functional reading needs of the educable mentally retarded. The teacher must target other specific reading competencies needed by a student based upon their degree of functionality. These additional reading competencies can be determined by an analysis of the reading skills found necessary for a learner to function successfully in the current and possible subsequent environments. Some procedures for the systematic analysis of environments for functional curriculum goals have been described in Chapter XI. Because of the deficits exhibited by retarded learners in word-attack skills, specific vocabulary words found in these environments may need to be taught directly to the learner.

Reading Skills

Most tests, texts, and reading systems divide the reading process into three major components: word-attack skills, sight-word vocabulary, and comprehension. Actually, these three areas probably constitute the basic core of questions which a teacher should address when assessing a new student. Specifically:
1. What kinds of word-attack skills does he possess and which ones does he rely on most heavily?
2. What is the extent of his sight-word vocabulary?
3. What is the extent of his comprehension skills?

Word-Attack Skills

Word-attack skills include that set of techniques which enables a learner to decode an unknown word so that he can pronounce it and understand it in the proper context (Gillespie and Johnson, 1974). These skills are normally categorized under the headings: phonics, structural analysis, contextual clues, and configuration clues.

PHONICS. The purpose of phonics instruction "is to help the child develop the ability to work out the pronunciation (or approximate pronunciation) of printed word symbols which at the moment he does not know as sight words" (Heilman, 1972, p. 245). There are two basic approaches to teaching phonics—analytic and synthetic (Bagford, 1972). The synthetic approach emphasizes sound blending and the teaching of sounds for certain letters. The analytic approach starts with a pool of 75 to 100 sight words from which the letter sounds are taught. Research appears to favor the synthetic approach. In terms of the efficacy of phonics instruction with mentally retarded the research is supportive (French, 1950; Hegge, 1934; Warner, 1967). It should not be the sole source strategy for reading instruction. The decision to utilize phonics instruction and the amount of phonics instruction should be based upon the strengths and weaknesses of the learner.

STRUCTURAL ANALYSIS. Structural analysis deals with the structure of the word rather than the elements of sound. Structural analysis includes:

1. Compound words
2. Prefixes and suffixes
3. Root words
4. Syllabication

The student combines prefixes and suffixes with base words to change the meanings of the root words. The emphasis is on the meaning of the prefixes and suffixes as clues to identifying unknown words.

CONTEXT CLUES. When using context clues, the student uses the information in the text to identify unknown words. The student is taught to look for certain clues, such as synonyms, comparisons, or contrasts. The reader "guesses" the unknown word based upon the context.

The "cloze" procedure is a commonly used technique for assessing the extent to which a student uses context. It is also a procedure used to teach students to use context. Figure 9.1 shows a passage which has been modified to exemplify the cloze procedure. Normally every fifth word from a 250-300 word passage is deleted in the passage. Generally, the procedure should not be used with students below the fourth grade reading level.

Sight-Word Vocabulary

Sight words are those printed words which are identified automatically by the learner. The learner does not exhibit "delay" in identifying those words but calls them when they are "flashed." Hesitation or even immediate correction should not be accepted as a demonstration by the learner as mastery of sight words. Sight words should be presented on "flash" cards to the student at a rate of one syllable per second (i.e., one syllable words should be flashed for one second, two syllable words for two seconds, etc.). The teacher should put the words into two piles (mastery and nonmastery) as they are called by the learner. A record should then be maintained regarding the number of sight words identified and a listing of the mastered and

Figure 9.1
Sample Reading Passage Written in a Cloze Format[1]

Joe and Bob decided _____ embark on a diving _____ to look for lobster. _____ they were new to _____ area, they first had _____ find out the laws _____ regulations concerning lobster fishing. _____ found out some interesting _____. The lobsters had to _____ taken in season, had _____ be a certain size, _____ had to be taken _____ hand. Fortunately this was _____ season for diving for _____.

They found a reef _____ was said to have _____. After anchoring their small _____, the two boys put on _____ snorkels, masks, and fins _____ jumped into the water. _____ hour of searching did _____ produce any lobster although _____ of beautiful fish were _____. The lobster certainly _____ fun even though a _____ lobster was not to _____ found on the reef.

[1]Adapted from J. E. Sedlak, *IEP: Educational Diagnostic Inventories*, Belle Vernon, PA: National Press, 1978. Used with permission.

nonmastered words. The printing of words on the flash cards should be in primary type or clear manuscript print.

Selecting the words to be used to assess the extent of sight-word vocabulary can be done in a variety of ways. The selection of these words will be guided to some extent by the age, ability, and needs of the student. A portion of the sight-word vocabulary of the secondary aged student should be based upon functional words found in the environment and vocational placements. Figure 9.2 contains a listing of these words. For the primary aged learner, words such as the 220 Dolch word list is an excellent starting point for sight words. Sight-word lists can also be taken from basal-reading texts as a part of an Informal Reading Inventory (IRI). Specific procedures to be followed in the construction of this word list are contained in the section on IRI's.

Comprehension Skills

Reading comprehension is probably one of the most important and yet least understood skills in the reading process. All authorities would agree that the ultimate goal of a reading program is the development of these skills but there is disagreement on the procedure for achieving this end. Some authorities favor an emphasis on comprehen-

Figure 9.2
Environmentally Specific Reading Vocabulary

Traffic/Business Signs
Stop
Yield
One way
Speed limit
No parking
Bus stop
Handicapped

Clothing or Material Care
Do not iron
Do not bleach
Dry clean only
Laundry
Delicate cycle
Permanent press

Machine and Equipment Operation
Operation/operator
Power on/off
Discard
Remove
Insert
Cover
Attach
Keep way from heat
Flammable/inflammable

Emergency Assistance Signs
Police
Hospital
Fire station
Ambulance
Rescue squad
Emergency room

Restroom Signs
Boys/girls
Men/women
Gentlemen/ladies
Guys/gals
Restroom
Toilet

Environmental Warning Signs
Danger/dangerous
High voltage
Condemned
Wet paint
Wet floor
Slippery when wet
Poison
Do not swallow
Explosives
Caution
Hazardous
Dead end
Low clearance
No trespassing
Keep out
No smoking
Do not touch
Do not enter

Direction Signs
In/out
Enter/exit
Up/down
Left/right
Entrance
Turn
One way

Figure 9.2 (Con't)

Health service	Over/under/through
Doctor	Push/pull
Telephone	Walk/don't walk

Vocational Signs

Authorized personnel only
Employees only
Pay here
Open/closed
Elevator
Stairs
Out of order
Express lane only
Cashier
Check out
Manager

sion in the early stages of reading instruction while others emphasize the sound-symbol relationships. Most would agree that comprehension is related to language and that problems in reading comprehension may be as much a "thinking" problem as it is a reading problem (Moffett, 1968). The teacher needs to partial out the reading-comprehension problem from the oral language comprehension problems. Inherent in such an analysis the teacher will need to consider:

1. The past experiences of the reader
2. The content of the written passage
3. The syntax of the written passages
4. The vocabulary of the written passages
5. The oral language comprehension of the learner
6. The questions being asked to assess comprehension

Any one or combination of these could be a factor in a reading comprehension problem.

The development of comprehension skills requires a teacher's awareness of each of these variables. The teacher needs to be particularly aware of the questions being asked to assess a learner's comprehension of a written passage.

There are several "models" for the teaching of reading comprehension and each of these rely heavily on a hierarchy of questions.

Harris (1970) has recommended that comprehension be taught to achieve the following skills for a learner:
1. Ability to find answers to specific (factual) questions
2. Reading for main ideas
3. Reading to follow a sequence of events
4. Reading to note and recall details
5. Grasping the author's plan
6. Following printed directions

Informal Reading Assessment

Informal Reading Inventory

The Informal Reading Inventory (IRI) is used by teachers to establish a student's reading level in regard to placement in a basal reading series and selection of reading materials for the learner. Through it the teacher can determine the learner's independent, instructional, frustrational, and good listening levels in reading. The IRI consists of a series of paragraphs taken from a basal reading series (preferably the one used in the room and arranged in increasing order of difficulty). The student reads passages orally and silently as the teacher records errors. To construct an IRI a teacher should:
1. Select two 60 to 120 word passages from each level of a basal reading series, preferably from the latter half of the book.
2. Retype these passages onto separate sheets.
3. Construct five comprehension questions for each passage. Different levels of questions should be written, e.g. factual, main idea, vocabulary, inferential, sequencing, and vocabulary.
4. Compile a list of vocabulary words from each level, selecting every fifth new word. (You could also choose every fifth word from the reading passages and eliminate duplicates.)
5. Type vocabulary words on a sheet.
6. Construct a scoring sheet. It could merely be a copy of the passages and vocabulary words onto which the teacher can code errors.

Administering and Scoring

Administering and scoring an IRI is not a mechanical process. The results will only be useful if the evaluator understands the reading process and the analysis of errors. To administer the inventory, follow these steps:

1. Have student read vocabulary words first (words in isolation).
2. Record all errors (e.g., substitutions, hesitations, omissions). See Figure 9.3 for a sample marking system.
3. Stop when the student misses 25% of the words on one level. Self-corrections are not errors.
4. Have student read silently the passage for the highest level where vocabulary recognition was 100%.
5. Record beginning and ending time for passage.
6. Ask and record comprehension-question responses.
7. Have student read passage aloud and record errors. Figure 9.3 depicts a common set of symbols which can be used for "error" marking.
8. Use second passage as a reliability check if needed.
9. If comprehension is less than 50% and oral reading shows a lack of rhythm, meaningless word substitutions, and word-recognition difficulties, the learner should stop oral reading.
10. Teacher should then read aloud the parallel passage for the last level and ask comprehension questions. The teacher should continue until the comprehension-question errors drop below 75%.

The "guidelines" for establishing the independent, instructional, frustration, and listening levels are as follows:

Independent — Student reads in a natural conversational tone with few word recognition errors (e.g., 99–100% accuracy). Comprehension is 80–90% or above. This level indicates the complexity of material a learner can handle independently.

Instructional — Student reads with 90% word recognition and comprehends 60–75% of the questions. This level indicates where a learner can be placed for instruction.

Frustrational — Student reads with a lack of rhythm and makes meaningless word substitutions. Word recognition is less than 90% and comprehension is less than 60%. This level indicates material is too difficult even with teacher guidance.

Listening— Student responds correctly to at least 60–70% of the comprehension questions asked. This level indicates the vocabulary and syntactic structure is understood by the learner.

Figure 9.3
Sample System for Marking Errors in IRIs

Type of Error	Description	Marking
Assistance	Teacher had to supply word after 5 seconds	*Underline words* aided
Hesitations	Learner hesitated at word but teacher did not have to supply assistance	Check (✓) above hesitated word
Additions/Insertions	Learner inserts word not on page	Put in word or word parts with caret ( )
Mispronunciation	Learner does not accurately pronounce word	Phonetically write in learner's pronunciation
Omissions	Learner leaves out a word or words and reads on	Circle (○) the omitted words or punctuation
Order reversals	Learner inverts word order	Mark reversals with this symbol:
Regressions	Learner reads word(s) and then rereads them	Put a wavy line under word(s) repeated
Self-corrections	Learner makes a mistake but corrects it spontaneously	Write "sc" above word
Substitutions	Learner reads one word as another	Underline the omitted word and write in the given one

ANALYSIS. The analysis of the reading errors should be based upon the *nature* of the errors rather than solely the *number* of the errors (Goodman, 1965). Substitution and omission "miscues" may be acceptable linguistically and conceptually. For example, substituting the word "pet" for "dog" or "football team" for "Pittsburgh Steelers" may be both conceptually and linguistically correct in a passage and may not be counted as an error since the meaning of the passage was not obliterated by the substitution. In traditional error analyses, self-corrections and repetitions are generally coded as "errors" but could also be viewed as an opportunity on the part of the learner to gain subsequent meaning in a passage (Brown, 1975). The types of errors (or miscues) should be analyzed by category in order to determine if the nature of the "error" is linguistic, cognitive, or graphic (Hammill and Bartel, 1978).

CLOZE PROCEDURE. The cloze procedure is both an instructional and an assessment strategy. Graded passages are used just as in the IRI but these passages are somewhat longer, i.e., 250 to 300 words in length. Every fifth word is deleted from the passage and substituted with lines of uniform length. The student can read the passage either orally or silently and supply the missing word for the "blank." When done silently, the student normally supplies the missing word in writing. Ekwall (1976) suggests the following guidelines for determining a student's reading level:

Independent—57% or more of the deleted words correct

Instructional—44% to 56% correct

Frustrational—43% or less correct

Issues related to the cloze procedure involve whether the student must substitute the exact word for the blank or if a synonym is acceptable. We believe that a linguistically and conceptually correct substitution should be acceptable. The cloze procedure can be modified and used by the teacher in ways other than the preceding. The following are some suggestions.

1. Delete only verbs from passages or some other part of speech to determine if student error is sensitive to this dimension.
2. Insert first letter of deleted words as an added clue.
3. Have length of line approximate length of deleted word.
4. Supply correct answer and two or three foils from which the learner must select the correct word.

5. Delete words from verbal problems in mathematics and require word rather than numerical answers (Sedlak, 1974).
6. Use in subject areas such as science and social studies to assess comprehension (Gilliland, 1978).
7. Use it when teacher orally reads passages and deletes words.

Reading and the Variant-English Speaker

A great deal of attention has been drawn to the use of variant English and its relationship to reading achievement and reading instruction. The basic question raised is to what extent, if any, does variant English interfere with a child's ability to learn to read. Rigg (1978) and Cunningham (1976–1977) found that *teacher's reaction* to dialect is a major factor as to whether or not a child exhibits problems in learning to read. If the teacher views the dialect pronunciation as a reading "error," the child will probably encounter problems in learning to read. Teachers who recognize the dialect pronunciation and realize that it has not interfered with the comprehension of the passage will continue on in the lesson. Phonological differences need not be corrected (Cohen and Plaskon, 1980). The purpose of reading is to extract meaning from the printed word and not simply the sounds of letters and words. Goodman (1965) has discussed the need to recognize reading "miscues" and not always to label these miscues as "errors." The variant-English speaker may "translate" a written passage when reading it orally into his dialect. Examples of such translations are:
1. "Ms. Thomson she be my teacher" for "Mrs. Thomson is my teacher."
2. "Bill he jump over the fence" for "Bill jumped over the fence."
3. "John he be going home on the bus" for "John is going home on the bus."
Cohen and Plaskon (1980) point out that the learner who is rearranging the syntax of the sentence to fit his dialect is performing a complex task and should not be penalized since the deep structure (meaning) of the sentence is unchanged. Somervill (1975) points out that such style switching should be viewed as a positive feature revealing a learner's growth in reading competence.

In terms of which instructional method in reading is "best" for the variant-English speaker the research is sparse but the authors would recommend that both the Direct Instruction Approach and the

Language Experience Approach hold great promise. Both methods contain procedures which are supportive of the dialectical differences and follow recognized principles of effective instruction. Both approaches are described in the next section.

Reading Approaches

Special education teachers use a variety of procedures and systems in the teaching of reading to the retarded. There is no singularly superior method (Kirk, Kliebhan, and Lerner, 1978). Heilman (1977) notes that virtually every method and procedure has been successful with some children and unsuccessful with others. Therefore, it is recommended that no single approach be used with all learners in a class. Successful reading instruction is based upon teacher versatility in selecting materials and techniques for helping children who are experiencing specific reading difficulties. In fact, the skill of the teacher is regarded by many as being more important than the efficacy of a specific approach. This segment then will describe some of the more commonly used approaches to the teaching of reading and any related shortcomings. Special education teachers need to be aware of these approaches so that they can judicially select a program for a learner.

Basal Readers

Most primary and intermediate grade teachers throughout the United States use a graded basal-reading series as foundation of their reading program. Basal readers offer a sequential and interrelated set of books and materials ranging from readiness up to sixth or eighth grade levels. They also have a teacher's manual which presents detailed lesson plans for the development of each story. The content of the stories at one time were quite sterile but in recent years the settings of stories have included apartments, trailer parks, and urban areas. Characters have changed to minimize racism and sexism (Gillespie-Silver, 1979). Another significant change noted by Wallace (1981) was the addition of word-analysis approaches as opposed to sole reliance on sight-word approaches.

Some advantages of a basal-reading program according to Wilson and Hall (1972) include:

1. Controlled vocabulary
2. Sequentially developed skills
3. Decoding and comprehension are stressed
4. Colorful, attractive materials
5. Teacher's guide with step-by-step outlines for each lesson
6. Supplemental workbooks and related materials

Disadvantages of the approach have been offered by a number of writers (Gillespie-Silver, 1979; Heilman, 1972, 1977; Kaluger and Kolson, 1978; Niemeyer, 1965; Wilson and Hall, 1972). These include:

1. Provisions for individual differences are usually limited to the usual three levels.
2. The material continues to be dull and repetitive.
3. Encourages group instruction and de-emphasizes individual needs.
4. Special education students have frequently been in the same basal reader year after year with little growth and greater resistance to reading.
5. Minimal variety of sentence structures.
6. Language patterns are simpler than the oral-language patterns of the learner.
7. Highly structured, inflexible program.
8. Themes of stories being incompatible with interests and reading abilities of older youngsters.

Language Experience Approach

The Language Experience Approach (LEA) is a multifaceted system which integrates the development of listening, speaking, writing, and reading skills. It can be used in the first grade up through junior high school. Student-created stories serve as the basis for reading instruction. The teacher writes down sentences and stories dictated by the student. In the early grades these stories are normally done in small groups with different students contributing different sentences to the story. In later years a student will create the entire story and dictate it into a tape recorder, to another student, or to a teacher or volunteer. At this level, the student might also write the entire story himself with the teacher correcting grammar and spelling. When the story is dictated, the teacher can discuss word choice, sentence structure, and different sounds of words and letters but generally does not change the story. Instruction in phonics and vocabulary evolves as students begin to need these skills in writing and reading their own material or that of other students (Spache and Spache, 1977). Copies are kept of each day's story and are used for review. In this way a sight vocabulary of commonly used words is developed. All related activities must be developed by the teacher.

When used with variant-English speakers, the stories are generally written using standard spellings and standard English syntax. For example, if the student dictates the sentence "My name be John and I lives in Carbondale," the teacher would write the sentence as "My name is John and I live in Carbondale." The teacher would then read the sentence aloud and have the student read the sentence aloud. His reading of the sentence in the variant-English form would be accepted with the comment "That's right" and the rereading of the sentence by the teacher once again in the standard form. This rereading is for the purpose of modeling and feedback to the learner. Nondialectical miscues would be corrected by the teacher.

The strengths of the approach are:
1. The content of stories is based upon student experiences.
2. All vocabulary is within the speaking and listening vocabulary of the learners.
3. Syntax and sentence structures are familiar to the learners.
4. Students can relate reading to a communication process.
5. Emphasis is on comprehension.

Weaknesses of the approach have been cited by Heilman (1972) and these include:
1. Uncontrolled vocabulary.
2. Great demand is placed on teacher time.
3. Requires a well trained teacher.
4. Basic sight words may not be repeated often enough.

Fernald Approach

The Fernald approach is a multisensory system developed by Grace Fernald (1943) to be used primarily with students who have encountered repeated failure in learning to read. The system is also referred to as the VATK system—visual, auditory, tactile, and kinesthetic. Beginning instruction revolves around words the learner wishes to learn. As the student learns to write these words, stories are composed by the student using the words. The teacher writes any of the words for the learner he cannot spell. All new words are learned by the VATK procedure. The story is typed and used for subsequent reading instruction.

STAGE 1. The learner selects a word which the teacher writes in cursive or manuscript large enough so that it can be traced with a finger. The student then looks at the word (visual), says the word (auditory), traces the word (tactile), and copies the word (kinesthetic). He continues until he can correctly produce the word from memory. The student may also trace the word in the air for practice. The word is then added to a story and to an alphabet box of new words.

STAGE 2. All features remain the same except that the learner no longer traces the word. He looks at the word, pronounces it, and writes it from memory. He maintains his word box, discarding words as they are mastered.

STAGE 3. The word is no longer written for the learner. He merely locates a word on the page, says it, and writes it. Words are no longer self-selected at this stage. Reading from books rather than self-made stories is emphasized.

STAGE 4. New words are learned on the basis of the stack of sight words which the student has mastered. Reading materials are books which are of interest to the learner.

The VATK method has been effective with retarded learners (McCarthy and Oliver, 1965). Authorities are unsure as to why the method works but it has been hypothesized that it is the result of attention and concentration which is made to each word rather than the tracing or writing (Johnson, 1963; Morris, 1958). There have also been a variety of authors and researchers who have modified VATK procedures with beneficial results (Cawley, Goodstein, and Burrow, 1972; Johnson, 1966; Monroe, 1932).

Direct Instruction

The Direct Instruction approach in the teaching of reading requires instruction in essential reading skills through the most effective and efficient means. The basic source of information in the Direct Instruction approach can be found in Carnine and Silbert (1979). The approach can be described in relationship to each of the following components:

1.   Organization of instruction
2.   Program design
3.   Presentation techniques

Organization of instruction deals with the efficient use of time in the teaching process. Scheduling, arranging materials, and engaged time in reading are dealt with in this component. Teachers need to schedule sufficient time and follow the schedule to ensure that possible instructional time is not wasted. Materials used in the teaching need to be arranged and organized to make efficient use of time. Both the arrangement of teacher materials and student materials is critical. Brophy and Evertson (1976) found that students made significant academic gain in classrooms where:

1.   Each student knew what his assignment was.
2.   If he needed help, he could get it from the teacher or from some designated person.
3.   He was accountable for completing the assignment appropriately because he knew his work would be checked.

Independent work is placed in folders on students desks. Teachers should use colored clips or other markers indicating groups or different pages in the teacher's guides.

Program design involves the precise specification of objectives of essential skills, devising problem-solving strategies, developing teaching procedures, selecting appropriate examples, providing sufficient and appropriate practice, and properly sequencing skills. The scope of reading skills is evaluated and nonessential skills are eliminated. Objectives are written in relation to skills and not to global functioning levels. Strategies are taught which a learner can use to pronounce new words or derive meaning from a passage. In the teaching procedures, a format is followed which specifies "what to say, what words to emphasize, what to ask, how to signal, how to correct appropriately, etc." (p. 15). Student failure is considered teacher failure. Careful selection of examples is important and providing sufficient and appropriate practice of a skill is also essential. Guidelines for the sequencing of skills are as follows:

1.   Preskills of a strategy are taught before the strategy itself is presented.
2.   Instances that are consistent with a strategy are introduced before exceptions.
3.   High utility skills are introduced before less useful ones.
4.   Easy skills are taught before more difficult ones.
5.   Strategies and information that are likely to be confused are not introduced at the same time. (Carnine and Silbert, 1979, p. 17)

The reader should note that these guidelines are quite compatible with the instructional strategies described in Chapter III.

Presentation techniques involve small-group instruction, unison oral responding, signaling, pacing, monitoring, diagnosis and correction, and motivation. Groups of five to ten students are taught for one half hour each day. Students are seated in a semicircle within two feet of the teacher. Unison oral responding requires all students to actively respond to questions. Questions are used frequently throughout the lesson. Signals are cues given by the teacher to students indicating that they should make a response. The signal can be a clap, hand drop, or change in voice inflection. Pacing refers to the rate of presentations. Fast-paced, short presentations are advocated. Monitoring involves far more than simply noting correct and incorrect responses. The teacher also watches eyes and mouths to be sure students are focusing on the proper stimuli and responding appropriately. Attention to the proper seating of high-responding and low-responding youngsters is also critical. Students are questioned individually as well as in groups but only after adequate group practice. Close monitoring is essential to avoid student confusion and problems. The correction procedure involves: praise, modeling, response to a parallel task, and then a delay test. The final component of the presentation techniques deals with motivation. Frequent pats, handshakes, and physical contact are given for successful reading. The fact that the lessons are well planned and structured maximizes the probability that the students will be successful.

The direct-instruction system places high demands on a teacher and emphasizes accepted teaching practices. It is a highly effective system which has demonstrated achievement gains with low-income learners and variant-English speakers (McDonald, 1976; Tickunoff, Berliner, and Rist, 1975).

Functional Analysis Model

Sidman and Cresson (1973) analyzed single-word reading into six observable tasks, two of which were *receptive*, two *associative*, and two *expressive* with respect to language. The six tasks for single-word reading were:

1. Auditory comprehension—teacher *states* word, learner points to *picture*.
2. Auditory reception—teacher *states* word, learner choses

printed word.

3. Reading comprehension 1—teacher shows *picture*, learner choses *printed word*.
4. Reading comprehension 2—teacher shows *printed word*, learner choses *picture*.
5. Picture naming—teacher shows *picture*, learner *states* word.
6. Oral reading—teacher shows *printed word*, learner *states* word.

The model argues that each of the six tasks need not be taught to a learner in order for a learner to demonstrate competence in *all* tasks. The six tasks show a transitive equivalence relation. Wulz and Hollis (1979) and Sidman and Tailby (1982) demonstrated that if the teacher taught students to a criterion in tasks 1 and 2 (auditory comprehension and auditory reception) that handicapped students were able to transfer what they learned to tasks 3 and 4. If either task 5 or 6 was taught, the other would transfer to the untaught task. Hollis (1982) further indicates that the strategy is equally applicable to sentences, as well as single words.

Knowledge of this procedure of stimulus organization is important for a teacher of the retarded since it demonstrates a savings of instructional time. This functional analysis model demonstrates some of the essential and less essential tasks needed in teaching handicapped students to read.

Linguistic Approaches

The linguistic approach is based upon a "whole-word" approach to the teaching of reading. The principle of "minimal change" is emphasized with initial instruction consisting of three letter words using a consonant-vowel-consonant (cvc) pattern using short vowels (e.g., fan, pan, ran, can). Letters and sound equivalents are not presented in isolation but as total words. Most linguistic readers have no pictures or illustrations. Emphasis is placed on learning the essential mechanics of reading with little attention to comprehension. Vocabulary is controlled through the phonetic regularity of the words rather than through frequency of usage (Myers and Hammill, 1976). A logical progression of words are introduced, with regular forms being taught first. Rhyming words and stories which use these words are the basis for the student acquiring familiarity with printed words. The major advantage of the system is the frequent repetition of words, the use of the principle of "minimal change" as a learning-to-learn strategy, and the relationships between words in terms of pronunciation. Disadvantages include the de-emphasis on comprehension, the incompatibility between the learner's oral language and the system, and the assumption that learners will "discover" the letter-sound relationships (Kirk, Kliebhan, and Lerner, 1978).

Instructional Strategies for Teaching Selected Skills

Sight Words

Neef, Iwata, and Page (1977) found that the presence of known items in a list of unknown items served to facilitate the acquisition of the unknown words. The presence of the known items appeared to act as a reinforcing agent and was not as frustrating to the learner than when all sight words on the list were unknown. They therefore recommended that both known and unknown words should be presented in lists when sight words are being taught.

Hendricksen, Roberts, and Shores (1978) were able to increase the sight-word vocabulary of two primary aged disabled readers by modeling basic sight words. The two-step procedure followed was to: (a) show the learner a sight word on a flash card and say "This word is _____" and then (b) to ask the learner "What word is this?" They found this procedure to be superior to first asking the student to name the word and then telling him the word.

Oral Reading

Having students silently read material (prereading) before being asked to read aloud is a commonly used instructional strategy. Lovitt, Eaton, Kirwood, and Pelander (1971) found that using this strategy resulted in decreased oral-reading errors.

Word-attack Strategies

The deficient reader may rely heavily on a single word-attack strategy when decoding words and give up in frustration when it fails to "unlock" the pronunciation of the word. Hansen and Eaton (1978) used a series of corrective feedback statements to teach five mildly handicapped boys to expand their word-attack strategies. The corrective sequence used was as follows:

Step 1. Tell student he has miscalled a word and to "try another way."

Step 2. Tell student to finish reading the sentence and to guess the word.

Step 3. Tell the student to break the word into parts and pronounce each.

Step 4. Teacher covers parts of the word and asks student to decode each.

Step 5. Locate sound(s) in word student is miscalling. Isolate this letter or combination and ask "what sound does _____ make?"

Step 6. Provide the correct word to the student.

Reading Rate

"Stress accuracy first and then speed" is a basic instructional principle. Speed becomes important in reading as in most skills so that the student can complete an assignment in a reasonable period of time. Harris and Sipay (1971) suggest four strategies for increasing word perception.

1. Abundant practice of the most commonly used words.
2. Time reading of selections, using reinforcement and continuous charting of progress.
3. "Flashing of words and phrases with a gradual reduction in exposure time.
4. Controlled reading through presentations such as a language master.

Summary

The following rules are offered as a summary of the major points addressed in this chapter and also Chapter II in relating general strategies to the teaching of reading. These rules are based upon the "general" characteristics of the mentally retarded in reading. Neither all characteristics nor all rules apply to all mentally retarded learners.

1. Material to be read should be within the conceptual and experiential levels of the learner.
2. Material should be of "high-interest" value to the learner and

functional.

3. Break the learning task into small attainable steps and program for successful experience to minimize the learner's "expectancy for failure."

4. Provide continuous feedback to the learner on performance and correct errors immediately.

5. Be sure the student is attending to the relevant characteristics of words and sentences and maximize the differences of words presented by analyzing distinctive features.

6. Provide opportunities throughout the day (spaced review/distributed practice) for the student to practice recognition of sight words, reading, or use of a phonics rule.

7. Provide the learner with sight words in different type styles and locations to maximize generalization and transfer of the skill.

8. Remember, the end product of learning to read is comprehension of printed material.

Remember this . . .

1. Written communication is the most difficult of the language arts skills for mentally retarded learners.

2. Written expression is not simply talk written down.

3. Spelling is the weakest of the written language arts skills for the mentally retarded.

4. The most commonly used activities for teaching spelling are the least effective.

5. Peer tutoring is an effective activity for teaching new spelling words.

CHAPTER X

Written Expression Including Spelling

Written expression is the most sophisticated of the language arts skills. It is also generally the last of the language arts skills in which the EMR learner will achieve mastery. Written expression requires or subsumes several needed skills.

1. handwriting (manuscript or cursive);
2. spelling;
3. vocabulary;
4. syntax;
5. sentence composition;
6. punctuation.

Written expression should not be viewed merely as a graphic reflection of oral language. Four of the six preceding components are essential in written expression but are not common to oral language. Syntax and vocabulary are the only common elements. Our oral language is characterized by numerous stops, hesitations, incomplete and "run-on" sentences. Such weaknesses are allowable in spoken language but are viewed as serious errors when committed to paper.

Written Expression of the Retarded

Durrell and Sullivan (1958) studied the abilities of retarded children in the areas of reading, writing, speaking, and listening. Of the four areas, the children were found to be poorest in writing. They attributed poor writing ability mainly to a spelling deficiency. Cart-

wright (1968) and Sedlak and Cartwright (1972) have noted the following characteristics of writing samples from educable mentally retarded
students:
1. More spelling errors than their mental age (MA) or chronological age (CA) peers.
2. More grammatical errors (e.g., punctuation, syntax, and
   usage) than their MA or CA peers.
3. More restricted written vocabulary than their MA peers.
4. Shorter sentences and shorter compositions than their CA
   peers.

Analysis of Writing Samples

Figure 10.1 depicts some facsimiles of written language examples
produced by EMR students. The three students show marked differences in their abilities to express their thoughts in written form. All
three youngsters were in junior high at the time these stories were written. There should be no doubt in the readers mind that different sets
of objectives need to be set for each of these individuals in regard to
their written language programs. Each needs an individualized educational program in written communication skills. The focus of Joe's program should be on the development of spelling skills, punctuation
(primarily capitalization), sentence construction and sentence combining skills. Joe's printing is neat and even shows some innovation (note
the circled "i's"). He also appears to show good sequencing in his story.
Cathy's story is almost incomprehensible. With some effort you
could read the story and make sense from it. Cathy needs to write short
sentences which express a single thought. Spelling and punctuation
need to be stressed in these exercises. She probably should dictate
a sentence aloud into a tape recorder before attempting to write it.
The teacher might also explore the use of manuscript printing rather
than cursive writing in her written communication.
Michael has a better sense of sentences than Joe but still needs
additional help. The spelling is the greatest detracting element in the
story. Improved handwriting skills would help the legibility of the composition. Michael's program should include functional spelling and
handwriting.
Many of the deficiencies in the written expression of the retarded
appear to be skill deficits rather than being conceptual in nature and

these should be directly amenable to correction through systematic instruction. Isolating the principle problems and then targeting written expression objectives has been shown to be effective in enhancing writing skills (Brigham, Graubard, and Stans, 1972; Hansen and Lovitt, 1973).

Cartwright (1969) has suggested the use of an error-analysis chart as one means for systematically pinpointing written language deficits. Use of such analyses of a student's errors allows specific objectives to be written which address the deficit area. Areas of error analysis suggested by Cartwright in the analysis chart include:

Verbs: form, agreement, tense
Pronouns: antecedent, usage
Words: omissions, additions, substitutions, substandard
Sentences: incomplete, run-on
Punctuation: periods, commas, apostrophe, other
Capitals: sentence, proper nouns, overuse
Modifiers
Plurals

The goal of writing instruction is not to produce novelists but rather to develop functional communication skills. Examples of functional writing skills would include making lists (shopping, chores, phone numbers, etc.), signature, writing a check, completing application forms, writing a note to a teacher, postman, repairman and the like, addressing an envelope, writing a letter, and writing directions.

Error Analysis and Variant English Speakers

Error analysis has been discussed throughout this book. In the area of written expression with the variant English speaker not only the presence of an error needs to be determined but also the cause of the error. Errors in written expression could be the result of structural language differences in the dialect or variant English speech differences. For the variant English speaker many phonological features of words will not be accurately represented in standard written form. Examples of this error source are exemplified by the spelling of "pin" for "pen," "hem" for "him," "sin" for "sing," "pud" for "put," "goin" for "going," and "foe" for "four." In contrast, differences in syntax could account for the omission of the suffix "-ed," use of "a" rather than "an," and the reordering or omission of words in sentences. These types of

Figure 10.1

Samples of Three EMR Students' Stories About a Picture

Joe

① It looks like the family is getting ready for a picket. the mother is piting the basket the little girl is giveing the dog something to get and the farther and boy are getting the baseball things together.
② it looks like the family is on its way but they for/ got there pet dog.
③ the family stops and the boy gets out and the dog jumps up on him and the boy and the dog gets back in the car.
④ the mother is cooking the little girl is getting the food out the farther and boy and dog are playing baseball.

errors need to be differentiated from the errors which represent deficiencies in spelling skills or skills in mechanics. Figure 10.2 shows several sentences. Analyze them according to the types of errors we have discussed. Circle the spelling errors or grammatical/mechanical errors attributable to speech differences and underline the spelling errors or grammatical/mechanical errors attributable to skill deficits.

Figure 10.1 (Con't)

Cathy

[handwritten sample]

mother sinting the tabbat to eat
let go whil or mathe sby.
side further she want to get lon
with heavr work

thay are going into town to du
some shop the dog run into stiet
he want to with tham but
cont tch him with tham.

the boy jumpfout over the car
after dog father want to if
you did get the car we ging
lend.

mother and jane are rooky
sterer aot gaur sfoather you
toshople ire mathe to git did
tutith ner thik.

Experience Charts and Stories

Most individuals are comfortable talking about things they know or have done. For this reason, experience stories are an excellent technique for use in early writing experiences. One major purpose of an experience story is to teach the student to organize ideas. The

Figure 10.1 (Con't)

Michael

The Family Piance

The Famaly dicitted to go on a trip. One day yo the sack a lunch. And they got every thing in the car. they decided in gang to the Piance ground for some fun. Well when every one was in the door the dog went out to the side walk and Bill had to get out and chain the dog up.

teacher accomplishes this by leading the learner through a logical presentation by a series of questions. These experience stories in writing, parallel the language experience approach in reading. Sentences should be short and vocabulary should be kept simple. A small number of sentences should be used but each should contribute significantly to the story. There should be a deliberate attempt to build in a repetition of sight words. Steps to follow in the creation and use of an experience chart are:

1. Select a topic (planning a trip, picture, classroom activities).
2. Discuss the topic with each student contributing ideas.
3. Probe students through questions for a title of the story.
4. Print or write title on chart or board large enough for all to see.

5. In early stories, keep one sentence per line.
6. Through questions, have students contribute sentences to the story.
7. Teacher should read the story aloud after it is completed.
8. Have students read aloud story and copy story.

One of the goals of writing is communication. Sharing stories, notes, letters, or directions between students is one means of providing students with feedback on their style and organization. When reading someone else's writing the learner becomes attuned to omitted words, spelling, legible (or illegible) handwriting, phrasing and organization and realizes the value which others put on these aspects of writing.

Figure 10.2
Samples of Dialectical and Mechanical Written Language Errors

1. He be trying to get home.
2. i ask hem if he be goin?
3. I never had no trouble with nobody
4. Ef you wants to go you can
5. him shoes our od en durte.

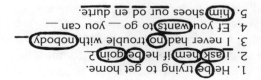

Answers:

Handwriting

While it would be convenient to assume that EMR students have a specific deficit that makes good handwriting an unachievable goal, the truth is that the fault lies not with these students but with ourselves (Milone and Wasylyk, 1981). Not only special education teachers but teachers as a group, have not been trained to teach handwriting. Decent handwriting is a skill that can have many far-reaching consequences. In school, good penmanship means that the student's work will be neat and legible and in mainstreamed classes such work will enhance the image of the EMR student and consequently serve to correct certain misconceptions surrounding these students. Also, in school, the students with good handwriting will be asked to help with various school art projects and may be able to tutor younger students in this skill area. In the work environment, good handwriting means that the individual can fill out applications and forms, take notes, or deliver messages with success.

Handwriting must be taught directly to the students. EMR learners acquire skills through incidental learning at a lesser rate than the students in regular classes and even those students do not acquire penmanship skills unless taught. Direct instruction of handwriting will effectively outweigh any factor which might serve to hinder the acquisition of this skill. However, not only must handwriting be taught but the student must understand that the teacher believes it to be a very important skill.

The Lesson

The handwriting lesson should be a scheduled daily activity and should last about fifteen minutes. Students who need additional instruction should receive it at intervals during the day and not as part of an extended class. Students should be taught to sit upright, with the lower back touching the seat back and the upper back and shoulders leaning forward. Elbows should be just off the edge of the desk and each student must be shown how to hold the pen or pencil. Plan a specific vocabulary of handwriting terms and use these terms consistently. Check with other teachers to be sure that the terms you are using are the same as those being used in the regular classes. Use the best quality paper available and make sure the lines are clear. Check the position of each student's paper and immediately correct improperly positioned paper (see Figure 10.3). Although the goal for each student is the ability to write with a standard pen or pencil, students may need to begin with the writing tool of their choice (markers, crayons, large pencils).

Both manuscript and cursive letters are constructed from certain basic strokes (see Figure 10.4). These basic strokes are relatively easy to learn and once mastered enable the student to approach complete letters and words. The student who has illegible handwriting can be helped through the mastery of these basic strokes to improve letter formations. Legibility, not necessarily perfection, should be the goal.

Figure 10.3
Paper Positions for Manuscript and Cursive Writing

PAPER POSITION (Manuscript)

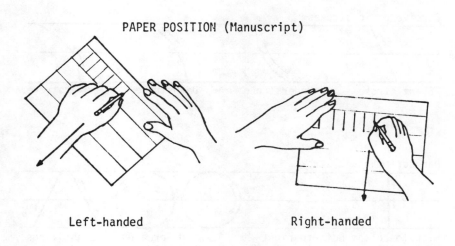

Left-handed   Right-handed

PAPER POSITION (Cursive)

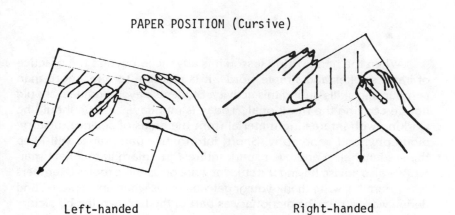

Left-handed   Right-handed

Figure 10.4
Basic Strokes of Cursive and Manuscript Writing

Cursive basic strokes

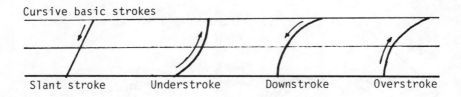

Slant stroke   Understroke   Downstroke   Overstroke

Manuscript basic strokes

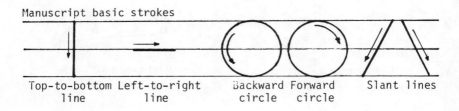

Top-to-bottom Left-to-right   Backward Forward   Slant lines
    line   line   circle circle

When the handwriting lesson has advanced beyond the practice of basic strokes and simple words, it is possible to offer more than penmanship skills during this activity. Students beyond grade 3 should not be copying the traditional "Today is Monday . . ." but should be working with interesting material from the areas of science, history, biography, and geography. Short, informative paragraphs will keep the students alert and even spark interest in unfamiliar subject matter. We also advise having the student write on specific topics (Members of My Family), write thank-you or get-well notes when appropriate, and define words from the dictionary as part of the handwriting curricula. In this way, they will be kept from a total dependence on the "copy from a model" approach and encouraged to perceive that the skill of handwriting goes beyond the "handwriting period." As an extension of this, every teacher should set criteria for the acceptability of hand-writing in all written assignments.

Do not forget the power of surrounding the students with examples of good handwriting, praising students who are achieving the goals of good penmanship, and allowing learners the opportunity to evaluate their own writing.

Teaching of Spelling

Spelling is one of the most difficult skills of the language arts program which needs to be learned. While it is a major problem for many school children (Horn, 1969) there is no concensus as to why a word is difficult to spell. There is also an absence of agreement on how difficult words should be taught (Cahen, Craun, and Johnson, 1971). Unfortunately, some of the most commonly used methods are also the least effective (Haring, Lovitt, Eaton, and Hansen, 1978). Traditional spelling workbooks teach spelling and related language arts skills simultaneously. While these related skills (e.g., dictionary usage, word building, word meaning) are valuable, they may cause confusion and difficulties for the retarded learner and detract from the primary purpose, which is learning to spell specified sets of words. Hansen (1973) has described a procedure called "program slicing" as a means of breaking down a generalized textbook into small steps or units. Basically, this involves reorganizing words in a graded speller according to common dimensions. Pretesting is done on each group of words and only unknown words are taught. There is a fixed set of activities which is followed by the students each week and the reading of "directions" is minimized.

Selection of Words

The words for a student's spelling program can be derived from a variety of sources: standard spelling books, basal readers, basic "survival" word lists, word lists based upon word frequency (Carroll, Davies, and Richman, 1971), "demon" spelling lists, words from other textbooks used in class, words a student wishes to learn, or from misspellings on written work or words frequently used. There are pros and cons which can be offered for each of the selection procedures. For example, many words chosen for inclusion in spelling texts are infrequently practiced in everyday writing tasks; on the other hand, the words generally are grouped by some common properties, have specified activities, require less work for the teacher, and make mainstreaming easier if the student is in a graded spelling book used by the rest of the school. The teacher's decision as to which option to follow (or combination) will need to be guided by an understanding of the overall spending goals for the student and the prognosis for achieving the goals.

In the first 2 to 3 weeks of school we would recommend that the words contained in Figure 10.5 be assessed and taught by the teacher before beginning the regular spelling program. This list contains frequently used word formats in students' writing and provides a baseline for the teacher in spelling instruction. The authors have noted that students correctly spell words such as "elephant," "knickers," and "snoopy" on their weekly tests but repeatedly misspell "they" (thay), "who" (how), "was" (wus), and related high-frequency words.

For the primary aged student, spelling words should be taken from a set which the student encounters in his reading. This will probably entail gathering words from the basal-reading series, the Dolch Word List, or from experience stories. For secondary age students, the core of words needs to be functional and derived from the environments in which the student lives, words related to employment and social situations should have a high priority. Spelling words might be best derived from misspellings in written assignments which stress a functional topic such as a thank-you note, party invitation, shopping list, employment form, directions, or note to a teacher, doctor, paper boy, or mailman.

Assessment of Spelling Skills

There are a number of norm-referenced spelling tests, some of which have diagnostic properties. Most of these, however, will merely provide the teacher with grade-level-equivalent information and little else. As mentioned in the chapter on assessment, norm-referenced tests provide little in the way of specific guidelines for instruction and all need to be followed by informal assessment procedures. In the area of spelling, such an assessment should follow from an analysis of a student's error patterns in written work, by the analysis of error patterns found on the norm-referenced tests, or by an analysis of error patterns found in a teacher-constructed spelling test composed of

Figure 10.5
The 100 Most Commonly Written Words

1. I	26. if	51. which	76. come
2. the	27. all	52. some	77. were
3. and	28. so	53. has	78. no
4. to	29. me	54. or	79. how
5. a	30. was	55. there	80. did
6. you	31. very	56. us	81. think
7. of	32. my	57. good	82. say
8. in	33. had	58. know	83. please
9. we	34. our	59. just	84. him
10. for	35. from	60. by	85. his
11. it	36. am	61. up	86. got
12. that	37. one	62. day	87. over
13. is	38. time	63. much	88. make
14. your	39. he	64. out	89. may
15. have	40. get	65. her	90. received
16. will	41. do	66. order	91. before
17. be	42. been	67. yours	92. two
18. are	43. letter	68. now	93. send
19. not	44. can	69. well	94. after
20. as	45. would	70. an	95. work
21. at	46. she	71. here	96. could
22. this	47. when	72. them	97. dear
23. with	48. about	73. see	98. made
24. but	49. they	74. go	99. glad
25. on	50. any	75. what	100. like

Adapted from Earnest A. Horn, "A Basic Writing Vocabulary of 10,000 Most Commonly Used Words in Writing," *University of Iowa Monograph in Education*, 1926, First Series, No. 4, Iowa City, Iowa.

words based upon specific spelling rules. Areas of attention which should be observed are:
   1. Omission of silent letters (e.g., *tak* for *take*)
   2. Omission of sounded letters (e.g., *personl* for *personal*)
   3. Omission of a doubled letter (e.g., *fil* for *fill*)
   4. Doubling (e.g., *untill* for *until*)
   5. Addition of a single letter (e.g., *backe* for *bake*)

6. Transposition or partial reversal (e.g., *pickel* for *pickle*)
7. Phonetic substitution for a vowel (e.g., *injoy* for *enjoy*)
8. Phonetic substitution for a consonant (e.g., *prizon* for *prison*)
9. Phonetic substitution for a syllable (e.g., *stopt* for *stopped*)
10. Phonetic substitution for a word (e.g., *weary* for *very*)
11. Nonphonetic substitution for a letter (e.g., *reword* for *reward*)
12. Nonphonetic substitution for a consonant (e.g., *importent* for *important*)
13. Phonetic spelling of nonphonetic words (e.g., *kwik* for *quick*)

Fixed Word Lists

The most commonly used word arrangement for the teaching of spelling is the fixed word list. In this procedure a set of words is presented and learned as a unit. Graded spelling texts follow this format. Different sets of words are assigned each week with perhaps a review or retention test given every six weeks. The set of words presented in any given list may be partially or totally unknown to the students. Words which are missed on Friday's test generally are ignored or perhaps added to a "missed-word" list from which the student should practice and review. This procedure works well for *most* students but it does not ensure spelling mastery for *all* students. An alternative procedure is for each student to practice the words on the list until he/she is able to spell all the words correctly for two or three perfect tests and then proceed to the next list of words. "Dictation" for practice or tests can be accomplished by tape recording the word list on a cassette or on language-master cards. The student can self-correct the paper if it is practice and the teacher can correct it when it is a test.

Flow Word Lists

McGuigan (1975) has indicated that a major limitation of fixed word lists is that words on a fixed list are mastered at different rates by the students and that a student may spend unnecessary time practicing known words without being continually challenged by new ones. In order to circumvent this problem, McGuigan has suggested a procedure which uses a flow list. In this process, words are dropped from a pupil's daily-study and test-word lists when he learns them to criterion. New words are added as old words are deleted from the list.

The criterion commonly followed for moving words off the list is the successful spelling of the same word(s) on two consecutive days. This criterion can be modified for the entire class or for individual learners. Some students need more trials of overlearning in order to retain the skill over time than other students. By following this method each student in the room will be operating with a different group of words each day. New words are added in sequence from a master word list. Each student will need to maintain a record of his words either in a notebook or on a set of flash cards. The number of words on each student's daily list will vary according to the characteristics of the learner. Some students' lists will have five words while others might have ten or fifteen. The system works well if used in conjunction with peer tutoring. Some general rules of thumb for operating this system are:

1. Student should master at least one word per day, and if rate is below this level, reduce the words in the student's list.
2. Administer a retention test every one to two weeks by selecting mastered words at random. If the student misses a word, add it back onto his list. This add-a-word method results in students learning to spell new words faster and with greater retention than with fixed word lists (Hansen, 1978).

Instructional Strategies for Teaching Spelling

PEER TEACHING. Harris (1973) found that being a tutor or being a tutee resulted in similar successful acquisition levels of new spelling words and was superior to independent study. Students should be divided into pairs and given a set number of words (fifteen to twenty). The tutor should:

1. Dictate each word from a flash card to the tutee
2. Give feedback if a word is correct and show correct spelling if a word is wrong
3. Deposit each word into a mastery or nonmastery box
4. Recycle nonmastered words

Students should reverse roles after ten minutes of practice. The tutee should write the words and not merely spell them aloud.

HOME-BOUND TUTORING. Broden, Beasley, and Hall (1978) found that parents can carry out a tutoring intervention similar to the preceding with highly effective results. The teacher should have the student put spelling words on cards on Monday and take them home. The teacher should send home a written step-by-step procedure for tutoring the child on the words. Steps 1 through 4 in the example above would provide sufficient detail for a parent to carry out the tutoring.

POSITIVE PRACTICE. The use of *varied* positive-practice activities such as finding each spelling word in the dictionary, writing the definition for the words, use the words in sentences, etc., was found to be effective in raising weekly spelling-test scores but only when there was a *variety* of positive consequences delivered for spelling achievement (Foxx and Jones, 1978). Suggestions for these consequences included prizes, positive written comments, and posting high scores or the names of high scorers. In the absence of a contingency for spelling achievement these "related activities" will have minimal effect on spelling achievement.

IMITATION PLUS MODELING. For students with spelling problems and attention deficits, imitation plus modeling may be an effective strategy. It involves the following steps: (1) reading a word to the student; (2) having the student write the word; (3) if spelled correctly, praising the learner; (4) if misspelled, having the teacher write an exact imitation of the misspelled word and saying "This is how you spelled the word" and then showing a correctly written model for the misspelled word and finally requiring the pupil to recopy the word from the model. Research by Kaufman, Hallahan, Hass, Brame, and Boren (1978) substantiates the use of this procedure.

SELF-CORRECTION. Allowing students to practice writing their spelling words from memory or diction and then having them self-correct their papers is a more effective strategy for enhancing student performance on weekly tests than allowing the teacher to correct the practice tests. Hansen and Lovitt (1974) found that self-correction facilitated acquisition of unknown words without a loss in retention. A second component to the effectiveness of self-correction was that students practiced their words daily, using this method and that they practiced until they got all words correct on two out of three trials. Two advantages of self-correction include the immediacy of feedback and the possible comparison of misspellings to the model in order to identify specific letter-order errors. If "cheating" is a problem in carrying out such a procedure, we would recommend that the self-correction be conducted in the view of the teacher with colored pens.

COVER-COPY-COMPARE. Under this strategy described by Hansen (1978), the student: (1) analyzes the distinctive features of a word (e.g., length, prefixes, suffixes, configuration); (2) writes the word with the model present and silently says each letter of the word as it is formed; (3) covers the word and writes it from memory; and (4) compares the written word to the model. The process is repeated until mastery is achieved.

Less Effective Strategies

The use of a midweek pretest with feedback but without specific teacher intervention does not result in increasing weekly test scores (Foxx and Jones, 1978). Simply recopying each misspelled word ten times does not result in increasing weekly test scores (Foxx and Jones, 1978). It can be effective if used with contingent reinforcers. Attending to the elements in a word and the distinctive features is critical. Strategies which force a student to attend to elements are those which appear to be most successful. Hanna, Hanna, Hodges, and Peterson (1971) have noted that the correspondence between phonemes and graphemes in the American Spelling System are consistent 80% of the time. Using a word-by-word approach to the teaching of spelling should be less efficient than teaching patterns and rules.

Lovitt (1973) found that students could readily be taught the rules but that they had difficulty in generalizing these rules to new words and determining the *exceptions* to the rules. If spelling rules are to constitute a part of a spelling program, the students must be provided with specific instructions on how and when to use spelling rules *and* their exceptions. In the absence of specific instruction and examples of these exceptions, rule learning will not be highly effective in training efficient spellings.

Other Suggestions for Spelling Instruction

Besides the specific procedures described in the preceding section, there are a variety of related teaching or caveats followed in spelling instruction. These include:
1. Being certain that the student can correctly pronounce each word
2. Requiring the student to define each word or use it in a sentence
3. Noting similarities between words
4. Noting differences in highly similar words
5. Teaching the phonetic rule and the exceptions
6. Differentiating between homonyms

7. Teaching the spelling of difficult words in syllables
8. Color coding prefixes, suffixes, or root words
9. Changing the initial consonant on root words or changing prefixes/suffixes for word building
10. Teaching new words using a multisensory approach (e.g., VAKT).

Summary

The overall goal of written expression is communication. To ensure this communication, the handwriting needs to be legible and the words spelled in a reasonably accurate manner. The written language program for many mentally retarded learners will be highly individualized. The analysis of errors in writing samples needs to consider not only the mechanical errors due to skill deficits but the grammatical errors as well which might be the result of differences in dialect used by a variant English speaker. In the teaching of spelling students will not incidentally learn the words but must be taught directly and given repeated opportunities to achieve mastery and overlearning.

Remember this . . .

1. A child spends a majority of the school day in listening type activities.

2. There are forty three sound patterns for the twenty six letters of the English alphabet.

3. The use of nonstandard English by a student in school may be related to an inability to recognize a need to shift styles rather than to an inability to use standard English.

4. Webbing is a strategy for facilitating oral language use and organizing ideas.

CHAPTER XI

Instruction in Listening and Speaking

    While most individuals consider the three R's as the basis of any academic curriculum, progress in these and related areas might be severely restricted if the listening and/or speaking skills of a student were deficient. Adults and children devote a large percentage of their time to listening activities. Listening to the radio, watching television, listening to the teacher explain directions or assignments, and conversations with friends and acquaintances consume a major portion of a day. In school-related tasks it has been estimated by Flanders (1970) that as much as 66% of a child's day is spent in auditory-related tasks. Burns and Broman (1975) report research which indicates adults spend about 42% of their waking hours in listening activities, 32% in conversations, 11% in writing, and 15% in reading. While these are rough estimates and subject to error, they do reflect the importance of listening and speaking skills from the vantage of percentage of time used. The development of listening skills is critical if we are to maximize the learning opportunities available to the mentally retarded. Lundsteen (1964) has demonstrated that listening skills can be improved. Equally important is the development of speaking skills since research has demonstrated that people make judgments and form positive or negative impressions regarding the intelligence of a speaker based upon their oral language skills (Labov, 1966). The concern before the teacher now is not whether the development of listening and speaking skills is an important area of the curriculum but rather how to best meet the needs of these children in regard to listening and speaking.

Language Development of the Mentally Retarded

The sequence of language development in the mentally retarded closely parallels that of nonretarded children but at a slower rate of acquisition. Speech difficulties are common for the mentally retarded. Spradlin (1963) found that articulation problems were related to intelligence test scores. While they have more speech-related problems than normal students, the differences are quantitative rather than qualitative. Their speaking vocabularies are more restricted than students of comparable chronological ages (McMillan, 1977). Dunn (1973) has noted that this deficit becomes increasingly serious as they mature since language differences between normal and mildly retarded learners become more pronounced. Not only the semantic features of their language show deficiencies but also the syntactical features. Semmel, Barritt, Bennett, and Perfetti (1968) found the language of the retarded to be less abstract than that of their nonretarded counterparts. Kirk and Gallagher (1979) reported that the mildly retarded use proportionately less complex sentence structures and descriptions in their oral communication. As a result the mildly retarded encounter more problems in communicating effectively with others. They need to use more sentences to convey an idea than a nonretarded person, thus it takes them more time to express an idea. They have great difficulty transmitting information which represents sequences of activities. Employers and other adults may react negatively to persons who have difficulty expressing themselves or who are slow to express an idea.

Dunn (1973) has indicated that oral language stimulation appears to be at least modestly effective with mildly retarded children. Webb and Kinde (1963) point out that oral language training needs to be intensive and systematic. The general conclusion which can be reached is that growth and change can be achieved but the possible extent of change is unknown. MacMillan (1977) has summarized the prognosis when he wrote, "The fact that they are capable of improving their performance if certain strategies are provided makes the outlook for teaching retarded children an optimistic one" (p. 360).

Components of Language

Before discussing some strategies for assessing or teaching listening and speaking skills the teacher must understand that language is a rule-governed system of behavior and composed of identifiable components. These components include:

1. Phonology
2. Morphology
3. Semantics
4. Syntax
5. Pragmatics

Phonology refers to the individual speech sounds (phonemes) and the rules that govern the sequence of those sounds. While the English alphabet contains twenty six letters, the phonological system contains forty three sound patterns. Nineteen of these are vowels and dipthongs and twenty four are consonants in the oral language system. The acquisition of these sounds follows a sequential developmental order which is acquired by an individual by age eight.

Morphology involves the smallest individual meaningful sound element in the language (morpheme) and the rules for combining these morphemes into words. Morphemes include root words as well as prefixes and suffixes. The word "girls" for example would contain two morphemes — "s" indicating plurality and "girl" indicating root word.

Semantics represents the meaning of words in a language. In terms of assessment we normally refer to a student's vocabulary development. Students acquire new words through interactions with their environment and having someone label the object or event relationship. The development of vocabulary is therefore highly related to experiences. The different types of words are broken into groupings called "form classes" (e.g., nouns, verbs, function words, adjectives, adverbs, etc.).

Syntax involves the use of the rules of the language in combining words into sentences. Syntax involves the placement of different types of words into the proper order to create meaningful sentences. This placement of words is rule based. Syntax is developed through experience with the language and repeated exposure. There is a progressive sequence of sentence development that occurs naturally as students get older. This sequence normally shows development from one-word utterances (e.g., "ball," "go") to two-word utterances (e.g., "shoe on," "daddy go") and telegraphic speech (e.g., "eat cookie now," "Johnny dog run car"). The first "formal sentences" are referred to as *kernel* sentences and differ from the telegraphic speech in that they contain function words (e.g., a, the, in, under). An example of a kernel

sentence is "The girl is kicking the boy." From the development of
kernel sentences the student passes into sentences which show
transformations or the combining of two or more sentences into one.
Transformations reflect greater linguistic maturity than single
sentences. For example, the kernel sentences, "The dog is brown,"
"The dog is chasing the ball," "The ball is red," can be combined into
the sentence "The brown dog is chasing the red ball," or into the
sentence "The dog that is brown is chasing the ball that is red." Using
either of these transformations would indicate a more mature use of
the language than the preceding short sentences. Combining kernel
sentences into "double-base" and "adjective" transformations is based
upon rules which can be specified.

Pragmatics is the ability to use the language code in the proper
social context (Bloom and Lahey, 1978; McLean and Snyder-McLean,
1979). The true functional power of oral language rests within the social
context in which it is used. Shifts in the roles taken by different
speakers and shifts in style from variant to standard English usage
are examples of aspects of the language which are studied in
pragmatics.

The teacher of the mentally retarded must be aware of these different components of the language system in order to be able to
specifically identify deficit areas and also to be able to plan a corrective program. Failure to recognize these different components of the
language system could result in a very global approach to the teaching
of aural/oral language skills. While such an approach might be acceptable for teaching a nonhandicapped child, teachers of the mentally
retarded need to focus on specific areas of deficit. The amount of incidental learning and skill transfer exhibited by nonhandicapped
learners is more restrictive in the retarded learner. Instruction must
be specific and systematic.

Assessment of Aural/Oral Language Skills

Any assessment of aural/oral language skills should be based
upon the five components of language explained in the earlier section. These components of language development can be assessed in-
formally by the teacher through naturalistic observation and recording
or teacher-constructed tests. These components can also be assessed
through formal measures. A listing and description of expressive and

receptive language scales are presented in Figure 11.1. Standardized tests are useful because they tell how a child compares with other children on the basis of his performance. They are relatively quick and easy to administer and lighten the burden of the evaluator. These tests however do not totally describe the child's language system. The norms allow for little flexibility in the administration of the test and yield scores based upon item pass/fail but are not necessarily analyzed by error types. It is the pattern of errors that can provide the teacher with valuable information. The functional use of language is the most important aspect of language assessment. Such an assessment is performed best through naturalistic observation. Naturalistic observation involves the following process:

1. Identifying the problem from the information available
2. Developing the hypotheses as to what is contributing to the difficulty
3. Gathering information through the observation of a child using: anecdotal records, frequency counts, time interval recording, or time samples
4. Proposing tentative solutions
5. Implementing solutions one at a time and keeping data
6. Evaluating results and if unsuccessful, try again

Oral Language and the Variant-English Speaker

An unusually high percentage of students from ethnic minority groups are found in special classes (Dunn, 1968; Mercer, 1973). Many of these students use a variant or nonstandard English in their oral communication. Writers disagree as to whether these differences should be viewed as *deficiencies* or as *difference*. In fact, such arguments have even resulted in lawsuits and court cases (Monteith, 1980; Robinson, 1981; Smithermon, 1981).

The deficit model implies that variant or nonstandard usage is associated with a cognitive limitation. Bereiter and Engelmann (1966) illustrate this view by their conclusions that nonstandard English speakers are unable to use "causal logic" due to an absence of an if-then structure, specified plurality forms, and the use of double negatives. The deficit model does not recognize the rule structure of the variant form of a language.

In contrast, the *difference* model (Baratz and Shuy, 1969) views

Figure 11.1
Expressive and Receptive Language Scales

Test/Publisher	Purpose	Age Range	Stimulus/Response	Scoring
		Receptive Language Tests		
Peabody Picture Vocabulary Test (PPVT), American Guidance Service, 1965, cost: $14.00	According to the manual, the purpose is "to provide an estimate of a subject's verbal intelligence through measuring his hearing vocabulary" (Dunn, 1965, p. 25). However, the test may more validly represent a child's vocabulary density.	2.0 to 18.0	Given four pictorially represented choices, the tester reads the single-word verbal stimulus with the carrier phrase "show me" or "point to . . ." Ex. point to table Ex. point to Edifice	A basal and ceiling is established, a raw score of number of correct responses is computed and converted into a mental-age score, intelligence quotient, or percentile equivalent. Administration time: 10-15 minutes
Assessment of Children's Language Comprehension (ACLC), Consulting Psychologist Press, 1973, cost: $13.50 for kit	The test is designed to determine the level at which a child is unable to decode and remember lexical items presented in increasing syntactical length and complexity. The nature of the test helps to isolate areas of difficulty. Complexity: 1 to 4 critical elements	Normative data from 3-0 to 5-5 years	When presented with spiral-bound line-drawn picture plates, the testee is to look at each of the pictorial stimuli presented on the plate while the examiner reads the verbal stimulus from the test form using a carrier phrase such as "point to" or "show me." Ex. Show me the "lady sitting" Ex. Point to "dog eating and cat sitting"	Part A (1 critical element) is scored by adding the number of correct responses. Parts B, C, and D are scored by computing a percent correct as well as a narrative description of error patterns. Administration time: Untimed test, 15-20 minutes for administration and scoring

Figure 11.1 (Con't)

Test/Publisher	Purpose	Age Range	Stimulus/Response	Scoring
Test for Auditory Comprehension of Language (TACL), Teaching Resources Corp., 5th ed., 1973, cost: $39.95	To determine the child's developmental level of auditory comprehension of vocabulary and linguistic structure. Information obtained can lead to guidelines for therapeutic intervention. Language categories measured are: (1) form class and function words, (2) morphological constructions, (3) grammatical categories, (4) syntactic structure. A screening form is available.	3.0 to 6.0	Given pictorially represented stimulus choices, the tester reads aloud the stimulus items and the child responds by pointing to the appropriate picture.	Responses scored as correct or incorrect, converting total raw score into an age-equivalent score and percentile rank. The entire test must be administered in order to utilize the normative data. Administration time: 20 minutes
Vocabulary Comprehension Scale, Teaching Resources Corp., 1975, cost: $40.00	Designed to assess comprehension of basic concepts such as pronouns, words of position (e.g. in, on), size (e.g. small, fat), quantity (e.g. all, less), and quality (e.g. hard, same).	Preschool to 6.0	Given toy objects (e.g. playhouse, cars, dolls, tea set, etc.) the examiner requests testee manipulation of specific object to appropriately represent the verbal command. e.g. (Make doll go up ladder) e.g. (Give me the big block)	Each item is scored pass/fail. The items within each category are ranked according to developmental age. The testee's performance level is compared to sample population yielding a rough index of developmental performance level. Administration time: 45 minutes

Figure 11.1 (Con't)

Test/Publisher	Purpose	Age Range	Stimulus/Response	Scoring
		Expressive Language Tests		
Environmental Language Inventory (ELI), Charles E. Merrill, 1978, cost: $7.95	To assess expressive language in three modes: initiation, conversation, and free play by analysis of semantic-grammatical rules underlying the testee's production of multiword phrases according to their semantic intent.	No age range limitations reported	Given assortment of non-linguistic stimuli (toys, object, edibles) the examiner elicits 24 stimulus sets, testing each rule three times, by manipulating the stimuli to stimulate spontaneous and initiated responses providing cues as necessary. e.g. Examiner makes doll fall down—child responds by watching. Examiner cues—"Tell me what happened" cuing up to an initiated response if necessary.	Response can be scored according to frequency, proportion, rank order of rule, mean length of utterance, and percent of intelligible/unintelligible words. Administration time: 30 minutes up to several sessions
Carrow Elicited Language Inventory (CELI), Teaching Resources Corp., 1974, cost: $50 for kit	The test is designed to measure a child's productive use of grammar. The testee's performance is compared with peer performance and can help determine the specific grammatical structures in error.	3.0 +		

Figure 11.1 (Con't)

Test/Publisher	Purpose	Age Range	Stimulus/Response	Scoring
CELI (cont.)	[Expressive test — imitative] Based on precept that a child can only accurately imitate structures within his grammatical repertoire.			
The Oral Language Sentence Imitation Screening Test (OLSIST) and The Oral Language Sentence Imitation Diagnostic Inventory (OLSIDI), Linguis Systems, Inc., 1977, cost: $79.00 complete test	The test assesses the child's syntactical performance and as an indicator of necessary further testing. The OLSIST provides initial indicators of a deficit and the OLSIDI provides a "deep test" of the particular language areas found deficient in the screening. Based on theory of language development described by Brown (1973).	Preschool +	Both tests are sentence imitation tasks where the examiner reads a sentence and asks the testee to "say exactly what I say."	The examiner records the testee's exact response. All word changes, omissions, or additions are scored as incorrect. A percentage-of-correctness score is computed as well as a mean length of imitated utterance. Administration time: OLSIST—10 minutes OLSIDI—5 minutes per subtest
Receptive and Expressive Language Tests				
Porch Index of Communicative Ability in Children (PICAC), Consulting Psychologists Press, 1975	A reliable and sensitive measure of a child's level of communicative functioning assessing levels by subtests classified by modality: verbal, gestural, reacting, auditory, visual, and graphic. The test can only be administered by	No limit	All but one subtest revolve around a set of 10 common objects. Stimuli and response criterion are based on the modality category being tested. 1. Verbal: "Tell me the name of each of these _____."	Responses scored on five dimensions: accuracy, responsiveness, completeness, promptness, and efficiency. Each response is ranked on a 16-point scale. Administration time: 1 hour

Figure 11.1 (Con't)

Test/Publisher	Purpose	Age Range	Stimulus/Response	Scoring
PICAC (cont.)	trained personnel. Results yield a level of communicative functioning, baseline data against which to measure progress over time and diagnostic, prognostic, and therapeutic information.		(single-word responses); "Tell me what you do with each of these" (sentence responses). 2. Gestural: "Show me what you do with each of these." 3. Reading: Child reads single words, words printed backwards, or sentences, in order to respond to placing the cards correctly. 4. Auditory: Child responds by following directions spoken by examiner. 5. Visual: Matching object to object and picture to object. 6. Graphic: Child is required to draw; copy words, geometric shapes, or pictures; write from dictation; or follow spoken directions by writing the answer.	

Figure 11.1 (Con't)

Test/Publisher	Purpose	Age Range	Stimulus/Response	Scoring
Preschool Language Scale (PLS), Charles E. Merrill Publishing Co., 1969, cost: $5.00	Designed to determine areas of strength and weakness or deficiencies of receptive and expressive language ability.	Any age child presumed to be functioning at a preschool or primary age.	The scale is administered in two parts by age level. Four items for each age level is presented testing auditory comprehension with pictures and objects and verbal ability by having the child name items, give home address, etc. Ex. "point to the wheels on the car" (picture of car) or following instructions given verbally "tell me your name and home address" "name six animals in one minute"	A "basal age" is established and test continues to point at which all four items are missed within an age level. Responses are scored according to the regulations of acceptability in the manual. Correct items are totaled yielding auditory-comprehension age, as well as a combined language age. The scores can be computed into quotients given the chronological age. Administration time: Dependent on establishment of basal age.
Northwestern Syntax Screening Test (NSST), Northwestern University Press, 1971, cost: $10.00	To identify those children between 3 and 8 years of age who are significantly deviant in syntactical development to warrant further investigation. The test serves a dual function of providing a screening measure for group assessment and to provide a quick estimate of syntactical development.	3.0 to 8.0	The same linguistic structures are tested at both a receptive and expressive level. Pictorial stimuli presented on 10 four-choice plates measure the receptive component with the examinee utilizing a pointing response. On the expressive component, the examiner shows a two-choice picture plate, provides a title without	A raw score of total correct answers is computed separately for both components and a percentile is calculated. Those children scoring more than 2 standard deviations below the mean are considered probably in need of language therapy and definitely in need of further language

Figure 11.1 (Con't)

Test/Publisher	Purpose	Age Range	Stimulus/Response	Scoring
NSST (cont.)			indicating the choice, and asks the child to point to the appropriate picture and name it.	testing. Administration time: 15 minutes

*Compiled by Sheila Davis

the variant-English form as rule based and systematic. Rather than viewing speakers of the variant-language form as "deficient" they are viewed as speaking a language with a different set of rules. The differences in dialect are much like the British view of American English. As Professor Higgins said in *My Fair Lady* regarding the use of proper English, "in America they haven't used it for years."

The study of variant-English speakers and their communication system would fall under the component of language called pragmatics. Teachers need to be aware of this language component and the aspects within it which comprise that area of study. Some of these aspects include the social environment, roles of the speakers, and shifts in styles.

Depending upon the social environment and the purpose of a communication exchange most speakers will shift to a level of language which is most appropriate for the setting. This range of shift can fall along a continuum from the very "proper" use of the English language (formal English) to the level of jargon, slang, or street language (informal English). Such style shifting is a natural and expected aspect of linguistic competence. Talking to friends after school is a social situation which calls for one level of language usage while a job interview or communication with authority figures (e.g., teacher, attorney, police, principal) would call for a different style of language.

Teaching students to shift between styles depending upon the social circumstances they encounter is an expected outcome of an oral language program for the mildly retarded variant-English speaker. Before learning to shift styles, however, the learner needs to be taught that different language styles exist and to receive training in formal or standard English. Our society categorizes individuals on the basis of how they talk. The use of variant-English forms in social situations requiring the use of formal English will call undue attention to an individual and shape the perceptions and impressions of others toward that individual. A major problem facing the mentally retarded is the "visibility" of the disability through their behavior. The goal of oral language training then is to minimize the differences between the speaker and the expectations of the individuals in the social setting.

Labov (1966) has listed a sequence of eight goals for communication instruction with the variant-English speaker:

1. Understand spoken English in order to learn from the teacher
2. Read and comprehend printed materials
3. Communicate to others in spoken English

4.   Express themselves in writing
5.   Use standard English for written communication
6.   Spell correctly
7.   Use standard English in oral communication
8.   Use appropriate pronunciation in order to avoid stigmatization

Cohen and Plaskon (1980) list eight principles which should guide teachers who are instructing mildly handicapped variant-English speakers:

1.   The "perfect" English speech form does not exist. A wide range of speech patterns are considered acceptable.
2.   The language standards of the child's environment/community are important.
3.   If the language style of the child's community differs from the standard form, "the child should be taught to recognize the difference and the parallel forms of the standard and variant forms" (p. 447).
4.   Formal grammar should not be taught. Instruction should focus on how we use language and not why we use it.
5.   Learners should be given ample opportunities daily to use the language and to express themselves.
6.   Opportunities for spontaneous dialogue and structural drills should be balanced.
7.   Expect students to make the transition through regular usage standard form after having sufficient opportunity to learn it.
8.   The plan to develop a continuum of styles should start in the early years but probably will not be fully attained until secondary school.

Do's and Don't's

The following set of do's and don't's should help you develop appropriate oral language objectives and intervention strategies for teaching the variant English speaker:

1.   Don't correct random errors in oral language.
2.   Don't start at the very beginning of language development.
3.   Don't constantly correct language and speech "errors."
4.   Do model appropriate use of English.
5.   Do provide sufficient practice on standard forms.

6. Do have planned activities for students to practice standard speech forms.
7. Do be aware of parallel variant and standard language patterns, and make students aware by translating between the two.
8. Do stress the "communication" aspect of language.

Techniques for Improving Speech

Speech and oral language are not terms which should be used interchangeably. Speech involves the sounds of the language and the intelligibility of those sounds, while oral language deals with the structure and content of the language. Problems with speech may interfere with the communication process in the same way that poor handwriting will interfere with the written communication of a message.

The most common types of speech problems are:
1. Articulation disorders
2. Voice disorders
3. Stuttering

Some of the more common assessment instruments used with these disorders are described in Figure 11.2.

Gearhart and Weishahn (1976) suggest that students with articulation problems should receive "ear training." Ear training involves specific instruction to the learner to discriminate between the error and the correct articulation. The error and then the correction are presented sequentially so that the student can hear the difference. As a part of this training, the student needs good speech models in the classroom. Close cooperation with the speech therapist is also essential.

For voice disorders, the teacher should reinforce proper modification of voice usage and the avoidance of vocal abuse. A reminder, such as a signal, of instances of voice abuse by the learner can also play a role in a corrective program.

To the authors' knowledge no one has a solution to the problem of stuttering. As such, the teacher should not be expecting a "cure" but rather be looking for a reduction of stuttering encounters. Reducing a learner's level of anxiety by carefully planning and structuring events and responses in the classroom is one means to reduce stuttering instances.

Figure 11.2
ARTICULATION (Phonological) ASSESSMENT*

Name/Publisher	Purpose	Age Range	Stimuli/Responses	Scoring
The Templin-Darley Tests of Articulation Bureau of Educational Research and Service Extension Division C-20 East Hall University of Iowa, Iowa City, Iowa 52242	The 141 item test samples consonants, vowels, diphthongs, and two and three consonant clusters. Single consonants are tested in the initial, medial and final positions of words. The test is designed to provide a detailed description and analysis of a child's articulatory skills.	3.0 to 8.0 years	Given a line drawn pictures, the student will verbally respond to the stimuli, "What is this?" There are 2 to 4 drawings each on 6 × 9 inch plates. A sentence form is provided for older children and a screening test is included.	Responses are scored on the test form as correct productions, substitutions, omissions, distortions, sounds with nasal emission of air and no responses. Norms are provided. Administration Time: 15 minutes
The Goldman-Fristoe Test of Articulation American Guidance Services, Inc. Publishers Bldg. Circle Pines, Minnesota 55014	The tests consist of 3 subtests that provide a means of sampling an individual's articulatory performance of sounds in words, and sounds in sentences as well as testing for stimulability.	2 yrs and older	44 stimulus items are contained. The subject is presented with a single item picture and responds verbally to the stimulus "What is this?" This procedure yields spontaneous single words. The subject is also presented with an activity picture and verbally responds to the stimulus "Tell me a story about this picture," yielding spontaneous, connected, conversational speech. Finally, a stimulability probe	The score form is color coded according to the position of the sounds in words. Vowels are not tested and no screening test is provided. There is no normative data. Administration Time: 10-12 minutes

Figure 11.2 (Con't)

Name/Publisher	Purpose	Age Range	Stimuli/Responses	Scoring
The Fisher-Logemann Test of Articulation Competence Houghton-Mifflin Co.110 Tremont Street Boston, Mass. 02107	The test is designed to assess 25 single consonants in initial, medial, and final positions of words, 22 consonant clusters, vowels; and diphthongs in a spontaneous single-word naming task.	2.0 to 6.0 years	of sounds in error are tested through an imitative test where the tester models the spoken word and the subject repeats it. The subject is presented with a color picture of a single item (2 to 3 pictures per page) and will respond verbally to the stimulus "What is this?" yielding spontaneous single word productions.	The scoring is performed in narrow transcription with the response forms organized to facilitate pattern analysis based on manner, place and voicing. No normative data is provided. Administration time: approximately 12 minutes
The Deep Test of Articulation Stanoix House, Inc. 3020 Chartier Ave. Pittsburgh, Penn. 15204	The test is a series of in depth contextual tests for individual phonemes designed to provide a collection of sound-specific measures beyond three-potion articulation testing.	not applicable	Given various combinations on line-drawn pictures representing monosyllabic words, the subject verbally responds to "Look at these two pictures and make them into one silly word—say the word." The subject responds with a bisyllabic word. Example: cup—sun Response: cupsun The presentation is system-	Each response is scored as correct or incorrect providing an indication of consistency of production and place of (blank). No normative data is provided. Screening test and sentence form are provided. Administration time: 5-10 minutes per test

Figure 11.2 (Con't)

Name/Publisher	Purpose	Age Range	Stimuli/Responses	Scoring
The Distinctive Feature Analysis of Misarticulations University Park Press 233 East Redwood St. Baltimore, Md. 21202	The purpose of distinctive feature analysis is to analyze consonant errors of a speech sample by a step by step sequence leading to the tabulation of a percentage of correct and incorrect usage of distinctive features across sounds. This procedure is appropriate only for those individuals with multiple articulation errors.	No specific range	atically arranged to provide opportunity for 60 items per target sound. One target sound per test. No specific test stimuli are included. Sounds can be elicited in single word context or in conversational, connected speech. The monograph describes the feature analysis procedures.	Features per sound are scored + or − for presence or absence of a feature. A percentage of correct and incorrect usage is tabulated. Guidelines for selecting a feature for training and suggestions for remediation are provided.

*Compiled by Sheila Davis

While the development of the speech therapy program is the primary responsibility of the speech therapist, the teacher becomes the extension of the therapist in the classroom in the delivery of the speech therapy program throughout the school day. In such a role relationship the teacher (and her staff) remain the primary delivery agent for services. The teacher should therefore feel comfortable in discussing the proposed program with the therapist and to seek advice on how to respond in different situations. Several "rules" which should guide the behavior of the teacher in a classroom with students who exhibit speech problems include:

1. *Do not* rebuke, embarrass, or reprimand the child for speaking poorly since such behavior could be modeled by other students in the class. *Do* establish an atmosphere for students to feel free to experiment with speech.
2. *Do* become a good speech model but *do not* overarticulate since such behavior will call undue attention to the speech problems.
3. *Do* set aside time in the schedule for specific practice in speech development. Tape recorders, language master, telephone, TalkBack®, and similar types of materials and devices can be used for these periods.

General Principles in Language Instruction

Lamberts (1978) has delineated the following principles in teaching language skills:

1. The behavior desired from the student must be *directly* derived from the objective.
2. The activities must be planned in a logical, easy-to-hard progression. Presentation of the *stimuli* must be sequenced as well as the *type of response* required from the learner.
3. The activities should allow for different types of responses from the learner (e.g., pointing, carrying out an action, imitating a model, etc.).
4. There must be different activities and different materials used for the same objective to promote generalization.

Oral Language Activities

The development of good oral language behavior by students is not possible unless the teacher gives them a chance to talk. The teacher's role is to provide the opportunities for interaction and to structure a theme or topic for spoken interchange. Cohen and Plaskon (1980) indicate that some fairly common topics and strategies used in stimulating oral communication skills include the following:

Storytelling
Oral reporting
Announcements
Memory games
Panel discussions
Explanations
Telephone use
Interviews
Debates
Drama

Cohen and Plaskon also point out that the atmosphere of many classrooms ". . . take on the characteristics of a college lecture hall in terms of opportunities for conversation, dialogue, and idea exchanges" (p. 221). They suggest that teachers do not know how to incorporate these activities into the daily classroom routine and make them exciting. One strategy which they suggest is that of "webbing."

Webbing requires that the class or teacher decide upon a particular theme or topic. Acceptable themes might be "water," "apples," "energy," "jobs," "friends," etc. Once the theme is determined the "web" begins. The leader (teacher) writes the issue, topic, or word on the board and encircles it. Students then generate related points, themes, or terms which can be tied to this central theme. These are written on the board, circled and attached to the central theme or related theme. Topics or words should be added to each central circle in a clockwise fashion. As ideas are presented there is bound to be some overlap. These overlaps should be connected with a line. Two simple webs are presented in Figures 11.3 and 11.4. The use of a web has many benefits. Among them are the following:

1. The exercise is a vocabulary builder.
2. It shows the interrelationship of ideas.
3. It is a systematic and graphic form of brainstorming.
4. It allows individuals to justify or explain their reasoning for a subcategory.
5. It allows for a free exchange of ideas between students.

6. Students engage in turn taking in its construction.
7. Students make decisions on "where" a topic should be placed in the web and "if" a topic should be placed in the web.
8. The strategy can be used to plan topics within a unit of study.
9. Webs can be used in subsequent lessons for elaborations.
10. Webs can be used as a "warm-up" activity for written exercises.

Vocabulary Training

The careful selection of words is of the utmost importance when your objective is to increase the expressive or receptive vocabulary of the learner. If you are working with young children, words which refer to objects ("ball," "table"), common actions ("stop," "go"), and object characteristics ("hot," "broken") should be taught before abstract entities ("yesterday," "next week") or relationships ("tallest," "in the middle"). For both expressive and receptive vocabulary training it is important that verbs, prepositions, adjectives, and adverbs are taught as well as nouns. Quite often there is a tendency to rely heavily on the teaching of nouns to the exclusion of other speech forms. Such a focus could delay the development of advanced syntactic forms such as phrases or transformations. The words selected should also be high frequency use words so that the student can have the opportunity to practice them. With older students the vocabulary taught should be vocationally related terms. Instruction should focus on the precise meaning of these words. Students should be required to spontaneously use these words orally as well as respond to them receptively.

Role Playing and Oral Communication

Role playing is an excellent strategy for practicing oral/aural communication skills since a student must not only be the transmitter of information but the receiver of information as well. Role playing is also good because it is such an "open" activity and can focus on a variety of topics in different subject areas. The chapters in this book on social skills, career education, and study and survival skills all present examples of role-playing situations which can be enacted in a classroom. While the activity is taking place the teacher has the opportunity to observe not only the oral/aural skills of the learners but also their problem-solving, comprehension, and planning skills.

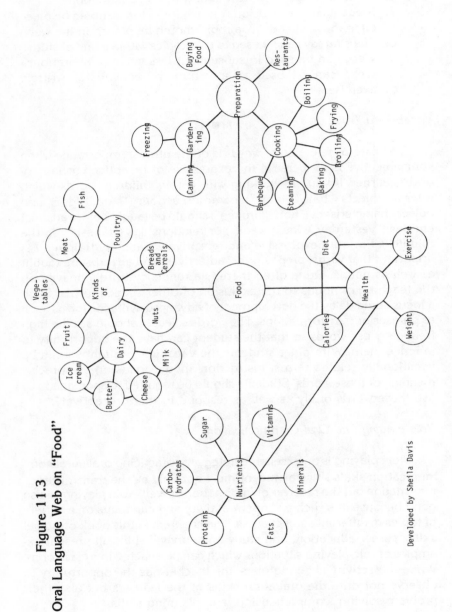

Figure 11.3
Oral Language Web on "Food"

Developed by Sheila Davis

Figure 11.4
Oral Language Web on "Jobs"

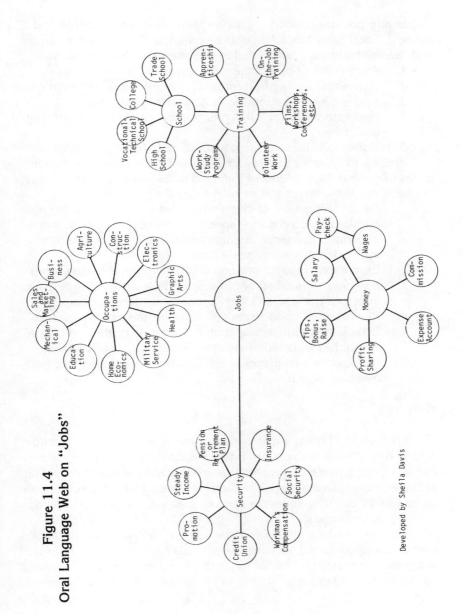

Developed by Sheila Davis

Listening Skills Needed by Learners

In any communication exchange there must be a listener and a speaker. Each party has a role in the exchange of information. Some skills and/or competencies needed by the listener include the following:
1. Attention to the speaker
2. Nonverbal signs of attention (e.g., head nod, eye fixation)
3. Verbal signs of attention (e.g., uh-ha, yeah, ok)
4. Understanding of the pragmatics (e.g., slang, formal discourse)
5. Knowledge that the topic has shifted in focus or orientation.

In order to enhance the listening skills of the learners, the teacher needs to remind the students of the need to listen and to stress listening behavior throughout the day. She can do this by:
1. Establishing a set of classroom rules whereby students are required to listen during specific times of the day (e.g. morning announcements, attendance taking, lunch counts, opening classroom exercises, etc.).
2. Eliminating distractions and distractive "noise" in the room.
3. Having a planned story or listening time each day where an interesting event or story is read and then questioned.
4. Reinforcing "good listening" through the use of rewards.
5. Establishing a listening center in an area of the room with earphones and either a tape recorder, language master, radio, or record player is set up with a structured (but fun) listening activity.

Summary

Listening and speaking activities represent about 75% of a child's school day. Proper instruction in these areas is therefore important. For the mentally retarded learner the teacher should not assume that information received aurally is actually retained. Listening skills need to be taught and developed in the same direct manner as spelling, reading, or arithmetic.

The way we talk affects the attitudes of individuals with whom we come into contact. Since one of our goals for the mentally retarded is a greater integration into society, behavioral deficits, such as an inability to switch language styles, will work against the realization of such a goal. A planned program of oral and aural skills throughout the school day is required to achieve some of the subtle behaviors required in oral/aural communication.

Remember this . . .

1. EMR learners may have a rote computational habit.

2. The four basic operations (addition, subtraction, multiplication, and division) are often incorrectly taught to the mentally retarded.

3. Calculators are an accepted alternative to hand computation.

4. Conceptually, there are at least four types of subtraction, three types of division, three types of multiplication, and two types of addition.

5. Understanding what a student is doing wrong might not tell you *why* he is doing it wrong.

CHAPTER XII

Teaching Arithmetic and Problem Solving

The majority of special educators now agree that children with handicaps in learning will profit from a meaningful, conceptual, rule-based approach to arithmetic instruction (Sedlak and Fitzmaurice, 1981). Changing demands of society have altered traditional priorities in the teaching of mathematics to the EMR learner. This chapter will explore some characteristics of the EMR learner in regard to arithmetic and give suggestions for a basic math curriculum.

Characteristics of the EMR Learner

Traditionally, the EMR learner exhibits one or more of the following characteristics when involved in mathematics:

1. Discrepancy between computational and reasoning skills
2. Deficit in problem-solving ability
3. A rote computational habit
4. Immature computational strategies
5. Reliance on faulty rules resulting in incomplete concept formation.

A closer look at the deficit in problem-solving ability may illustrate the specific difficulties encountered by these learners. EMR learners tend to exhibit inadequate verbal problem-solving skills, especially when such skills are measured by success in solving arithmetic word problems (Sedlak, 1974). Students have a tendency to rely on "tricks" in order to solve word problems. The teacher should scrutinize student work and observe carefully signs of any of the following strategies and note that they should be corrected:

1. If there are more than two numbers, add them.
2. If there are two numbers of approximately the same size, subtract the smaller from the larger.
3. If one number is relatively large compared to a second, divide. If the division answer has a remainder, cross out the work and multiply.
4. Look for "cue" words, e.g., left, all together, difference, total, etc. (Goodstein, Cawley, Gordon, and Helfgott, 1971).
5. Add all of the numbers. This strategy is referred to as the "rote computational habit" and is exhibited by at least one-third of all EMH learners (Sedlak and Schenck, 1980).

Each of these is a sign that the student is not actively processing verbal information but merely relying on tricks. This brief look at problem solving will hopefully serve notice to the teacher of the EMR learner. It is always necessary to look beyond the answer to a mathematical problem and examine the process by which the learner arrived at the result.

Content of Mathematics Instruction

Children with learning handicaps do not internalize incidental information at the same rate as nonhandicapped peers so that explicit instruction is always required. Further, rapid technological changes in society require instruction which facilitates generalization and transfer. Instruction in mathematics then must embrace many topics and on the next pages we will attempt to outline as much of that content as possible.

SETS. A set is a group in which all members have a common quality other than the fact that they belong to the same group. The set of whole numbers includes odd and even, while the set of even numbers includes numbers evenly divisible by two. Thus, instruction in sets involves joining classes and breaking down classes and noting qualities belonging to some member of two different classes.

PATTERNS. A pattern is a repeating sequence of elements (AA2AA2AA2). Patterns can be copied or made longer. EMR learners need to develop a sense of pattern and of "what comes next."

GEOMETRY. Geometry is concerned with position or location

in space. Some basic concepts that must be acquired are: open, closed; inside, outside; on, under, over, between; left, right; and so on. A knowledge of basic two-dimensional shapes (sphere, cube, cone, pyramid) provides the learner with an awareness of these shapes in the environment and a means of communicating about them.

MEASUREMENT. Topics to be covered in measurement should include time, temperature, weight, linear measure, volume, distances, etc. Familiarity with the metric system may need to be emphasized.

NUMBER AND OPERATIONS. Learners must be given a firm understanding of what a number is and the relationship between numbers. Major emphasis should be on basic mathematical facts and on the development of computational skills. Content in this area should include reading and writing number names, addition (with regrouping), subtraction (with regrouping), multiplication, division, and even/odd numbers.

FRACTIONS. Fractions are numbers that represent parts of a group or parts of a whole thing. Cooking (measuring), distances, and the weather forecast all involve the use of fractions. Basic to the understanding of fractions is an understanding of parts, wholes, and the part-whole relationship. Relationship of the size of the part to the size of the whole should be taught as well as the concept of equivalence classes, that is, what fraction of the same whole equals the same amount.

PROBLEM SOLVING. Problem solving promotes language, reading comprehension, reasoning skills, and skills in evaluation. Certain variables should be considered in a problem-solving program: types of numbers used, type of computation to be performed, reading level, format, extraneous information, grammatical constructions, and so on. Students must be taught to sift out significant information and to recognize situations where insufficient information has been supplied.

Finding Error Patterns

In Chapter II the topic of error patterns was introduced. Conceptual as well as skill deficits can be uncovered by the careful analysis of student errors. Study the problems shown in Figure 12.1 and the analysis of the error patterns which had developed. Try to identify the error patterns found in the problems in Figure 12.2.

Figure 12.1
Error Patterns for Two Learners

Barbara

8 1	2 1	5 11	2 11
693	325	726	434
− 248	− 151	− 349	− 276
445	1 474	2 487 $\times$	268 $\times$

1. Works from left to right.
2. Borrows from hundred's place if number in ten's position is too small.

Mary

	1	4	0 0
432	74	385	563
+ 265	+ 43	+ 667	+ 545
697	18	9116 $\times$	118 $\times$

1. Adds from left to right.
2. Carries the number in one's position.
3. Got second problem correct by accident.

Simply examining error patterns may lead you to understand what the student is doing wrong but not why he is doing it wrong. You may also be unable to see a pattern. In searching further you many need to talk to the learner and have him do the problem aloud. The following are some problems done by the daughter of the authors:

12	11	12	11	10
− 4	− 3	− 5	− 7	− 6
3 $_\times$	3 $_\times$	2 $_\times$	4	4

We could not figure out the pattern and so we asked her to explain how she arrived at those answers. She demonstrated for us how she does subtraction using her fingers. In her system all numbers greater than 10 are converted to base "5" with the right hand representing the units position. She then uses her left hand to "hold" each group of "5." Numbers are "borrowed" from the left hand in groups of "5" as needed. In doing each of the first three problems she had forgotten

Figure 12.2
Sample Problems with Error Patterns

Mike did the following problems. Look for a consistent error pattern.

```
   74        35        67        56
 + 56      + 92      + 18      + 97
 ─────     ─────     ─────     ─────
 1210       127       715      1413
```

Margie—Find the error pattern.

```
  8 1       6 1       7 1
  197       176       384
 − 43      − 23      − 59
 ─────     ─────     ─────
 1414      1413       325
```

Bill—Find the error pattern.

```
  3 4       3 3       4 5       5 6
   25       240       363       470
 − 21     − 205     − 341     − 443
 ─────    ──────    ──────    ──────
   13       130       112       120
```

Bob—Find the error pattern.

```
              1         5
   46        76        48
 × 24      × 32      × 57
 ─────     ─────     ─────
  184       152       336
  102       228       250
 ─────     ─────     ─────
 1204      2432      2836
```

Jim—Find the error pattern.

```
   233       221       231
 2/176     4/824     3/713
```

that she was still "holding" one group of "5" in her left hand after borrowing. That is why each of her answers was "5" less than the correct response. She realized her mistake immediately and corrected each.

Students may have extremely exotic explanations for their responses—even when they are wrong. The problem for the teacher is overcoming the logic.

Interactive Unit

Mathematics content is essentially the same for retarded learners as it is for the nonretarded. The critical element in regard to the mentally retarded is how to provide the instruction and circumvent the behavioral deficits unique to the learner. From this problematic situation evolved the Interactive Unit (IU), a systematic instructional system designed to accommodate the behavioral needs of the disabled learner (Cawley, Fitzmaurice, Goodstein, Lepore, Sedlak, and Althaus, 1976, 1977). The model is composed of eight cells, four of which identify teacher behaviors and four of which identify learner responses. There are sixteen possible behavioral interactions. The model allows either the teaching or the assessment of a concept through one or all of the behavioral combinations. Definitions of these cells can be found in Figure 12.3.

Sedlak and Fitzmaurice (1981) have delineated the advantages of the IU. According to these authors the IU allows a teacher to:

1. Partial out or teach around a disability
2. Provide repeated practice of a skill or concept with varied interactions to minimize boredom
3. Systematically hold constant a learner's response mode while varying the output
4. Systematically hold constant the input while varying the type of response to be made by the learner
5. Use manipulatives in a meaningful way and to follow a logical sequence of behaviors up to the graphic symbolic mode
6. Diagnostically look at a learner's understanding of skills and concepts in a way other than with a pencil and paper test (p. 485)

The IU is an excellent instructional system to follow for teasing out the error patterns in students' work in mathematics.

Teaching Specific Skills in Mathematics

This section will denote specific content and strategies for teaching operations, problem solving, calculator usage, measurement, money, and time-telling.

Figure 12.3
The Interactive Unit

Teacher	Construct (C)	Present (P)	State (S)	Graphically symbolize (GS)
Learner	Construct (C)	Identify (I)	State (S)	Graphically symbolize (GS)

Construct (C):   Teacher manipulates or uses objects to demonstrate

a math concept, and the learner uses objects to

demonstrate understanding.

Present (P):   Teacher presents the learner with a fixed visual

display composed of pictures or prearranged objects.

Identify (I):   Teacher asks learner questions with multiple-choice

answers using pictures.

State (S):   Spoken instructions, questions, and/or responses are

used.

Graphically

  Symbolize (GS):   Written or drawn symbolic sets of materials,

nonpictorial worksheets, and computational worksheets

are used; learner responds by writing.

Operations

Operations and problem solving are closely related. The relation-ship lies not in the computational aspects but rather in the concep-tual aspects. The four basic operations are often incorrectly taught to the mentally retarded because they are presented as rotely learned facts. Students are usually *not* taught that there are at least two types of addition, four types of subtraction, three types of multiplication, and three types of division. They are taught that subtraction is "take away" or "remainder." They learn that in solving a subtraction prob-lem you start with more but end up with less. When confronted with a problem such as:

John has 5 apples and Bill has 2.
How many more does John have than Bill?

The student cannot conceptualize this problem as subtraction because nothing is taken away. At the end of the problem both boys still have apples. The problem is asking for a comparison for which the student is unprepared to solve. Figure 12.4 lists the different types of addi-tion, subtraction, division, and multiplication and gives examples of each. It is best to teach each of these with pictures—preferably manipulatives. We recommend the use of small cards (two inches by two inches) which can be used as manipulatives depicting familiar ob-jects and then large mats of a related theme with which the manipulatives can be used. Figure 12.5 gives some examples. The teacher can draw or trace these objects onto a ditto master, run off copies, have students cut out objects and paste onto 2 " x 2 " oaktag cards.

PROBLEM SOLVING. Curriculum developers have not yet fo-cused adequate attention on teaching problem-solving skills. In the development of such programs, several variables should be considered: the size of numbers used, the type of computation to be performed, the sequence of operations, and the reading level. Less conventional factors, such as the format in which the information is presented, ex-traneous materials, grammatical constructions, and rules of logic to be applied also can enter into the solution of the problem.

Computation is incidental to problem solving. Of far greater im-portance are the types of information processing required in any prob-lem situation. Sifting out from a set of information those bits that are needed in a given situation is a necessary skill. Much of the literature

Figure 12.4
Types of Addition, Subtraction, Multiplication, and Division Problems

OPERATIONS IN MATH

Addition Types

1. Direct   Three bananas were growing on a tree. Overnight, two more bananas grew on the tree. How many are on the tree now?

2. Indirect   There are five apples left on the tree after Bill picked two. How many were on the tree (originally) before Bill picked some?

Subtraction Types

1. Remainder   There were five apples on the tree. Bill picked one. How many are there now? (Neutral Question)
How many are left? (Cued Question)

2. Negation   There are four pieces of fruit on the tree. Three are apples. How many are not apples?

3. Comparative   I have two baskets of strawberries.
This basket has five strawberries.
That basket has three strawberries.
How many more does this have than that?
How many less does this have than that?
Which has more?
How any more do I have to put in this basket so it will have as much as this basket has?

FRUIT TO FRUIT
I have six pieces of fruit (e.g. apples and bananas mixed) in this basket and four pieces of fruit in this basket.
     How many more do I have in basket 1 than in basket 2?
     How many more/fewer in basket 2?
     How many more apples in basket 1 than in basket 2?
     How many more apples in basket 2 than there are pieces of fruit in basket 1?

4. Indirect   I have five apples. I picked three from this tree and the rest from this tree. How many did I pick from the second tree?

Figure 12.4 (Con't)

Multiplication Types

1. Equal Units
   Addition
   I have three trees. Each of them has 3 oranges on it. How many oranges do I have?

2. Cartisian
   John has 3 Hawaiian shirts and 5 pairs of pants each of a different color. How many outfits can John have?

3. Array/Matrix
   There were 6 chars in each of 3 rows. How many chairs are there?

Division Types

1. Partitioning
   Tim has 15 bananas. He wants to put an equal number of bananas in each basket. How many will be put in each basket?

2. Measurement
   Bill has 15 bananas. He wants to put 5 bananas in each basket. How many baskets does he need?

3. Matrix/Array
   There are 48 chairs to be placed in the auditorium in 8 rows. How many chairs will be placed per row?

in verbal problem solving suggests that students do not always apply that skill. To recognize that some of the information is irrelevant to the question being posed is one skill; to realize that not enough information is provided to answer a question is yet another essential skill. Both must be developed.

Problem-solving activities should focus on relevant situations. Some limited research (Lydra and Church, 1964) indicates that having students find solutions to real classroom and home problems rather than solving simulated ones is highly effective in the development of these skills. Problem solving especially at the secondary level should cover a wide range of topics and of problem types. To this end, problems and topics such as those in Figure 12.6 can be used with the secondary EMR learner.

CALCULATOR USAGE. Shoppers in grocery stores regularly use calculators to estimate food costs, college students use them to do basic (and advanced) mathematics and statistics, fellow school teachers use them for balancing their checkbooks. In short, calculators are an accepted alternative to hand computation in society. Wrong answers are perceived as being far more stigmatizing than reliance on a calculator for correct computation. Initial instruction should focus on the meaning for each symbol on the calculator and its use:

CE—clear entry

C—clear entire display and also previous calculations

M + —add a value to the values in memory
M – —subtract a value from the value in memory
CM—clear memory (erases value in memory to zero)
MR or R—memory retrieval (displays the value in memory)
X—multiply
 – —subtract
 + —add
 ÷ —divide
 = —equals
 .—decimal
 ✓—square root

Figure 12.5
Problem Mats and Manipulative Cards

 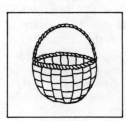 

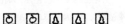 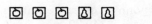 

Themes for Problem Mats	Common Objects for Manipulative Cards
baskets	fruit--apples, bananas, pears
house scene	vegetables--lettuce, tomato, carrots
street scene	clothing--shoes, ties, hats, coats
yard scene	transportation--cars, trucks, boats, planes
lunch boxes	tools--hammer, wrench, screw

Figure 12.6
Sample Topics and Word Problems for Secondary EMR Students

Topic	Problem	Comment
1. Planning a date	1. Bill wants to take Jennifer to the movies and then out for a pizza and soft drink. How much will the date cost?	1. Have the students supply the needed information and work the problem in small groups. The students also can plan for unexpected expenses on a date and add them to the problem.
2. Saving for a radio, stereo, TV, etc.	2. Steve cuts grass each week to earn money. He wants to save enough for a _____ that costs _____. He saves _____ dollars per week. How many weeks will it take him to save for the _____?	2. This problem requires that the students go to stores (or check advertisements) and price the cost of radio, TV, and stereo sets.
3. Painting a room	3. The label on the gallon of paint says it will cover 700 square feet. How many gallons will it take to paint his room?	3. Square measure could be dealt with under problem solving or this could be treated as just a straight measurement activity.
4. Payroll deductions	4. John's gross earnings were $140.00 per week. He had payroll deductions for Social Security and federal and state income taxes. What was his take-home pay? What was his normal hourly wage? What was his normal hourly wage after deductions?	4. The students have to find out about Social Security, federal and state withholding, etc.

Figure 12.6 (cont.)

Topic	Problem	Comment
5. Traveling	5. Bill wants to get to _____ (e.g., Pittsburgh). _____ is _____ miles from his house. About how long will it take to drive to _____?	5. The students may need to use a road atlas to help out here. They should base their plan on using interstates (faster) rather than secondary roads (slower).

The process of doing computation on a calculator differs from that in hand calculations. In hand computation, work generally is performed from right to left (e.g., addition of units, then tens, then hundreds); with a calculator, these intermediate steps are done by machine. For this reason, the process of calculator usage needs to be taught differently from traditional computational skills. A task analysis approach for assessment and instruction is recommended for such teaching (see Figure 12.7).

The number of steps into which each problem type will need to be divided is a function of the individual differences among students and the amount of difficulty they encounter doing the problems correctly with a calculator. To use these task analyses for assessment purposes, the teacher hands out the calculator and the problem and tells the student to solve it. The teacher observes as the student works and puts a " + " or " − " next to each step to indicate a correct or incorrect response. Each step of the task analysis is written as an observable behavior. The procedure thus can pinpoint at which step a problem exists. In some cases, a step in a task analysis may need to be broken down into smaller segments. That decision usually is made if a student has difficulty with a step. In all cases, the steps in a task analysis should be observable behaviors.

Caution: If calculator usage is taught, the skills of estimation and rounding must also be taught so that calculator usage does not become a rote process.

MEASUREMENT. Reading and using basic measurement instruments (e.g., yardstick, thermometer, bathroom scale, measuring

Figure 12.7
Task Analysis (TA) of Calculator Usage

Problem: 45
                 + 38

TA

1. Clear calculator by pressing "C"
2. Press key for numeral in tens place (e.g., 4)
3. Press key for numeral in units place (e.g., 5)
4. Press " + "
5. Press key for numeral in tens place (e.g., 3)
6. Press key for numeral in units place (e.g., 8)
7. Press " = "
8. Write or state numeral on display (83)

Problem: $4.53
              +   .62

TA

1. Clear calculator by pressing "C"
2. Press key for numeral in dollar position (e.g., 4)
3. Press "."
4. Press key for numeral in tens place (e.g., 5)
5. Press key for numeral in cents place (e.g., 3)
6. Press " + "
7. Press "."
8. Press key for numeral in tens place (e.g., 6)
9. Press key for numeral in cents place (e.g., 2)
10. Press " = "
11. Write or state numeral on display (5.15)

Problem: 9
                   5
                   6
                 + 4

TA

1. Clear calculator by pressing "C"
2. Press key for first numeral
3. Press " + "
4. Press key for next numeral

Figure 12.7 (Con't)

5. Press "+"
6. Press key for next numeral
7. Press "+"
8. Press key for last numeral
9. Press "="
10. Write or state numeral on display (24)

Problem: $37\overline{)543}$

TA

1. Clear calculator by pressing "C"
2. Press keys for numerals under the radical (543)
3. Press "÷"
4. Press keys for numerals in divisor (37)
5. Press "="
6. Write or state numeral on display (14.675675)

Problem: 7/8 × 25 =

TA

1. Clear calculator by pressing "C"
2. Press key for numeral in numerator (e.g., 7)
3. Press "÷"
4. Press key for numeral in denominator (e.g., 8)
5. Press "×"
6. Press keys for numeral in equation (e.g., 25)
7. Press "="
8. Write or state numeral on display (21.875)

Problem: $\dfrac{\$1.29}{16}$ (price per unit cost)

TA

1. Clear calculator by pressing "C"
2. Ignore $ sign
3. Press keys for numeral and decimal in numerator (e.g., 1→.→ 2→ 9)
4. Press "="
5. Press keys for numeral in denominator (e.g., 1→ 6)
6. Press "="
7. Write or state numeral on display (0.080625)

cup, etc.) is an essential skill. Measurement requires the active manipulation and use of these materials. The skills required can be broken down into a task analysis to form easily teachable steps. Figure 12.8 presents a checklist of the more commonly used measuring instruments. The teacher should observe students reading/using them, mark a " + " or " − " beside each on the list, then teach or reteach articles as needed.

Figure 12.8
Functional Measurement Checklist

Instrument
_____ yardstick (e.g., measures length of a line)
_____ ruler (one foot)
_____ tape measure
_____ bathroom scale
_____ produce scale
_____ odometer
_____ speedometer
_____ gasoline (fuel) gauge
_____ water temperature gauge
_____ fever thermometer
_____ house thermometer
_____ measuring cups
_____ measuring spoons
_____ clock or watch
_____ digital clock or watch
_____ oil dipstick
_____ calendar

MONEY. Making change or counting money is a necessary and functional skill in society. The skill should be taught and practiced with real money and should not be a paper and pencil exercise but rather one of actually handling the bills and coins. Counting by 1s, 5s, 10s, 25s, and 50s is one of the major prerequisites to making change. Knowledge of coinage equivalencies (e.g., 5 pennies = 1 nickel, 5 nickels = 1 quarter, etc.) is another prerequisite.

As with the calculator, the process of counting money or making change can be assessed using a task analysis format. Several examples of task analysis of functional math skills in the area of money handling are presented in Figures 12.9 and 12.10.

Figure 12.9
Task Analysis: Counting Money

Problem: Given a pile of change, the student will count the coins with 100% accuracy

1. Separates the coins into piles of common coinage (quarters with quarters, dimes with dimes, etc.).
2. Puts coins into $1.00 stacks, largest denominations first.
   _____ a. half dollars
   _____ b. quarters
   _____ c. dimes
   _____ d. nickels
   _____ e. pennies
3. Combines miscellaneous remaining coins into $1.00 stack(s).
4. Counts the number of dollar stacks.
5. Counts the value of remaining coins.
6. Writes or states total amount of change.

Figure 12.10
Task Analysis: Making Change

Problem: Given a $20.00 bill for × purchase, the student will give change.

1. Begins counting aloud from × in increments of the largest coin value needed to reach the next largest whole coinage value (or makes appropriate substitution).
2. Selects appropriate coins while counting.

Example: Given a $20.00 bill for a $12.63 purchase, the student will give change.

1. Counts aloud: $12.64, 12.65, 12.75, 13.00, 14.00, 15.00, 20.00.

2. Selects appropriate coins

Preferred	Alternative
a. pennies *2*	a. pennies *2*
b. nickels *0*	b. nickels *2*
c. dimes *1*	c. dimes *0*
d. quarters *1*	d. quarters *1*
e. half dollars *0*	e. half dollars *0*

Figure 12.10 (Con't)

3. Changes coin value as next whole coin value is reached (or marks appropriate substitution)
   a. nickels
   b. dimes
   c. quarters
   d. half dollars
4. Selects bills when even dollar amount is reached.
5. Changes bill value as next whole bill appropriate is reached.
6. Recounts aloud and follows steps 1-5 as change is given to a "customer."

3. Changes coin value in order
   a. nickels *0*   a. nickels *2*
   b. dimes *1*   b. dimes *0*
   c. quarters *1*   c. quarters *1*

4. Selects bills—3–$1.00 bills

5. Selects 1–$5.00 bill

6. Repeats steps 1–5.

Problem: Given × amount of money printed on a tape or calculator display, the student will count out this amount using the smallest (or a reasonable) number of coins and bills.

Example: Given the printed amount of $16.38 the student will count out this change using the smallest (or a reasonable) number of coins and bills.

1. Counts aloud up to × in increments of large bills followed by smaller bills and then large coin values followed by smaller coin values.

1. Counts aloud $10.00, 15.00, 16.00, 16.25, 16.35, 16.36, 16.37, 16.38.

2. Selects appropriate bill and coin values in order.

2. Selects appropriate bill and coin values in order.
   a. 10.00 *1*   a. 10.00 *0*
   b. 5.00 *1*   b. 5.00 *3*
   c. 1.00 *1*   c. 1.00 *1*
   d. .50 *0*   d. .50 *0*
   e. .25 *1*   e. .25 *1*
   f. .10 *1*   f. .10 *0*
   g. .05 *0*   g. .05 *2*
   h. .01 *3*   h. .01 *3*

3. Recounts aloud and follows steps 1 and 2 as change is given to a "customer."

3. Recounts aloud and follows steps 1 and 2 as change is given to a "customer."

TIME. Digital watches and clocks have changed the way students learn to tell time and also to write time notation. Using a traditional timepiece, the student "translated" the position of one hand into time notation. There also was a tendency to use phrasings such as "a quarter after," "a quarter to," and "half past the hour" in telling time since the segments of the clock were perceived as a pie graph. With digital clocks there is a greater tendency to state the time according to hours and minutes, e.g., 4:15, 4:45.

Digital clocks and watches therefore eliminate a step in the writing of time notation since no translation is necessary. It probably still is necessary for secondary students especially to be able to use and understand the traditional language of telling time but digital timepieces present an alternative.

For a more traditional view of the analysis of time-telling skills, see Figure 12.11.

Figure 12.11
Analysis of Time-Telling Skills

1. Identifying numerals from 1 to 12
2. Stating the numerals from 1 to 12 when presented
3. Identifying the hour hand
4. Identifying the minute hand
5. Counting from 1 to 60
6. Counting by 5s
7. Stating that both clock hands move but that the minute hand moves faster
8. Telling time to the hour by saying "_____ o'clock"
9. Telling time to the half hour by saying "_____: 30"
10. Telling time to the quarter hour by saying "half past _____"
11. Telling time to the quarter hour by saying "_____:15"
12. Telling time to the quarter hour by saying "quarter after _____"
13. Telling time to the quarter hour by saying "_____:45"
14. Telling time to the quarter hour by saying "quarter to _____"
15. Telling time to the minute
16. Writing time notation

Summary

EMH learners have special characteristics which must be given

consideration in the development of a basic math curriculum. When involved in mathematics, such learner characteristics include:
1. Discrepancy between computational and reasoning skills
2. Deficit in problem-solving ability
3. A rote computational habit
4. Immature computational strategies
5. Reliance on faulty roles resulting in incomplete concept formation

Analysis of error patterns will help the teacher focus on individual learner characteristics and provide appropriate instruction. Strategies for teaching operations, problem solving, calculator usage, measurement, and money and time telling also should serve to aid the teacher in the delivery of math instruction to the handicapped learner.

Remember this . . .

1. Mentally retarded students suffer from a content deficit which may be partly related to poor instructional planning.

2. Unit instruction can be used to integrate science, health, and social studies content into the math and language arts program.

3. American government and/or American history courses are generally needed for high school diplomas.

CHAPTER XIII

Unit Instruction in Content Subjects

Content subject areas include science, history, geography, and health/physical education/recreation. The inclusion of physical education and recreation in the category of a "content" subject may seem strange to the reader, but because of the learning characteristics of the EMH student and the task demands to be successful in these areas (e.g., knowing the rules of the game, how to keep score, learning the specific vocabulary, etc.), the authors feel that it is justified. Student failure in a mainstreamed physical education class may not be due to lack of physical prowess but rather a failure to follow the rules. As such, the provision of direct instruction in such an area would be quite appropriate. Mentally retarded children do not readily acquire information about their environments incidentally as do normal children (MacMillan, 1977). The implication for teachers then is that they should not assume that retarded students have learned certain skills or facts "on their own" as have nonretarded students.

Content subject areas are the "knowledge" base of a curriculum. It is through these subjects that a student learns about the role of government, how to read a map, why the weather and seasons change, how to stay healthy, what to do with their leisure time, and why the price of oil set by OPEC affects the price they pay at the gasoline pump. Mentally retarded students suffer immeasurable harm because of what we fail to teach them. Many of the psychoeducational tests which they are given rely heavily on a "content" base to control the difficulty of the test items. Student "failure" on these tests, to a great extent, is a reflection of what we have failed to teach them and not a manifestation of mental retardation per se. There are three principles which the authors adhere to in regard to the teaching of content subjects to the mentally retarded: (1) mentally retarded students need to be taught more, not less; (2) they need to be taught the content of science, social studies, and health to minimize their observed "content" deficiencies; and (3) they need to be taught efficiently within the allotted portion of time available in the school day.

Unit teaching adheres to these three principles and is the approach which the authors advise should be taken in teaching content subjects to the mentally retarded.

Unit Teaching

Unit teaching involves the systematic planning, integration, and teaching of several content and/or skill domains around a single theme. Such themes might involve energy usage, personal hygiene, safety, map reading, weather, government, or almost any range of topics. Throughout this book the authors have repeatedly mentioned the efficient use of time by teachers as being the single most critical variable in the delivery of instruction to handicapped learners. Unit teaching, by its very design, can be an excellent strategy for maximizing the use of instructional time. Contrary to an opinion expressed by some teachers of the handicapped, the inclusion of content subjects in the curriculum need not detract from instruction in the basic skills. Content subject matter when taught via a unit approach can provide many opportunities to teach and reinforce basic skills.

Disadvantages of Unit Instruction

Unit teaching is not without its flaws. Major criticisms center around the following issues (Meyen, 1972):
1. Lack of internal consistency and sequencing of skills within units
2. Failure of teachers to formulate a structure for teaching units
3. Lack of a consistent sequence of unit topics which is followed
4. Amount of preparation time which is required to develop a unit plan

The following discussion will provide some procedures for minimizing these problems.

Unit Organization

Meyen (1972) has suggested that units should be based upon six core areas of experiences. The unit should emphasize the integration of these areas into the unit topic. The integration of these areas into a unit maximizes the use of instructional time since the words used in spelling, the stories written in English, the vocabulary learned in reading, and the problems solved in arithmetic all relate to the theme of the unit. A separate period of time each day need not be spent for "unit instruction," but much of the information which needs to be conveyed in a unit can be delivered through the instruction in the basic skill areas. Meyen's "core" includes arithmetic concepts, communication skills, social competencies and health, safety, and vocational skills. Some unit themes may fit some aspects of this core better than others, and therefore, all units will not contain all aspects of the core.

In general, a unit should contain the following components:

1. Rationale. The rationale states the reason(s) the unit is being taught on a particular theme, to a particular group, at a particular time.
2. Specification of Subunits. Subunits are possible lessons related to a theme. For example, a unit on local government would include subunits on elected offices, appointed offices, local government employees, services, local ordinances/laws, taxes, how laws are passed, citizen rights and roles. These subunits are listed and then organized into a sequential pattern.
3. General Objectives. These objectives might correspond to the subunits. These would be considered the long-term objectives.
4. Core Activities. These are the activities in arithmetic, communication, health, safety, social, and vocational areas which correlate with the unit. For example, the unit on local government would contain core activities similar to those specified in Figure 13.1. These core activities are a critical component of the unit and as such should be well planned.

Selection of Topics for Units

The overriding principle which should influence what is taught should be relevant to adult adjustment and community living skills

Figure 13.1
Core Activities for Unit on Local Government

ARITHMETIC

1. Make a graph on use of local property taxes.
2. Discuss how the fair market value of a property is determined.
3. What is the cost to taxpayers for vandalism?

COMMUNICATION

1. Obtain interviews with the current and past mayors of the community and tape record the interviews.
2. Maintain a scrapbook of all information secured on local government.

HEALTH

1. What agencies in local government deal with health-related problems? Make a display to show this.
2. What local ordinances exist which affect health (e.g., sewers, water chlorination, garbage collection or disposal)? Go to the local government office and speak to an official.
3. Make a list of the health facilities in your community (private and public). Discuss what services they provide.

SAFETY

1. What ordinances exist which affect personal safety (e.g., licensing of pets, no bicycling on sidewalks, jay walking)?
2. What provisions have been made for safety (e.g., fences, footpaths, bicycle paths, overpasses)?
3. What hazards or potential hazards exist in the community (e.g., open pits, lakes, cliffs)?

SOCIAL

1. What are the local facilities for private and public recreation? Make a list of what activities are available in these facilities and the costs.
2. Write notes of thank you to all persons who helped you with this unit.

Figure 13.1 (Con't)

VOCATIONAL

1. What are the jobs or job titles held by people in local government? Make a display with their pictures and job responsibilities.
2. Using the Dictionary of Occupational Titles in your library, identify what government jobs might exist in other communities.
3. Find out how peope in local government secure their jobs and whether they are paid or unpaid positions.

(Turnbull and Schulz, 1979). A review of the curriculum development model using environmental analysis in Chapter VII is quite compatible with this principle. Unit instruction should focus on the practical application of science and social study information. Questions which should be considered include:

1. Will it help the student become more independent in the community, employment setting, and/or at home?
2. What is the jeopardy of the student not knowing this information?
3. Will the student be receiving this information from other sources? (Turnbull and Schulz, 1979, p. 260)

Sequencing Topics and Skills in Units

Attention to the proper sequencing of unit objectives and topics has several advantages. Among them are more rapid learning, elimination of content gaps, and less failure. Herlihy and Herlihy (1980) suggest that one means for sequencing subject matter by the classroom teacher is through the use of content checklists. Content checklists are scope and sequence charts available with most commercial series. Figure 13.2 provides some examples of commercial materials which might be encountered. These include a listing of the broad subject areas and subareas in a sequence. The analysis follows the same process as a task analysis except that the subject area is not skill based so much as it is hierarchical and concept based.

Figure 13.2
Examples of Secondary Level Materials in Content Subjects

GOVERNMENT/HISTORY/SOCIAL STUDIES		
Title	*Publisher*	*Level*
Exploring American Citizenship	Globe Book	7-13
The New Exploring American History	Globe Book	4-12
American Adventures	Scholastic Book Service	7-16
The American Nation: Adventure in Freedom	Follett	7-10
The New Exploring a Changing World	Globe Book	6-12
Short Stories in Law Education	Paul S. Amidon	7-12
Skills for Understanding Maps and Globes	Follett	4-12
The United States in the Making	Globe Book	6-12
The Human Expression: History of Peoples and Their Cultures	J.B. Lippincott	9-12
The Americans	Holt, Rinehart & Winston	7-9

SCIENCE		
Title	*Publisher*	*Level*
Pathways in Science	Globe Book	7-12
Science Workshop	Globe Book	4-12
Biology and Human Progress	Prentice-Hall	9-12
Me and My Environment	Hubbard	7-9
Spaceship Earth Series	Houghton Mifflin	7-9
The Wonders of Science Series	Steck-Vaughn	7-12

Figure 13.2 (Con't)

You and the Environment: An Investigative Approach	Houghton Mifflin	7-9
Me Now	Hubbard	4-8
Exploring and Understanding Series	Benefic Press	4-9

HEALTH/PHYSICAL EDUCATION/RECREATION

Title	Publisher	Level
Fine Motor Skills for Secondary	Kimbo Educational	9-12
Nutrition, Food, and the Consumer	Society for Visual Education	9-12
Nutrition and Good Health	Society for Visual Education	8-12
Cooperative Activities	Kimbo Educational	9-12
Taking Charge of Your Life	School Specialty Supply	7-12
Understanding Yourself	Steck-Vaughn	6-7
How We Grow	EBA Educational Media	6-9
Learn About Genetics	Xerox Educational Publications	5-10
Recreation and Leisure Time Series	Edmark Associates	6-12

American Government and United States History

Most school systems require successful completion of both an American government and a United States history class in order to qualify for high school graduation. While a high school diploma may not be in the future for all EMH students, those who do have the opportunity to qualify may have significant difficulty with these subject areas. Tutorial instruction from the special education teacher may provide some support for a youngster in such classes, but the development of supplemental materials is critical.

Project PASS, a Title IV-C project developed by the Livonia Public Schools in Michigan, has produced an extensive array of curriculum materials for the mildly handicapped child in these areas. Preliminary test data indicate that mildly handicapped students performed 22%

better with these materials than without them. All differences on individual modules were significant beyond the .05 level. The materials developed by Project PASS were independent of a specific series. The content was based upon a content analysis of the leading texts. Content from all these texts was rewritten and put into modules. Teachers then select the module topics which are covered by the particular areas in a specific textbook series. It is very difficult to locate well written supplementary materials such as these for the subjects of U.S. history and American government.

Each of the modules contains: vocabulary-controlled content sheets, glossary sheets, activity sheets, pre-tests, and post-tests. Samples of the formats used in these materials are in Figure 13.3. The materials are organized into a format which makes them nonthreatening to the students. Principles of effective instruction which have been followed in the design of the project and the materials are:

1. Instruction in small steps
2. Sufficient practice materials for key topics
3. Feedback to the learner
4. Meaningful (readable) material
5. Organization of material into meaningful units

The materials include fifty five topical modules in American government and ninety eight topical packets in United States history (see Figure 13.4 and Figure 13.5). The modules are nonconsumable and cost about $1.50 each. A teacher may purchase only those modules which are compatible with the series used by the district. Additional information on the materials can be secured from the Livonia Public School District, 15125 Farmington Road, Livonia, Michigan, 48154.

Science

Two science programs designed specifically for the educable mentally handicapped are the *Me Now* and the *Me and My Environment* programs published by Hubbard Scientific. The programs were developed through federal grant support and stressed a "hands-on" approach. *Me Now* is a biological science course of study while *Me and My Environment* deals with the physical sciences. The total package for each curriculum is quite expensive (over $1,000). The teacher's manuals and lesson guides, however, are quite affordable at about $25

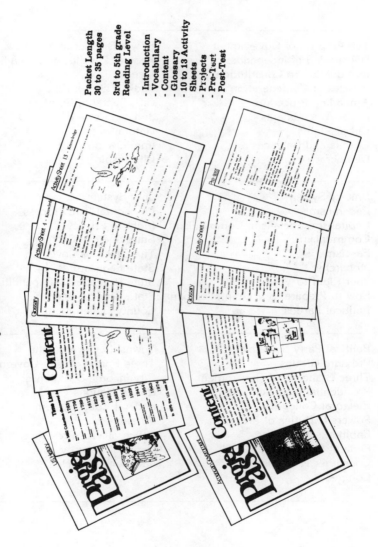

Figure 13.3
Sample PASS Format

Figure 13.4
Topics in American Government

The Purpose of Government	How a Bill Becomes a Law
Declaration of Independence	Federal Revenue & Expenditures
Introduction to Constitution	Income Tax
Articles of Confederation	Judicial System
Amending Procedure	U.S. Supreme Court
Major Amendments	Judicial Review
Bill of Rights	Naturalization
Checks and Balances	Immigration
Democracy	Citizenship

Unitary System	Jury System
Federalism	Procedural Due Process
Capitalism, Socialism, Communism	Right to Privacy
Communism	State Judicial System
Fascism	The Office of Governor
Monarchy	State Legislatures
Your Right to Vote	State Revenues & Expenditures
How to Prepare to Vote in Michigan	State & Local Services
Political Parties	County Government

Political Party Systems	Township Government
Pressure Groups	Three Forms of City Government
Three Branches of Government	City Income & Expenses
Presidential Qualifications	United Nations
Electoral College	Federal Court System
Powers & Duties of President	Foreign Policy
Cabinet	Office of Vice President
Federal Services	National Security
Consumer Protection	Law Related Packet
Congress	

Figure 13.5
Topics in U.S. History

Exploration
Colonial Policies
English Colonial Growth and
  Development
French-Indian War
The Road to Revolution
Factions in the Revolutionary War
Road to Victory

Flavor of the Conflict
  (Revolutionary War)
Declaration of Independence
The Articles of Confederation
Writing the Constitution
The Struggle for Ratification
Launching the New Nation
Keeping the New Nation
  Out of War
The Jefferson Era

War of 1812
Nationalism in the United States
The Age of Jackson
Two Major Issues during Jackson's
  Administration
Manifest Destiny (1840s–1850s)
Development of American Life
  (1820–1850)

Westward Migration (1820–1850)
Cultural Development in the Early
  1800s

Civil War Campaigns/Leaders
Civil War Results
Presidential Reconstruction
Congressional Reconstruction
The South During Reconstruction
The Development of Industrial
  America
Problems of Industrial America

Conquest of the West
Becoming a World Power
The Spanish-American War
U.S. Relations with Cuba, the
  Philippines & China after the
  Spanish-American War
United States and Latin America
  (Early 1900s)
Social & Political Reform
  (1890-1917)

The Progressive Movement
Federal Reform Effort
The General Causes of World War I
The United States Moves into
  World War I
U.S. Goals in World War I:
  The Fourteen Points
Major American Battles of WWI

Supporting the War Effort of WWI
Wilson and the Peace Treaties
  after WWI

Figure 13.5 (Con't)

Slavery in America
Sectional Problems
Pre-Civil War Decade
Civil War Advantages/Policy of
    Each Side
Civil War Strategy

The Golden Twenties: The
    Economy of the 1920s
Hoover and the Depression
FDR and the New Deal
Life during the Great Depression
The Labor Movement (1860s–1930s)
Evaluation of the New Deal
Foreign Policy in the 1930s
Rise of Dictators

The European Background of World
    War II
The Asian Background of WW II
The United States Enters WW II
Events in the U.S. during WW II
Treatment of Minority Groups
Fighting in North America and
    Europe: WW II

The U.S. in the Pacific in WW II
Wartime Conferences
Aftermath of WW II
The United Nations
The Immediate Post-War Period
The Beginning of the Cold War
The Containment Policy
The U.S. and the Soviet Union

The Roaring Twenties
Intolerance in the 1920s
The Role of Women in the 1920s
Foreign Policy in the Twenties

China & Korea after WW II
The U.S. & Cuba since 1950
Background of the Vietnam War
The Vietnam War
The U.S. & the Middle East
The Panama Canal
American Economy and Labor
    after World War II
The Loyalty Issue after WW II

Farming in America from WW II
    to the Present
The Civil Rights Struggle
Civil Rights Laws of the 1950s
    and 1960s
The Kennedy Administration
Changes in the Civil Rights
    Movement
Youth in Revolt

Watergate
The Energy Crisis
The Women's Movement
The Revolutionary War: Overview
The Civil War: Overview
World War I: Overview
The 1920s: Overview
The Depression: Overview
World War II: Overview

each. Many of the experiments and activities can be completed with materials other than those which are unique to the program. A listing of topics contained within each of these curricula is contained in Figure 13.6.

Figure 13.6
Topic Outline in ME NOW and ME AND MY ENVIRONMENT

Topics	Intended Audience	Components
ME NOW		
Digestion and Circulation	Grades 4-8, EMR	Teacher's guide
Respiration and Body Waste		Model of functioning torso
Movement, Support, and Sensory Perception		Student worksheets
		Posters, pictures, and slides
Growth and Development		Filmstrips
		Chemical and supplies kit
		Evaluation instrument
ME AND MY ENVIRONMENT		
Exploring My Environment	Junior High, EMR	Teacher's guide
Me as an Environment		Filmstrips
Energy Relationship in My Environment		Cassettes
		35-mm slides
Transfer and Cycling of Materials in My Environment		Game
		Posters and booklets
The Air and Water in My Environment		Chemical and supplies kit
		Progress sheets
		Student worksheets

Health

Units in health are related closely to some of the units which might be taught under the heading of science. The difference would primarily be whether the focus of instruction was on "scientific principles" or on the development of personal needs. The scientific approach would teach the student why things occur, while a health-oriented unit would focus on the development of good health habits with the rationale being social rather than scientific. Educational television often offers exceptional health units for a variety of ages. Program guides are usually available for the teacher, and video taping allows even more flexible use of these programs.

Unit topics in the area of health might include grooming, dental care, nutrition, child care, and sex education. All of these are functional areas. Students need information from each of these areas in order to live independently and to adjust to the adult world. A unit in sex education might cover the following topical areas:

1. Puberty and maturation
   a. Menstruation
   b. Body changes
   c. Emotional factors
2. Responsibilities and relationships
   a. Intercourse
   b. Pregnancy
   c. Masturbation
   d. Birth
   e. Abortion
3. Interpersonal relationships
   a. Dating
   b. Sex roles
   c. Feelings of men and women
   d. Love and sexual activity
4. Venereal diseases
   a. Syphilis
   b. Gonorrhea
   c. Herpes

Probably the best source of information is from the Sex Information and Education Council of the United States, 185 Broadway and 61st Street, New York, New York. Several recommendations made by this group in regard to sex education include the following guidelines:

1. Information should filter into the curriculum early.
2. Give direct, honest responses to questions.
3. Values and life styles of the students should be considered since they may differ from that of the teacher.
4. Teachers should listen as well as teach.
5. Plan instructional materials carefully.

The authors would also note that a meeting with the parents of the students probably should precede the initiation of the unit.

Physical Education and Recreation

The motor development of educable mentally retarded children approximates that of the normal learner. For this reason, the activities for physical education should be the same as for the regular student. The problems which arise in physical education and recreation activities are related to understanding and following rules and attending to the relevant characteristics of the physical education activity. Problems arise because a student does not follow the rules of the game rather than being related to poor physical fitness. To this end, the special education teacher may need to teach the rules of commonly played games and then through examples have students recognize violations to the rules. The teacher should plan units of instruction on use of leisure time, participatory sports, solitary leisure activities, sedentary leisure activities, and spectator sports. Each of these categories of units could overlap.

The critical features of units in these areas, however, are to teach students to use their leisure time and to expand their options for leisure time activities. One means of expanding the options is to actually teach students the rules of the game. For example, the game of football can be enjoyed either as a participant or as a spectator much better if the violations to the rules are understood. Each game has a specialized vocabulary which must be learned. An "off-side" penalty in football is different from the penalty by the same name in hockey or soccer. Some examples of specialized sports vocabulary which needs to be learned include clip, illegal motion, icing the puck, illegal block, intentional grounding, interference, foul ball, touchback, punt, goal, field goal, tripping, holding, delay of game, infield fly rule, fly ball, grounder, strike, bunt, drag bunt, net ball, inbounds, serve, net, wipeout, and bird.

There are also subtle rules of sports activities which need to be taught as sports etiquette. For example, bowlers on adjacent lanes should not bowl simultaneously; or when overtaking a cross-country skier, the skier should yell "track" as a warning. Violations to sports etiquette will further isolate mentally retarded individuals from the mainstream of society. Only through systematic instruction can the teacher be assured that some of these problems will be minimized. Figure 13.7 provides a list of a variety of physical education and recreation activities which might be incorporated into units.

Figure 13.7
Examples of Recreation and Physical Education Activities

CLASS A: Inanimate Objects

1. balloon	9. paper and pencil
2. baton	10. frisbee
3. blocks or logs	11. hula-hoop
4. bucket and shovel	12. balls
5. Etch-a-sketch	13. camera
6. binoculars	14. puppet
7. airplanes and gliders	15. marbles
8. trucks and cars	16. flashlight

CLASS B: Games

1. board games	9. relay races
2. tag	10. jigsaw puzzle
3. cards	11. steal the bacon
4. jump rope	12. musical chairs
5. tug-of-war	13. statues
6. Simon says	14. Mother, may I?
7. dominoes	15. arm wrestle
8. jacks	16. darts

CLASS C: Sports

1. hockey	9. swimming
2. baseball	10. handball
3. football	11. horseshoes

Figure 13.7 (Con't)

4. tennis
5. badmitton
6. basketball
7. golf
8. gymnastics

12. soccer
13. volleyball
14. track
15. skating
16. bowling

CLASS D: Hobbies

1. sewing
2. leatherworking
3. painting
4. pets
5. reading
6. collecting
7. plants
8. music (playing, singing, listening)

9. photography
10. working with clay
11. woodworking
12. cooking, baking, preserving
13. knitting
14. bird watching
15. crafts
16. model building

Summary

The mentally retarded student is hurt by what we fail to teach. The teacher has a limited amount of time each day to cover the basic curriculum areas of math and language arts. All too often content subject areas are included as time is available. By following a plan of unit instruction and also making maximum use of instructional television and well written curriculum supplements such as the Project PASS materials, a great deal of science, social studies, health and physical education information can be infused into the school day. Reading can be taught just as well using a social studies book or a newspaper as a basal reading series. The teacher must seek to create opportunities throughout the day for including these content areas into the base curriculum.

Remember this . . .

1. Career education and vocational education are not the same.

2. There are more than 23,000 job titles in the *Dictionary of Occupational Titles* (DOT).

3. Family life is a part of career education.

4. Social skill development is a critical part of career education.

CHAPTER XIV

Overview of Career Education

Cegelka (1981) reviewed current interpretations and official definitions of career education and found the following statements to reflect these positions:

1. Career education is a part of the total school curriculum.
2. Career education stresses awareness, attitude, and broad skills.
3. Career education is a means of assisting individuals to lead productive lives.
4. Career education is interested in preparing the individual to be a successful member of society whether paid or as a volunteer.
5. Career education focuses on the citizen, family life, leisure time, volunteer work, and paid employment.

Therefore career education is designed to give students an awareness of the possibilities available to them in the community in terms of work, family, citizenship, and leisure time while vocational education teaches specific job skills such as welding, typing, or computer operation (Faas, 1980). Obviously, the dimensions of a vocational education curriculum lie outside the scope of this text and we will not attempt to deal with this aspect of the secondary curriculum. We will instead direct your attention to a career education orientation and in that context discuss career awareness and basic curriculum goals.

Basic Curriculum Goals

Once again we must draw your attention to the fact that EMH learners must be taught a wide variety of skills and this is as true in the career education area as in the traditional curriculum areas of math and reading. With current accepted definitions of career education including family, work, and leisure time components, the basic curriculum will want to include the following goals:

1. To be familiar with the world of work (see under Career Awareness)
2. To be able to deal with social interactions that require a verbal response
3. To be able to deal with work interactions that require a verbal response
4. To be able to deal with criticism interactions both when offering and accepting criticism
5. To be able to deal with compliments both as the giver and the recipient
6. To be able to deal with home situations that require action and/or a verbal response
7. To be familiar with types of jobs found in society (see under Career Awareness)

All seven goals must actually and actively be taught beginning in early elementary schools and continuing through the secondary years. Goals one and seven have been addressed in the Career Awareness section so that this portion will deal in the main with goals two through six.

Social Interactions

Verbal social interactions are a part of normal life but what a child may be able to "get away with" may not enhance the personal or career development of an adolescent or adult. Figure 14.1 presents a sample of typical social interactions for which an adult must develop an appropriate response. Students who learn to cope with such social situations will be better prepared to take their place in adult society. Classroom teachers can have students role play these interactions, model, or discuss them. Different situations can be selected for use with different age groups while all should be taught or reviewed in the late elementary and secondary years.

Figure 14.1
Sample Social Interactions

1. You are working and someone says "hello," you should say . . .
2. Your supervisor says to you, "How are you today?" You should say . . .
3. You are introduced to a new employee. You should say . . .
4. During a break a friend sits down next to you and starts talking to you about the workshop picnic that you both went to. What should you say?
5. The bus driver says to you, "Hi, how's it going?" You say . . .
6. While you are working a friend comes up and says hello. You say . . .
7. Your boss brings someone over to your work area and says, "I would like you to meet Paul, he is a new employee." You say . . .
8. Your boss comes up to you and says, "Sure is hot today." You say . . .
9. It is lunch time and your friends are talking about a movie that you saw. You say . . .
10. Someone new comes up to you and says, "Hi, I'm Sue." You should say . . .
11. When someone waves and says "hello," you should say . . .
12. Someone says "See you later." You say . . .
13. You are talking with a friend at work and he/she says "Better go, it's getting late." You say . . .
14. Someone comments to you that the price of pop in the machine has gone up. You say . . .
15. When you see someone new at work, you should say . . .
16. You are walking to work and see your boss. You should say . . .
17. A new person is working at your work table. This is the first time you see him/her. You say . . .
18. You are talking to another employee and it is time for you to get back to work. You say . . .
19. You are happy to see an old friend that stopped by to visit. It is almost break time. You should say . . .
20. When you are working and another employee wants to talk to you, you should say . . .
21. You are listening to another worker and someone else interrupts. You should say . . .
22. You are waiting to have a job interview and see someone you know. You say . . .
23. Someone walks up to your work area and just looks at you. You should say . . .

Figure 14.1 (Con't)

24. Another worker is getting ready to go home. You say . . .
25. You are waiting for the bus to go home after work and see your boss. You should say . . .
26. When you get to work in the morning, you see a group of your friends. You say . . .
27. You notice that someone new is looking for your work supervisor. You should say . . .

Adapted from C.N. Schloss and P.J. Schloss, *Independent Living Skills*, (Austin, TX: Pro Ed, 1985).

Work Interactions

The ability to cope successfully with the variety of interactions that occur in the work world may mean the difference between employment and unemployment for adolescents and adults. Have students role play the sample work interactions suggested in Figure 14.2 and have them develop some of their own. Students may wish to use these to create a short skit which can be performed for others in the school. Bulletin boards can be developed by the students to offer appropriate suggestions for dealing with any of these situations. Allow students to realize that there may be many possible and appropriate responses to these situations and that they must decide what response suits their particular situation.

Figure 14.2
Sample Work Interactions

1. When at work, you run out of things to do. You see your supervisor and say . . .
2. You are at work and cannot find your supervisor to ask for help. You see a friend and say . . .
3. How would you ask someone to help you lift a heavy box at work?
4. You need to find a box to put your work in. How would you ask for help?
5. You just spilled some pop in the lunch room and need a mop. You say . . .
6. You need to ask your supervisor if you can leave early to see a doctor. You say . . .
7. You are having trouble doing a difficult job and don't know what to do. You raise your hand and a supervisor comes to your work area. You ask . . .

Figure 14.2 (Con't)

8. You would like to take next Thursday off because your parents will be visiting. You see your boss and say . . .
9. You are in a new work area and need to use the restroom. You can't find it and see another employee. You say . . .
10. You are in the supply room and can't find a pail. You see another employee who is busy sweeping. You say . . .
11. After work you ned to go to the post office and don't know where it is. You say . . .
12. There are no paper towels in the restroom. You see a supervisor and say . . .
13. You are working and make a mistake and don't know what to do. You raise your hand and the supervisor comes over to your work area. You say . . .
14. Another worker is bothering you and you need help from your supervisor. You raise your hand and when called on, you say . . .
15. Another employee asks to borrow 50¢ to buy some pop. You say . . .
16. When talking with your boss, he/she asks if you would like some coffee. You say . . .
17. Your boss walks by and notices some garbage on the floor and asks you to pick it up. You say . . .
18. You are asked where the restroom is. You say . . .
19. Another employee asks you if you know where the supervisor is. You say . . .
20. You're asked to help another employee to stack up some boxes. You say . . .
21. Your boss asked you, "Would you like to do another job today?" You say . . .
22. Someone asks you to help them and you're busy. You should say . . .
23. A new employee asks you to sit with him/her to eat lunch. You say . . .
24. You are asked what your name is and where do you live. You say . . .
25. When asked, "How do you like your job?" You say . . .
26. You are asked by your supervisor to show another employee how to do a job. You say . . .
27. At break your boss says, "Going to the picnic tomorrow?" You say . . .

Adapted from C.N. Schloss and P.J. Schloss, *Independent Living Skills*, (Austin, TX: Pro Ed, 1985).

Criticism Interactions

We may not like it but accepting criticism is a necessary skill. Even the most perfect person will find that "someone out there" does not approve of his or her aspirations toward perfection. EMH learners may be especially sensitive to criticism directed toward them and at the same time insensitive to their criticism of others. Offer criticism in the classroom in an appropriate way and accept criticism in the same spirit. Explain to students who deliver criticism in an offensive fashion that such a delivery antagonizes or crushes the individual to whom it is addressed and then work on appropriate means of delivering necessary criticism. Figure 14.3 lists 30 possible criticism role playing situations, and these can be used to teach students the whys and hows of criticism.

Figure 14.3
Sample Criticism Interactions

1. Another employee is not dressed properly for work. You say . . .
2. You are helping another empoyee stacking boxes and he/she is not doing their share of work. You say . . .
3. Another employee keeps bothering you while you are trying to work. You say . . .
4. You don't like the way someone is acting during break. You should say . . .
5. How do you tell someone that you don't like the way they're dressed?
6. Someone is talking real loud at your work station. You should say . . .
7. Someone accidentally bumps into you while you are working. You say . . .
8. Another worker keeps talking to you while you are working. You say . . .
9. You see another employee smoking in the work area. You go up to the employee and say . . .
10. You are waiting in line to get on the bus after work and someone cuts in line. You say . . .
11. If someone keeps touching you, you should say . . .
12. During break another employee takes your pop. You should say . . .
13. You are sweeping the work floor with another employee. The other

Figure 14.3 (Con't)

employee keeps stopping and talking to others. This bothers you. You go up to the person and say . . .

14. You are working and your supervisor says, "Hey, you need to speed up!" You say . . .
15. You are told by your boss, "I don't like the way you've been acting!" You say . . .
16. Another employee calls you a "jerk." You say . . .
17. You are having trouble keeping up with your work. Your boss tells you to "keep up or you'll be out of a job." You say . . .
18. Your boss tells you that you are spending more time talking than working and says "speed up." You say . . .
19. You were just yelled at for fighting on the job. You say to your supervisor . . .
20. Your supervisor is upset because you left your work area without permission. You say . . .
21. Another worker complained that you are bothering other workers. Your supervisor mentions this to you and tells you that this has to stop. You say . . .
22. You keep leaving your work undone and are told by your boss that you must finish one job before starting another. You say . . .
23. When you get to work another employee tells you that they don't like what you are wearing. You say . . .
24. Another worker tells you that you are a pretty slow worker. You say . . .
25. You are told by your boss that you "better get your rear end moving or you'll be out of a job." You say . . .
26. Your supervisor has been finding errors in your work and tells you about it. You say . . .
27. Your boss comes up and says, "Speed up, this needs to get done today!" You say . . .

Adapted from C.N. Schloss and P.J. Schloss, *Independent Living Skills,* (Austin, TX: Pro Ed, 1985).

Compliment Interactions

Compliments can present difficulties whether we are delivering or receiving them. On the other hand, the recipients of sincere compliments not only feel better about themselves but also tend to view the individual who is delivering the compliment in a positive light. It is wise, therefore, to teach students how to deliver compliments and how to receive them. Figure 14.4 lists some possible compliment situations for classroom use. See Chapter VIII, "Study and Survival Skills," for more information on compliments.

Figure 14.4
Sample Compliment Interactions

1. You like what someone is wearing. You say . . .
2. Tell another employee that you enjoy working with them.
3. You like what someone said in class. You say . . .
4. You really enjoy working for your boss. You would say . . .
5. You really enjoyed an activity at work. You go up to the person in charge and say . . .
6. You were having problems in doing your work and asked your boss for help. He/she helped you and you really liked it. You should say . . .
7. Another employee helps you lift some heavy boxes. You really appreciate their help. You say . . .
8. When you think someone has done a good job, you should say . . .
9. You noticed that another employee did a really good job today. You say . . .
10. Another employee got a hair cut that you really like. You say . . .
11. Your boss helped you today when you were having some problems. You say . . .
12. Your counselor gave you a ride home because you stayed after to talk. You said . . .
13. You really enjoy working with another employee. You say . . .
14. You needed some help in doing your work and your boss helped you. You should say . . .
15. When someone tells me that they like what I'm wearing, I should say . . .
16. Your counselor says, "I hear you have been doing real good at work." You say . . .
17. Another employee tells you that you are a good friend. You say . . .
18. You were just told that were a good employee. You say . . .
19. Your boss told you, "I really enjoy you working here." You say . . .
20. When you are busy at work and you're told that you are doing a good job, you should say . . .
21. Your boss says, "You're doing great, keep up the good work." You say . . .
22. Your counselor tells you that your behavior has been really good. You say . . .

Figure 14.4 (Con't)

23. When you tell someone that they did a good job, they should say . . .
24. You were just told that you would be getting a raise because you are an excellent worker. You say . . .
25. You just helped your boss in straightening some boxes. He/she tells you that your help was appreciated. You say . . .
26. Your boss asked you to work late because they needed some extra help. Your boss said, "I really appreciate your help, thanks." You said . . .
27. Another employee complimented you for never getting mad. You say . . .

Adapted from C.N. Schloss and P.J. Schloss, *Independent Living Skills*, (Austin, TX: Pro Ed, 1985).

Home Interactions

All of us spend a great deal of time at home, and if we can deal with the situations that arise in the home, our time spent there will be more rewarding. Students often have not thought about how their home behavior influences others in the home or how the behavior of a mother and/or father in the home influences the behavior and manners of the children in that home. When using the sample home interactions in Figure 14.5, focus on the results of behaviors and how courtesy in the home can result in positive changes in that environment. Use the home interactions in a role-playing format and also assign students to role play or discuss certain situations at home.

Career Awareness

The focus of career awareness is making learners familiar with the world of work and all types of jobs found in society. Learners need to be aware of the many options available and the levels within each occupation. The development of this awareness should begin immediately after students enter school and continue through their secondary education. In order for the learner to assimilate a basic understanding of the world of work, certain components of that world must be identified and explored. A brief discussion of these components will comprise the next paragraphs.

Figure 14.5
Sample Home Interactions

1. Your mother tells you to take out the garbage. You say . . .
2. Your sister wants to borrow your sweatshirt and you have never worn it. You say . . .
3. While you are taking a nap, the phone rings. You think your Dad is home. You . . .
4. It is after school and your mother has left a fresh batch of cookies out to cool. You decide to . . .
5. The dog has shredded the Sunday newspaper. You will . . .
6. You are supposed to clean your room and you have just been invited to go skating. You . . .
7. Grandfather plans to plant his garden on Saturday. You usually help him but you want to watch TV. You . . .
8. You used the car last. Mom just ran out of gas and came in the house yelling "Who didn't buy gas?" You . . .
9. You decide to make a cup of coffee and you know that Mom is in the next room sewing. You . . .
10. You just got home from school. Mom is sick in bed and there are dirty dishes in the sink. You . . .
11. Dad is in a bad mood and you are tired of your brother messing up your room. You had planned to talk to Dad about it. You . . .
12. Your teenage son wants to try out for soccer. You are afraid he won't do his chores so you . . .
13. Aunt Ann and Uncle Joe are coming for the weekend. They are supposed to stay in your room but they stayed there last visit. You . . .
14. Your 10 year old daughter expects a big birthday party but you can't afford that. You . . .
15. A new family moved in next door and you aren't sure that they speak English. You . . .
16. Mom and Dad have spent the day painting the house. It's supper time and you . . .
17. Your teenage daughter won't get up in the morning. You . . .
18. The sidewalk needs to be shoveled again and you've done it three times already. You . . .
19. Your hushand/wife never helps wash the car. You . . .
20. Your mother won't give you money for the new jeans you want. You decide to . . .
21. The neighbors say you play your stereo too loud. You . . .
22. Your teenage son lost his driver's license for speeding. You . . .

Figure 14.5 (Con't)

23. The bathroom is always a mess and your Mom calls a family meeting. You say . . .
24. The Boy Scouts had a meeting and left a big mess. You . . .
25. All of your friends have a certain type of gym shoes and you want the same but your Dad says its a waste of money. You . . .
26. Grandmother always asks you embarrassing questions so you . . .
27. Your daughter wants to date an older man. You . . .
28. You have been invited to go to Florida with friends but your parents don't think its a good idea. You . . .
29. Your Dad smokes too much. You . . .
30. Two of your friends are in trouble with the police and your family wants you to break off these friendships. You . . .

Adapted from C.N. Schloss and P.J. Schloss, *Independent Living Skills*, (Austin, TX: Pro Ed, 1985).

Personal Values

Personal needs and values can be met by work, and students must be made aware of this aspect of work while at the same time learning that work will not necessarily meet all of their needs. Therefore, one goal of a career awareness program should be to identify values and needs such as positive self-concept, independence, success, self-sufficiency, financial goals, fulfillment, status, and self-worth, all of which can be met by work. Students could discuss their current values and how their needs could be met through work. Students will need to be exposed to the decisions and choices of others as well as what needs and values have not been met through certain career choices and how they might be met in different careers or through use of leisure time.

Society and Work

Students must learn that all jobs contribute to society and all work has its own dignity. You will want to discuss a wide array of jobs with your class showing how workers from all occupational categories contribute positively to society. Be sure to include jobs that require various amounts of skill and training so that it will be clear to the learner that all workers can produce services or goods that help people to meet their needs. Other concepts that may be explored at this time could include how workers are interdependent and the rewards of different careers.

Financial Aspects

Students need an understanding of the differences among jobs in respect to pay. Necessary to this understanding is an appreciation of factors such as skill, training, education, need, and supply of workers. Collecting information on the hourly, weekly, or monthly wages of various occupations and comparing such wages to the other factors (e.g., training, education) should encourage discussion among students and increase knowledge about career options.

Work Habits

Employees are expected to be able to follow directions, whether given verbally or in writing. Therefore, teaching students to deal with both simple and complex directions not only makes them more successful in school but also promotes a valuable work habit. The ability to get along with supervisors and co-workers is another important work habit. Teachers must provide students with the opportunity to work cooperatively and teach social and personal skills to their students. Games, discussion, role playing, class projects, and team sports can all contribute to this process. The ability to work safely and at an appropriate rate, while producing quality work, is especially important to the EMH worker (learner). Frequent discussion, study, and exploration of these components will enhance the employability of EMR learners. Finally, the classroom offers many opportunities to teach students the importance of punctuality and regular attendance. Structure your classroom so that students learn to take pride in being prompt and attending school on a regular basis. Guest speakers from the community may reinforce these habits by defining company policy as well as explaining what loss of work time means in terms of dollars and production.

Seeking Employment

Students need an awareness of sources of information about possible jobs. Newspaper ads, job announcements, employment agencies, and "word-of-mouth" are all likely sources, and students must be taught to use them. Students must be aware of the different types of job place-ment services available in the area and state. Next, the ability to cope with application forms must be mastered. Students must not only understand how to interpret the form but also they must know how to use and spell words needed for successful completion of the form. Finally, students must be prepared for the interview process in terms of speaking on the phone, dressing appropriately, and handling the questions of the interviewer. Role playing, films, discussion, and guest speakers can all contribute to these competencies.

Job Applications

Exposure to the vocabulary of job or employment applications and to the forms themselves will benefit all EMH learners and should be included in any curriculum. Figure 14.6 presents some basic vocabulary words used on most job application forms. Students must

Figure 14.6
Basic Job Application Vocabulary

Word/Abbreviation	*Meaning*
SS#, SSN, Soc. Sec. No.	Social Security Number
Marital Status	Married, single, divorced, separated, widowed
Spouse	Name of husband or wife
Dependents	People you support (e.g. wife, children, parents)
Applicant	Your name, person applying for job
Address	Place where you live
Signature	Your signed name
References	Names of people who can tell about your character or work skills
N/A	Not applicable; does not apply
Maiden Name	A woman's last name before marriage
Occupation	What you do for a living
Zip	Zip code number
A/C	Area code of telephone number

be taught to read the words and their abbreviations as well as to understand their meanings. These words can be a part of a spelling or English lesson and can also be worked into crossword puzzles and bulletin boards. Teacher and students should add to this list whenever possible.

The job application forms seen in Figure 14.7 and Figure 14.8 are samples that may be used to give students practice. Students and teacher may also develop their own forms or use actual forms from local businesses and employment agencies. Students should practice completing such forms giving accurate and appropriate information as well as using correct spelling and punctuation.

Types of Jobs

Elementary EMH students should be informed about major job categories which may be seen as white or blue collar, skilled versus unskilled, or classified according to training or education required for the position. A wise teacher might begin to link a student's developing skills and strengths to a variety of careers by such statements as "Good handwriting is important for hospital work" or "The skill of reading would be useful to a mechanic when he needs to use a car manual." Secondary aged students will require more specific information about types of careers, and such guides as the *Dictionary of Occupational Titles* (DOT) or the *Occupational Outlook Handbook* may be used for this purpose.

Figure 14.7
Job Application R

Name _____ Date of Birth _____

Address _____

Marital Status _____ SS# _____

Education_____

Telephone #_____ Years Experience _____

References _____

_____

Signature _____

Figure 14.8
Job Application X

Name_____ D.O.B._____

SS#_____ Marital Status_____

Employment Experience: (1)_____

(2)_____

(3)_____

Health_____ Vision_____ Hearing_____

Education:_____

Telephone_____ Spouse_____

Community Organizations: (1)_____

(2)_____

(3)_____

Current Occupation_____

Number of Children_____ Names: _____

_____

_____

Transportation_____

Would you be available on weekends? _____

Would you prefer: night shift_____ day shift_____

Have you served in the armed services? _____

Signature_____

The U.S. Office of Education has developed a cluster scheme that is most frequently used in school-based career education programs.

The fifteen clusters are:
1. Personal Services
2. Health Services
3. Construction
4. Manufacturing
5. Transportation
6. Agri-Business and Natural Resources
7. Public Services
8. Environment
9. Hospitality and Recreation
10. Fine Arts and Humanities
11. Communications and Media
12. Marketing and Distribution
13. Marine Science
14. Business/Office
15. Consumer and Homemaking Education

These clusters accommodate the more than 23,000 job titles found in the *Dictionary of Occupational Titles* (DOT). For specific jobs see Figure 14.9. Jobs within each cluster range from the highly skilled to the unskilled, and all are derived from a common core which provides the foundation for development of skills which are applicable to a group of related jobs.

These and related materials can be found in your school library which should be used as a career guidance resource center. The school or county librarian may have a career pamphlet file that can be used by students seeking career information. Films, filmstrips, newspapers, and magazines can be used to explore different occupation clusters. Bring in guest speakers from the local employment agency and ask the school counselor to present information on careers to your class. Encourage students to talk with members of the community in order to obtain career information and allow time for the exchange of job information during the school day.

Classroom Strategies

The following is a list of ideas or approaches for integrating career education into your classroom activities. These ideas are only a beginning as your own creativity and that of your students will give you many

Figure 14.9
Job Clusters
(U.S. Office of Education)

1. *Personal Services*

   Beautician
   Shoe Repairman
   Social Worker
   Insurance Agent
   Refrigeration, Air Conditioning
     and Heating Mechanic
   TV Repairman
   Radio Repairman
   Rabbi
   Tailor

   Babysitter
   Priest
   Missionary
   Furniture Upholsterer
   Barber
   Cleaner and Laundry Manager
   Telephone Operator
   Minister
   Mortician

2. *Health Services*

   Psychologist
   Doctor
   Orderly
   Practical Nurse
   Occupational Therapist
   Medical Secretary and Librarian
   Veterinarian
   Dentist
   Laboratory Technician
   Chiropractor
   Anesthesiologist
   Speech Pathologist

   Optometrist
   Pharmacist
   Podiatrist
   Laundry and Sterilizer
   Osteopath
   Psychiatrist
   Nurse
   X-Ray Technician
   Nurse's Aide
   Hospital Administrator
   Dental Technician
   Dental Hygienist
   Bacteriologist

3. *Construction*

   Mobile Home Builder
   Architect
   Plumber
   Plasterer
   Mason
   Bricklayer
   Printer
   Industrial Designer
   Cabinet Worker
   Roofer

   Surveyor
   Paperhanger
   Pipefitter
   Engineer
   Draftsman
   Carpenter
   Electrician
   Excavator
   Cement Mason
   Heavy Equipment Operator

Figure 14.9 (Con't)

4. *Manufacturing*

Machine Operator
Machine Maintenance
Electronic Engineer
Assembly Line Operator
Mobile Home Assembler
Welder

Industrial Traffic Manager
Industrial Designer
Sheet Metal Worker
Skilled Tradesman
Tool and Die Operator
Chemist
Mechanical Engineer

5. *Transportation*

Truck Driver
Pilot
Body and Fender Repairman
Traffic Control Manager
    — Airlines
Aerospace Engineer
Station Agent

Brakeman
Locomotive Engineer
Service Station Manager and
    Attendant
Auto Mechanic
Bus and Taxi Driver
Conductor

6. *Agri-Business and Natural Resources*

Farmer
Dairyman
Feed Store Manager
Miner
Soil Conservationist
Agricultural Engineer
Agronomist
Petroleum and Natural Gas
    Production Worker
Farm Manager

Poultryman
Petroleum Engineer
Rancher
Butcher
Farm Equipment Salesperson
Farm Agent
Fish and Game Manager
Mining Engineer
Wildlife Manager

7. *Public Service*

Kindergarten-Elementary Teacher
State Policeman
Janitor
Certified Public Accountant
School Administrator
Food and Drug Inspector
Court Recorder
Fireman
Urban Planner

Lawyer
Counselor — School, Employ-
    ment, Rehabilitation
Refuse Collector
Junior and Senior High
    Teacher
Government Service
Civil Engineer
Librarian

Figure 14.9 (Con't)

City Policeman
Nursery School Teacher

Court Bailiff
Military
Probation Officer

8. *Environment*

Forest Ranger
Gardener
Landscape Architect
Camp Counselor
Fish and Game Warden
Horticulturist
Park Ranger
Tree Surgeon
Geophysicist

Range Manager
Recycling Operator
Naturalist
Meteorologist
Biologist
Forestry Aide
Geologist
Environmental Engineer

9. *Hospitality and Recreation*

Stewardess
Restaurant Manager
Social Director
Waitress
Restaurant Hostess
Travel Agent
Dietician
Swimming Pool Manager
Hotel-Motel Manager

Waiter
Short Order Cook
Steward
Cook
Chef
Golf Pro
Cashier
Baker
Athlete

10. *Fine Arts and Humanities*

Professional Musician
Dancer
Author
Literary Writer
Music Critic
Art Critic
Actress
Conductor
Sign Painter
Music Director
Stage Designer
Composer
Orchestra Leader
Free-lance Artist

Cartoonist
Singer
Playwright
Music Arranger
Fashion Designer
Commercial Artist
Music Teacher
Poet
Piano Technician
Radio and TV Director
Actor
Film Editor
Jeweler
Singing Teacher

Figure 14.9 (Con't)

Floral Designer   Orchestrator
Sculptor

11. *Communications and Media*

    Journalist   Radio-TV Announcer
    Technical Writer   Electronic Technician
    Audio-control Technician   Lighting Technician
    Proofreader   Foreign Correspondent
    Staff Programmer   Sportscaster
    Sound Engineer   Maintenance Technician
    Script Writer   Reporter
    Newswriter   Transmitter Technician
    Photoengraver   Printer
    Photographer   Video Technician
    Lecturer

12. *Marketing and Distribution*

    Salesman   Consumer Product Seller
    Statistician   Systems Analyst
    Packaging and Designer   Sales Engineer
    Marketing Researcher   Economist
    Production and Control Position   Sales Supervisor
                                         Wholesale and Retail
                                             Distributor

13. *Marine Science*

    Marine Biologist   Physicist
    Seaman   Aquatic Biologist
    Commercial Fisherman   Marine Geologist
    Geophysicist

14. *Business/Office*

    Office Manager   Trailer Salesman
    Personnel Director   Bank Teller
    Advertising Worker   Receptionist
    Data Processor   Stenographer
    Computer Operator   Computer Programmer
    Public Relations Worker   Bookkeeper
    Accountant   Key Punch Operator
    Secretary   Purchasing Agent
    File Clerk   Bank Management

Figure 14.9 (Con't)

15. *Consumer and Homemaking Education*

Interior Decorator   Drapery Maker
Appliance Demonstrator   Credit Interviewer
Home Demonstration Agent   Seamstress
Price Control Agent   Fashion Coordinator
Milliner   Model
Homemaker   Extension Agent
Nutritionist   Home Economist

other approaches. Within each grouping, ideas are listed in a sequential order.

1. Matching job to interests
   a. Students compile a list of words that relate to a specific job or career.
   b. Students list their courses and tell how each related to possible future jobs.
   c. Students write a paragraph describing what an ideal job would be like.
   d. Students list three things they like to do. Then they list jobs that relate to these activities.
2. Bulletin boards, etc.
   a. Student-of-the-Week Bulletin Board is prepared by the students and is decorated with pictures and information (favorite book, goals, TV show, family member, food, talent, hobbies) about that student.
   b. Teacher prepares a "feelings" chart which lists approximately ten feelings or moods. Student points to feeling that is present that day and discusses how it developed and where it could lead.
   c. Teacher or students cut pictures of clothing and shoes from magazines and newspapers. Students make posters matching appropriate clothing to work in specific occupations.
   d. Students prepare career bulleting boards.
3. Work futures and images
   a. Students find newspaper and magazine articles that discuss the futures of different types of jobs.
   b. Teacher states stereotypes of different jobs and students

try to support or refute these stereotypes. Students may do this by interviewing people who hold the particular jobs under discussion.

c. Grandparents of students come to class and talk about how careers have changed.

d. In English or reading the students read fiction or nonfiction where themes concern work.

4. Categories of work

a. Students make a list of all types of workers that they see in action on a field trip.

b. Students walk through the community and compile a list of jobs that allow people to work outdoors.

c. Students divide the year into seasons and tell how these affect certain jobs.

d. Students are divided into teams. The team that can list the most careers wins.

e. Students make up a commercial and present it to the class. Class decides who might purchase this product or service.

5. Decision making

a. Teacher prepares "decision" type stories and offers students three or four alternatives. Students discuss their choices.

b. Students pretend they are traveling to Maine. They may take twenty pounds of luggage. Students are given a list of items they may wish to take and the weight of each. Students discuss possible consequences of their choices.

c. Students work with computer simulation of a wagon train trip. Students are confronted with choices and results.

d. Students are given problem situations which occur in certain jobs and asked to respond to them. Example: A carpenter is asked to figure the cost of adding paneling to a room. The sheets of paneling cost $8.97 each, and he needs thirteen of them.

6. Financial planning

a. Students are given copies of mail-order catalogs (Sears, Penney's) and are told they have a $75 clothing and shoe allowance. Students select choices and discuss.

b. Students study grocery store ads in local paper and decide where to shop.

c. Students are given a list of grocery items they must purchase. They study the grocery store ads in the newspaper and decide where to shop.

d. Students are given a "paycheck" and a list of bills to pay and a list of items available for sale. They plan a budget.

7. Is it right for you?

a. Teacher prepares lists of jobs. Students tell what could happen if the person who had that job could not do math or could not read.

b. Teacher assigns each student five jobs and students list types of equipment used by the people who work at these jobs.

c. Students come to school dressed like a worker in a certain career and tell the class about that career.

d. Students invite their parents to come and discuss the role and work of a homemaker.

8. Looking for work

a. Representatives from the local social security office come to the classroom to tell about the social security system and how to get a card.

b. Students read the classified ads in the newspaper and
   1) divide the jobs into categories,
   2) determine educational requirements of the jobs, and
   3) select one job and "practice" applying for it.

Summary

Career education functions as a part of the total school curriculum from early elementary school through the secondary years. Career education encompasses awareness, attitudes, and skills which prepare the individual to be successful in the home and in the work place. Many EMH students will never make the connection between the social and academic expectations of their school years and the broader world of work and family life unless they are able to participate in a curriculum which draws all of these expectations and activities together. Prepare your students now for the challenges that will arise and for participation in the mainstream of adult life.

Bibliography

Atkinson, R.C. Mnemotechnics in Second-Language Learning. *American Psychologist*, 1975, *30*, 821–828.

Ausubel, D.P. In Defense of Advance Organizers; A Reply to Critics. *Review of Educational Research*, 1978, *48*, 215–258.

Bagford, J. The Role in Teaching in Reading. In W. H. Miller (Ed.), *Elementary Reading Today: Selected Articles.* New York: Holt, Rinehart & Winston, 1972.

Baratz, J.D., and Shuy, R.W. (Eds.). *Teaching Black Children to Read.* Washington Center for Applied Linguistics, 1969.

Bereiter, C., and Engelmann, S. *Teaching Disadvantaged Children in the Preschool.* Englewood Cliffs, NJ: Prentice-Hall, 1966.

Black, J.E., and Burns, R. *Time in School Learning: An Instructional Psychologist's Perspective.* Paper presented at the annual meeting of the American Educational Research Association, Washington, D.C., 1975.

Blake, K.A. *Teaching the Retarded.* Englewood Cliffs, NJ: Prentice-Hall, Inc., 1974.

Blake, K.A. Amount of Material and Retarded and Normal Pupils' Learning. *Journal of Research and Development in Education*, 1975, *8*, 128–136.

Blessing, K., and Cook, J. *Class Size and Teacher Aides as Factors in the Achievement of the Educable Mentally Retarded. Final Report.* Bureau for the Education of the Handicapped, August 1970 (Grant #EG–30626620–1978).

Bliesmer, E.P., Reading Abilities of Bright and Dull Children of Comparable Mental Ages. *Readings on Reading.* Scranton, PA: International Textbook Co., 1969.

Bloom, L., and Lahey, M. *Language Development and Language Disorders.* New York: John Wiley & Sons, 1978.

Bond, G.L., and Dykstra, R. *The First Grade Reading Studies: Findings of Individual Investigations.* Newark, Del.: International Reading Association, 1967.

Boomer, L. Special education paraprofessionals: a guide for teachers. *Teaching Exceptional Children*, 1980, *12*, 46-49.

Borkowski, J.G., and Wanschura, T.B. Mediational Processes in the Retarded.

International Review of Research in Mental Retardation (Vol. 7). New York: Academic Press, 1974.

Brigham, T., Graubard, P., and Stans, A. Analysis of the Effects of Sequential Reinforcement Contingencies on Aspects of Composition. *Journal of Applied Behavior Analysis*, 1972, *5*, 421–429.

Broden, M., Beasley, A., and Hall, R.V. In-Class Spelling Performance. *Behavior Modification*, 1978, *2*, 511–529.

Brolin, D., Durand, R., Kromer, K., and Muller, P. Post-School Adjustment of Educable Retarded Students. *Education and Training of the Mentally Retarded*, 1975, *10*(3), 144–149.

Brophy, J.E., and Evertson, C.M. *Learning from Teaching: A Developmental Perspective.* Boston: Allyn and Bacon, 1976.

Brown, A.L. The Role of Strategic Behavior in Retardate Memory. *International Review of Research in Mental Retardation* (Vol. 7). New York: Academic Press, 1974.

Brown, L., Branston, M.B., Baumgart, D., Vincent, L., Falvey, M., and Schroeder, J. Utilizing the Characteristics of a Variety of Current and Subsequent Least Restrictive Environments as Factors in the Development of Curricular Content for Severely Handicapped Students. *AAESPH Review*, 1979, *4*(4), 407–424.

Brown, V. Programs, Materials and Techniques. *Journal of Learning Disabilities*, 1975, *8*, 605–612.

Bruekner, L.J., and Bond, G.L. *Diagnosis and Treatment of Learning Difficulties.* New York: Appleton-Century-Crofts, 1955.

Budoff, M. Learning Potential: A Supplementary Procedure for Assessing the Ability to Reason. *Seminars in Psychiatry*, 1969, *1*, 278–290.

Budoff, M. Learning Potential as a Supplementary Strategy to Psychometric Diagnosis. *Learning Disorders* (Vol. 3). Seattle, WA: Special Child Publications, 1968.

Burns, P., and Broman, B. *The Language Arts in Childhood Education.* Chicago, IL: Rand McNally, 1975.

Cahen, L.S., Craun, M.J., and Johnson, S.K. Spelling Difficulty: A Survey of the Research. *Review of Educational Research*, 1971, *41*(4), 281–301.

Campione, J.C. and Brown, A.L. Memory and Metamemory Development in Educable Retarded Children. *Perspectives on the Development of Memory and Cognition.* Hillsdale, N.J.: Lawrence Erlbaum, 1977.

Carnine, D., and Silbert, J. *Direct Instruction Reading.* Columbus, Ohio: Charles E. Merrill Publishing Co., 1979.

Carroll, J. A Model of School Learning. *Teachers College Record*, 1963, *64*, 723–733.

Carroll, J.B., Davies, P., and Richman, B. *The American Heritage Word Frequency Book*. Boston: Houghton Mifflin, 1971.

Cartwright, G.P. Written Language Abilities of Educable Mentally Retarded and Normal Children. *American Journal of Mental Deficiency*, 1968, *16*, 312–319.

Cartwright, G.P. The Relationship between Sequences of Instruction and Mental Abilities of Retarded Children. *American Educational Research Journal*, 1971, *8*, 143–150.

Cartwright, G.P. Written Expression and Spelling. *Teacher Diagnosis of Educational Difficulties* (pp. 95–117). Columbus, OH: Charles E. Merrill, 1969.

Cawley, J.F., Goodstein, H.A., and Burrow, W.H. *The Slow Learner and the Reading Problem*. Springfield, IL: Charles C. Thomas Co., 1972.

Cawley, J.F., Goodstein, H.A., Fitzmaurice, A.M., Lepore, A., Sedlak, R.A., and Althaus, V. *Project MATH: Mathematics Activities for Teaching the handicapped: Level I and II*. Tulsa, OK: Educational Process Corp., 1976.

Cegelka, P.T. Career Education. *Handbook of Special Education*. Englewood Cliffs, NJ: Prentice-Hall, 1981.

Chaffin, J., Maxwell, B., and Thompson, B. ARC-ED Curriculum: The Applications of Videogame Formats to Educational Software. *Exceptional Children*, 1982, *49*(2), 173–180.

Cohen, S.B., and Plaskon, S.P. *Language Arts for the Mildly Handicapped*. Columbus, OH: Charles E. Merrill, 1980.

Cunningham, P.M. Teacher's Correction Responses to Black-Dialect Miscues which are Non-Meaning-Changing. *Reading Research Quarterly*, 1976–77, *4*, 637–653.

David, J. Summer Study: *A Two-Part Investigation of the Impact of Exposure to Schooling on Achievement Growth*. Unpublished Doctoral Dissertation, Harvard University, 1974.

Dunn, L. Special Education for the Mildly Retarded: Is Much of it Justifiable? *Exceptional Children*, 1968, *35*, 5–22.

Dunn, L.M. Children with Mild General Learning Disabilities. *Exceptional Children in the Schools* (2d ed.). New York: Holt, Rinehart and Winston, 1973.

Dunn, L.M. (Ed.). *Exceptional Children in the Schools: Special Education in Transition* (2d ed.). New York: Holt, Rinehart, and Winston, 1973.

Dunn, L.M. A Comparison of Reading Processes of Mentally Retarded Boys of the Same MA. Studies of Reading and Arithmetic in Mentally Retarded Boys. *Monograph of the Society for Research in Child Development*, 1954, *19*, 7–99.

Durrell, D.D., and Sullivan, H.B. *Language Achievements of Mentally Retarded Children* (U.S.O.E. Cooperative Research Project No. 014). Boston: Boston University, 1958.

Ekwall, E.E. *Diagnosis and Remediation of the Disabled Reader*. Boston: Allyn & Bacon, 1976.

Ellis, N.R., Pryer, M.W., and Barnett, C.D. Motor Learning and Retention in Normals and Defectives. *Perceptual and Motor Skills*, 1960, *10*, 83–91.

Faas, L.A. *Children with Learning Problems: A Handbook for Teachers*. Boston: Houghton Mifflin Company, 1980.

Fernald, G.M.: *Remedial Techniques in Basic School Subjects*. New York: McGraw-Hill Book Co., 1943.

Fisher, C., Filby, N., and Marliave, R. *Instructional Time and Student Achievement in Second Grade Reading and Mathematics*. Paper presented at the annual meeting of the American Educational Research Association, New York, 1977.

Flanders, N. *Analyzing Teaching Behavior*. Reading, PA: Addison-Wesley, 1970.

Floyd, W.D. *An Analysis of the Oral Questioning Activity in Selected Colorado Primary Classrooms* (Doctoral Dissertation, Colorado State College). Ann Arbor, MI: University Microfilms No. 60–6253, 1960.

Fredericks, H.D., Anderson, R., Baldwin, D.L., Grove, D., Moore, W., Moore, M., and Beaird, J. *The Identification of Competencies of Teachers of the Severely Handicapped*. Project Report, 1978 (Grant #EG–0–74–2775).

French, E.L. Reading Disability and Mental Deficiency: A Preliminary Report. *Training School Bulletin*, 1950, *47*, 47–57.

Foxx, R.M., and Jones, J.R. A Remediation Program for Increasing the Spelling Achievement of Elementary and Junior High School Students. *Behavior Modification*, 1978, *2*(2), 211–230.

Gardner, W.I. *Learning and Behavior Characteristics of Exceptional Children and Youth: A Humanistic Approach*. Boston: Allyn & Bacon, 1977.

Garrison, M., and Hammill, D.D. Who are the Retarded? *Exceptional Children*, 1971, *38*, 13–20.

Gates, A.I. *Interest and Ability in Reading*. New York: The Macmillan Co., 1930.

Gearhart, B.R., and Weishahn, M.W. *The Handicapped Child in the Regular Classroom*. St. Louis, MO: C.V. Mosby, 1976.

Gillespie, P.H., and Johnson, L.E. *Teaching Reading to the Mildly Handicapped Child*. Columbus, OH: Charles E. Merrill, 1974.

Gillespie-Silver, P. *Teaching Reading to Children with Special Needs*. Columbus, OH: Charles E. Merrill, 1979.

Gilliland, H. *A Practical Guide to Remedial Reading* (2d ed.). Columbus, OH: Charles E. Merrill, 1978.

Goodman, K. A Linguistic Study of Cues and Miscues in Reading. *Elementary English Review*, 1965, *42*, 639–643.

Goodstein, H.A., Cawley, J.F., Gordon, S., and Helfgott, J. Verbal Problem Solving among Educable Mentally Retarded Children. *American Journal of Mental Deficiency*, 1971, *76*, 238–241.

Guzak, F.J. Teacher Questioning and Reading. *The Reading Teacher*, 1967, *21*, 227–234.

Hammill, D.D., and Bartel, M.R. *Teaching Children with Learning and Behavior Problems* (2d ed.). Boston: Allyn & Bacon, 1978.

Hanna, P.R., Hanna, J.S., Hodges, R.E., and Peterson, D.J. *Power to Spell.* Boston: Houghton Mifflin, 1971.

Hansen, C.L. Writing Skills. *The Fourth R: Research in the Classroom* (pp. 93–126). Columbus, OH: Charles E. Merrill, 1978.

Hansen, C.L., and Lovitt, T.C. *Effects of Feedback in Content and Mechanics of Writing.* Paper read at NIE Symposium, Seattle, WA, July 1973.

Hansen, C.L., and Eaton, M.D. Reading. *The Fourth R: Research in the Classroom.* Columbus, OH: Charles E. Merrill, 1978.

Hansen, C.L. Program Slicing: A Tool for Individualizing Instruction. *Education and Training of the Mentally Retarded*, 1973, *8*, 153–158.

Haring, N.G., Lovitt, T.C., Eaton, M.D., and Hansen, C.L. *The Fourth R: Research in the Classroom.* Columbus, OH: Charles E. Merrill, 1978.

Harris, A., and Sipay, E.R. *How to Increase your Reading Ability* (6th ed.). New York: David McKay, 1975.

Harris, A.J. *How to Increase Reading Ability.* New York: David McKay Co., 1970.

Harris, V.W. Effects of Peer Tutoring, Homework, and Consequences upon the Academic Performance of Elementary School Children. *Dissertation Abstracts International*, 1973, *33*, 11-A, 6175.

Harter, S., and Zigler, E. The Assessment of Effectance of Motivation in Normal and Retarded Children. *Developmental Psychology*, 1974, *10*, 169–180.

Hegge, T.G. Special Reading Disability with Particular Reference to the Mentally Deficient. *American Journal of Mental Deficiency*, 1934, *39*, 224.

Heilman, A.W. *Principles and Practices of Teaching Reading* (3d ed.). Columbus, OH: Charles E. Merrill Publishing Co., 1972.

Hendricksen, J., Roberts, M., and Shores, R.E. Antecedent and Contingent Modeling to Teach Basic Sight Vocabulary to Learning Disabled Children. *Journal of Learning Disabilities*, 1978, *11*(8), 524–528.

Herlihy, J.G., and Herlihy, M.T. *Mainstreaming in the Social Studies.* (Bulletin 62). Washington, DC: National Council for Social Studies, 1980. (ERIC Document Reproduction Service No. ED 186 346).

Hobson, V. Hansen, 269 F. Supp. 401 (D.D.C. 1967, affirmed Sub nom. Smuck V. Hobson, 408 F. 3d 175 (D.C. Cir 1969).

Hollis, J.H. *A Language and Reading Model for the Mentally Retarded.* Paper

Presented at the 6th IASSMD Congress, Toronto, Ontario, Canada, August 22–26, 1982.

Horacek, T. The Discipline Dilemma. *Today's Education*, April/May 1979, *68*, 20–21.

Horn, E.A. A Basic Writing Vocabulary of 10,000 Most Commonly Used Words in Writing. *University of Iowa Monograph in Education*, 1926, (First Series, No. 4). Iowa City, IA.

Huddle, D.D. Work Performance of Trainable Adults as Influenced by Competition, Cooperation and Monetary Reward. *American Journal of Mental Deficiency*, 1967, *72*, 198–211.

Hunkins, F.P. *The Influence of Analysis and Evaluation Questions on Achievement in Sixth Grade Social Studies*. Paper presented at the annual meeting of the American Educational Research Association, New York, 1967.

Johnson, G.O. *Education for the Slow Learners*. Englewood Cliffs, NJ: Prentice-Hall, Inc., 1963.

Johnson, M.S. Tracing and Kinesthetic Techniques. *The Disabled Reader*. Baltimore, MD: Johns Hopkins Press, 1966.

Jordan, T.E. *The Mentally Retarded* (4th ed.). Columbus, OH: Charles E. Merrill, 1976.

Kaluger, G., and Kolson, C.J. *Reading and Learning Disabilities* (2d ed.). Columbus, OH: Charles E. Merrill, 1978.

Kauffman, J.M., Hallahan, D.P., Hass, K., Brame, T., and Boren, R. Imitating Children's Terrors to Improve Their Spelling Performance. *Journal of Learning Disabilities*, 1978, *11*(4), 217–222.

Kirk, S., and Gallagher, J. *Educating Exceptional Children*. Boston: Houghton Mifflin, 1979.

Kirk, S.A., Kliebhan, S.J., and Lerner, J.S. *Teaching Reading to Slow and Disabled Learners*. Boston: Houghton Mifflin, 1978.

Labov, W. *The Social Stratification of English in New York City*. Washington, D.C.: Center for Applied Linguistics, 1966.

Lamberts, F. *P.L. 94–142 and the IEP: A Guide for Teachers of Children with Special Language Needs*. DeKalb: Northern Illinois University, 1978.

Lathrop, A. The Terrible Ten in Educational Programming. *Educational Computer Magazine*, 1982, *2*, 34–36.

Lenneberg, E.H. *Biological Foundations of Language*. New York: Wiley, 1967.

Levin, J.R. What We have Learned about Maximizing what Children Learn? *Cognitive Learning in Children: Theories and Strategies.* New York: Academic Press, 1976.

Levin, J.R., McCormick, C.B., Miller, G.E., Berry, J.K., and Pressley, M. Mnemonic versus Nonmnemonic Vocabulary-Learning Strategies for Children. *American Educational Research Journal*, 1982, *19*, 121–136.

Levin, J.R., Shriberg, Z.K., Miller, G.E., McCormick, C.B., and Levin, B.B. The Keyword Method in the Classroom: How to Remember the States and their Capitals. *Elementary School Journal*, 1980, *80*, 185–191.

Lewinsohn, P.M. and Danaher, B.G., and Kikel, S. Visual Imagery as a Mnemonic Aid for Brain-Injured Persons. *Journal of Consulting and Clinical Psychology*, 1977, *45*, 717–723.

Lovitt, T., Eaton, M., Kirkwood, M., and Pelander, J. Effects of Various Reinforcement Contingencies on Oral Reading Rate. *A New Direction for Education: Behavior Analysis.* University of Kansas, 1971.

Lovitt, T.C. *Using Applied Behavior Analysis Procedures to Evaluate Spelling Instructional Techniques with Learning Disabled Youngsters.* Unpublished manuscript, University of Washington, Seattle, WA, 1973.

Lundsteen, S. Teaching and Testing Critical Listening Skills in the Fifth and Sixth Grades. *Elementary English*, 1964, *41*, 743–747.

Lydra, W.J., and Church, R.S. Direct, Practical Arithmetic Experiences and Success in Solving Realistic Verbal 'Reasoning' Problems in Arithmetic. *The Journal of Educational Research*, 1964, *57*, 530–533.

MacMillan, D.L. The Problem of Motivation in the Education of the Mentally Retarded. *Exceptional Children*, 1971, *37*, 579–586.

MacMillan, D.L. Paired-Associate Learning as a Function of Explicitness of a Mediational Set by EMR and Non-retarded Children. *American Journal of Mental Deficiency*, 1972, *76*, 686–691.

MacMillan, D.L. *Mental Retardation in School and Society.* Boston: Little Brown, 1977.

MacMillan, D.L., and Borthwick, S. The New EMR Population: Can They be Mainstreamed? *Mental Retardation*, 1980, *18*, 155–158.

MacMillan, D.L., and Keogh, B.K. Normal and Retarded Children's Expectancy for Failure. *Developmental Psychology*, 1971, *4*, 343–348.

McAfee, J.K., and Mann, L. The Prognosis for Mildly Handicapped Students. *The Mildly Handicapped Student*, New York: Grune & Stratton, 1982.

McCall, R.B., Appelbaum, M.I., and Hogartz, P.S. Developmental Changes in Mental Performance. Monographs of the Society for Research in Child Development, 1973, *38* (Sec. No. 150).

McCarver, R.B., and Craig, E.M. Placement of the Retarded in the Community: Prognosis and Outcome. N.R. Ellis, *International Review of Research in*

Mental Retardation (Vol. 7). New York: Academic Press, 1974.

McCarthy, W., and Oliver, J. Some Tactile-Kinesthetic procedures for Teaching Reading to Slow Learning Children. *Exceptional Children*, 1965, *31*, 419–421.

McDonald, F.J. Beginning Teacher Evaluation Study, Phase II: Executive Summary. Princeton, N.J.: Educational Testing Service, 1976.

McGeoch, J.A., and Irion, A.L. *The Psychology of Human Learning* (2nd ed.) New York: Longmans-Green, 1952.

McGuigan, C.A. The Effects of a Flowing Words List Vs. Fixed Words Lists and the Implementation of Procedures in the Add-A-Word Spelling Program. (Working Paper No. 52). Seattle: University of Washington, Experimental Education Unit, 1975.

McLean, J.E., and Snyder-McLean, L.K. Transactional Approach to Early Language Training. Columbus, Ohio: Charles E. Merrill, 1978.

Meyen, E.L. Preparation of Life Experience Units for Teaching the Educable Mentally Retarded. Strategies for Teaching Exceptional Children (pp. 200–222), Denver: Lane, 1972.

Mercer, C.D., and Mercer, A.R. The Development and Use of Self-Correcting Materials With Exceptional Children. *Teaching Exceptional Children*, 1978, *11*, (1), 6–11.

Mercer, J.R. *Labeling the Mentally Retarded*. Berkeley: University of California Press, 1973.

Milone, M.N., and Wasylyk, T.M. Handwriting in Special Education. *Teaching Exceptional Children*, 1981, *14* (2), 58–61.

Moffet, J. *A Student-Centered Language Arts Curriculum Grades 11–13: A Handbook for Teachers*. Boston: Houghton Mifflin Co., 1968.

Monroe, M. *Children Who Cannot Read*. Chicago: University of Chicago Press, 1932.

Monteith, M.K. Implications of the Ann Arbor Decision: Black English and the Reading Teacher. *Journal of Reading*, 1980, *23*, 556–559.

Morris, J. Teaching Children to Read. *Educational Research*, 1958, *1*, 38–39.

Moyer, J.R. *An Exploratory Study of Questioning in the Instructional Processes in Selected Elementary Schools* (Doctoral Dissertation, Columbia University). Ann Arbor, Mich.: University Microfilms No. 66–2661, 1966.

Myers, P., and Hammill, D. *Methods of Learning Disorders*. New York: John Wiley & Sons, 1969.

Neef, N.A., Iwata, B.A., and Page, T.J. The Effects of Known-Item Interspersal on Acquisition and Retention of Spelling and Sight-Reading Words. *Journal of Applied Behavior Analysis*, 1977, *10*, 738.

Niemeyer, J.H. The Bank Street Readers: Support for Movement Toward an Integrated Society. *The Reading Teacher*, 1965, pp. 542–545.

Norwell, G.W. *The Reading Interests of Young People.* Lexington, Mass.: D.C. Heath, 1950.

O'Connor, N., and Hermelin, B. Recall in Normals and Sub-Normals of Like Mental Age. *Journal of Abnormal and Social Psychology,* 1963, *66,* 81–84.

Page, E.B. Teacher Comments and Student Performance. *Studies in Educational Psychology.* Waltham, Mass.: Blaisdell Publishing Co., 1968.

Pancsofar, E.L., Bates, P., and Sedlak, R. The development of task analysis for vocational training with severely handicapped students, *Illinois Council for Exceptional Children Quarterly,* 1982, 31, 20-23.

Phelps, H.R. Post-School Adjustment of Mentally Retarded Children in Selected Ohio Cities. *Exceptional Children,* 1956, *23,* 58–62.

Popham, W.J., and Baker, E.L. *Planning an Instructional Sequence.* Englewood Cliffs, N.J.: Prentice-Hall, 1970.

Rigg, P. Dialect and/in/for Reading. *Language Arts.* 1978, *55,* 285–290.

Robertson-Tchabo, E.A., Hansman, C.P., and Arenberg, D. A Classical Mnemonic for Older Learners: A Trip That Works! *Educational Gerontology,* 1976, *1,* 215–226.

Robinson, H.B., and Robinson, N. Mental Retardation. *Carmichael's Manual of Child Psychology* (3rd ed.). (vol. 11). New York: John Wiley & Sons, Inc., 1970.

Robinson, N.M., and Robinson, H.B. *The Mentally Retarded Child: A Psychological Approach* (2nd ed.). New York: McGraw-Hill, 1976.

Robinson, P.C. The Black English issue. *Education Leadership,* 1980–81, *38,* 474–475.

Sabatino, D.A., and Lanning-Ventura, S. Functional Teaching: Survival Skills and Tutoring. *A Handbook of Diagnostic and Prescriptive Teaching.* Rockville, Md.: Aspen, 1982.

Salend, S.F. Active Academic Games: The Aim of the Game is Mainstreaming. *Teaching Exceptional Children,* 1979, *12,* 3–6.

Salvia, J., and Ysseldyke, J.E. *Assessment in Special and Remedial Education* (2nd ed.). Boston: Houghton Mifflin Co., 1981.

Schloss, C.N. and Schloss, P.J. Independent living skills. In P.J. Schloss and C.N. Schloss (Ed.) *Handbook of Intervention forms for secondary special educators.* Austin, TX: PRO-ED, 1985.

Schortinghuis, N., and Frohman, A. A Comparison of Paraprofessional and Professional Success with Preschool Children. *Journal of Learning Disabilities*, 1974, *7*, 62–64.

Schreiber, J.E. *Teacher's Question-Asking Techniques in Social Studies*, (Doctoral dissertation, University Microfilms No. 67–9099, 1967).

Schumaker, J.B., Hovell, M.F., and Sherman, J.A. An Analysis of Daily Report Cards and Parent-Managed Privileges in the Improvement of Adolescent's Classroom Performance. *Journal of Applied Behavior Analysis*, 1977, *10*, 645–655.

Sedlak, R.A. Performance of Good and Poor Problem Solvers on Arithmetic Word Problems Presented in a Modified Cloze Format. *The Journal of Educational Research*, 1974, *10*, 467–471.

Sedlak, R.A., Sun, D., and Harper, J. *Use of Calculators to Enhance Problem Solving and Computation Skills of Mildly Handicapped Children*. Unpublished manuscript, Southern Illinois University, 1982.

Sedlak, R.A., and Fitzmaurice, A. Teaching arithmetic. In J.M. Kauffman and D.A. Hallahan, (Editors), *Handbook of Special Education*. Englewood Cliffs, N.J.: Prentice-Hall, Inc., 1981.

Sedlak, R.A., and Schenk, W.E. Verbal Problem Solving of EMH Learners. *Carolina Journal of Educational Research*, 1980, *1*, 1–10.

Sedlak, R.A., and Cartwright, G.P. Written Language Abilities of EMR and Nonretarded Children with the Same Mental Ages. *American Journal of Mental Deficiency*, 1972, *77*, 95–99.

Sedlak, R.A. Effectiveness of Paraprofessionals in Training for Working with Disabled Students. Unpublished manuscript, Southern Illinois University. Carbondale, Illinois, 1982.

Semmel, M., Barritt, L., Bennett, S., and Perfetti, C. A Grammatical Analysis of Word Associations of Educable Mentally Retarded and Normal Children. *American Journal of Mental Deficiency*, 1968, *72*, 567–576.

Sidman, M., and Cresson, O. Reading and Crossmodal Transfer of Stimulus Equivalences in Severe Retardation. *American Journal of Mental Deficiency*, 1973, *77*, 515–523.

Simches, G., and Bohn, R.J. Issues in Curriculum: Research and Responsibility. *Mental Retardation*, 1963, *1* (2), 84–87.

Skeels, H.M. Adult Status of Children with Contrasting Early Life Experiences: A Follow up Study. *Monographs of the Society for Research in Child Development*, 1966, *31* (3) (Series No. 105).

Smith, R.M. *An Introduction to Mental Retardation*. New York: McGraw-Hill, 1971.

Smitherman, G. "What go round come round": King in Perspective. *Harvard Educational Review*, 1981, *5*, 40–56.

Somervill, M.A. Dialect and Reading: A Review of Alternative Solutions. *Review of Educational Research*, 1975, *45*, 247–262.

Spache, G.D., and Spache, E.B. *Reading in the Elementary School* (4th ed.) Boston: Allyn & Bacon, 1977.

Spradlin, J.E. Language and Communication of Mental Defectives. *Handbook of Mental Deficiency.* New York: McGraw-Hill, 1963.

Stauffer, R.G. *The First Grade Reading Studies: Findings of Individual Investigations.* Newark, Del.: International Reading Association, 1967.

Steppe-Jones, C. *Inservice training of teachers to work effectively with paraprofessionals.* Unpublished doctoral dissertation Carbondale, IL: Southern Illinois University, 1981.

Sternberg, L., and Sedlak, R. The Use of Computational Worksheets: A Cloak of Teacher and Learner Competence. *New York State Mathematics Teachers Journal,* 1981, *31,* 17–20.

Tickunoff, W., Berliner, D.C., and Rist, R.C. *An Ethnographic Study of the Forty Classrooms of the Beginning Teacher Evaluation Study Known Sample* (Technical Report No. 75–10–5). San Francisco: Far West Laboratory for Educational Research and Development, October, 1975.

Todd, D., Scott, R., Bostow, D., and Alexander, S. Modifications of the Excessive Inappropriate Classroom Behavior of Two Elementary School Students using Home-Based Consequences and Daily Report Card Procedures. *Journal of Applied Behavior Analysis,* 1976, *9,* 106.

Turnbull, A.P., and Schultz, J.B. *Mainstreaming Handicapped Students: A Guide for the Classroom Teacher.* Boston: Allyn & Bacon, 1979.

Tymitz, B. Instructional Aspects of the IEP: An Analysis of Teachers' Skills and Needs. *Educational Technology,* 1980, September, 13–20.

Tymitz-Wolf, B. Guidelines for Assessing IEP Goals and Objectives. *Teaching Exceptional Children,* 1982, *14* (5), 198–201.

U.S. Office of Education. Estimated Number of Handicapped Children Served and Unserved by Type of Handicap. Bureau of Education for the Handicapped, March 4, 1975.

Wallace, G. Teaching Reading. *Handbook of Special Education.* Englewood Cliffs, N.J.: Prentice-Hall, 1981.

Warner, D. *Experimental Phonetic Reading Programs for Exceptional Pupils.* Los Angeles: California University, 1967.

Webb, C.E., and Kinde, S. Speech, Language and Hearing of the Mentally Retarded. *Mental Retardation.* Chicago: Aldine Publishing, 1967.

Wehman, P., and McLaughlin, P.J. *Program Development in Special Education.* New York: McGraw-Hill, 1981.

Wilson, R.M., and Hall, M. *Reading and the Elementary School Child: Theory and Practice for Teachers*. New York: Van Nostrand Reinhold Co., 1972.

Wright, L., and Willis, C. Reminiscence in Normals and Defectives. *American Journal of Mental Deficiency*, 1969, *73*, 700–702.

Wulz, S.V., and Hollis, J.H. Word Recognition: A Task-Based Definition for Testing and Teaching. *The Reading Teacher*, 1979, *32*, 779–786.

Zeaman, D., and House, B.J. The Role of Attention in Retardate Discrimination Learning. *Handbook of Mental Deficiency*. New York: McGraw-Hill, 1963.

Zigler, E. Research on Personality Structure in the Retardate. *International Review of Research in Mental Retardation* (Vol. 1). New York: Academic Press, 1966.

Zigler, E. *Training the Intellect Versus Development of the Child*. Paper read at the annual meeting of the American Educational Research Association, Los Angeles, 1968.

Zigler, E., and Butterfield, E.C. Motivational Aspects of Changes in IQ Test Performance of Culturally Deprived Nursery School Children. *Child Development*, 1968, *39*, 1–14.

Author Index

Subject Index

Mainstreaming, 15-16
Management, 85-97
Manipulatives, 132-133
Maps, 164-165
Mathematics:
 calculators, 105-106
 content, 252-253
 error patterns (see Error analysis)
 learner characteristics, 251-252
 teaching, 256-270
 Me and My Environment, 285
 Me Now, 285
 Measurement (see Mathematics,
  Teaching)
 Memory, 10
 Mental retardation, definition, 3, 4
  5, 6 (see also Educable mentally
  retarded)
 Microcomputers, 110-120
 instruction, 113-116
 parts, 111
 selection, 112-113
 software, 114-116, 121
 use, 119-120
Minimal change, 61
Mnemonics, 66-69
Modeling, 91
Money (see Mathematics, Teaching)
Morphology, 227

Negative reinforcement (see
 Management)
Nonstandard assessment strategies,
 35-36, (see also Assessment)
Notes, to parents (see Management)
Nutrition, 173

Opaque projectors, 143-144
Operations (see Mathematics, Teaching)
Organization of lessons, 60-62
Outlines (see Study methods)
Overhead projectors, 143-144
Overlearning, 70-73

Paraprofessionals, 97-102
 effectiveness, 102
 interview, 97-99
 in the classroom, 99-101
Parents, 95-97
P-A-T (see Study methods)
Peer teaching (see Spelling)
Phonics (see Word-attack skills)
Phonology, 227
Physical education, 287-289
Positive and negative examples, 66-67
Positive practice (see Spelling)
Positive reinforcement (see
 Management)
Practice, 58-60
Pragmatics, 228
Prevalence (see Educable mentally
 retarded)
Problem solving (see Mathematics,
 Teaching)
Programmed instruction, 110
Project PASS, 279-284
Punishment (see Management)

Qualitative information (see
 Assessment)
Quantitative information (see
Assessment)
Question and answer (see Study
 methods)
Questioning, 62-64

Reading:
 approaches, 193-200
 characteristics, 181-182
 goals, 182-183
 instructional strategies, 200-201
 skills, 183-188
Recreation (see Physical education)
Reinforcement, 65-66, 85-86, 88-90
 (see also Management)
Reminiscence, 73
Report cards, 95-96
Response cost (see Management)

Retention, 57, 70-74
Revelation of objectives, 58

Safety signs, 167-169
Schedules, 80-84
Science, 280, 285
Self-control, 90
Self-correcting materials, 139-143
Self-correction (see Spelling)
Semantics, 227
Speech, 239-243
Sequencing of objectives and
    information, 61
Short-term objectives, 153-156
Sight word vocabulary, 184-185
Social interactions, 292-294
Social skills, 167, 170-172, 292-299
Spaced review, 73
Speak and Math, 108-109
Speak and Read, 108-109
Speak and Spell, 108-109
Specific instruction (for transfer), 74
Spelling, 215-222
    assessment, 216-218
    fixed word lists, 218
    flow word lists, 218-219
    instruction, 219-222
    selection of word, 215-216
Structural analysis (see Word-attack
    skills)
Study methods, 165-166
Study-Rest-Study-Rest (see Study
    methods)
Survey Q 3 R (see Study methods)
Survival skills, 166-178
Syntax, 227-228

Task analysis, 42-46
Teacher attention, 90
Teacher responsibilities, 18, 19
Teaching, 13, 53, 54, 62-70
Teaching steps, size of, 61
Technology, 105
Television, 144-145

Testing (see Assessment)
Time (see Mathematics, Teaching)
Time-out (see Management)
Token systems (see Management)
Transfer, 55, 57, 73-74
Transparencies, 143-144

Unit teaching, 274-289
U.S. history, 279-280

Variable-speed tape recorder, 106
VATK system (see Reading Approaches)
Video cameras, 120
Video cassette recorders, 120

Work-attack skills, 183-184
Work interaction, 294-295
Worksheets, 127-132
Writing, analysis of, 206-207
Written expression, of the retarded
    205-211

DATE DUE

MR 17 '89			
DE 08 '89			
MY 30 '90			
GAYLORD			PRINTED IN U.S.A.